ARGENTINA

ARGENTINA

DEMOCRACY ON TRIAL

Daniel Poneman

PARAGON HOUSE PUBLISHERS

New York

Published in the United States by

PARAGON HOUSE PUBLISHERS
2 Hammarskjöld Plaza
New York, N.Y. 10017
Copyright 1987 by Daniel Poneman

Photograph credits: República Argentina, Presidencia de la Nación, *Perón: cuatro años de su gobierno* (Buenos Aires: Subsecretaría de Información, 1950) (photographs numbered 1 and 2); República Argentina, Presidencia de la Nación, Secretaría de Información Pública (photographs numbered 3, 4, 7, 8, 9, 11, 12, 13 and 14); República Argentina, Presidencia de la Nación, *Democracia y su Presidente* (Buenos Aires: Secretaría de Información Pública, 1984) (photographs 10 and 15); Associated Press (photograph 5); Sygma (photograph 6).

Book interior designed by A. Christopher Simon.

Library of Congress Cataloging-in-Publication Data

Poneman, Daniel.
  Argentina : democracy on trial.

  Bibliography:
  Includes index.
  1. Argentina—Politics and government—
1943–   . 2. Representative government and
representation—Argentina—History—20th century.
3. Civil-military relations—Argentina—History—
20th century. 4. Argentina—Economic conditions—
1945–   . 5. National characteristics,
Argentine.   I. Title.
F2849.P64   1987   320.982   86–25146
ISBN 0–913729–56–6

To Susan

This republic possesses all the requisite conditions to become, with the passage of time, one of the great nations of the earth. Its territory is immense and fertile, its surface being equal to that of all Europe save Russia; it is capable of supporting with care at least 100 million human beings; almost every climate is to be found within its limits, and, consequently, it can yield all products, from those of the tropics to those of the polar regions. Its rivers and its mountains are among the greatest of the globe. As its maritime frontier it has the Atlantic, which brings it into contact with the whole world.

CARLOS PELLEGRINI
President of Argentina, 1890–1892

Contents

Acknowledgments

This book could not have been completed without the generous support of many. I am deeply grateful to Steven Paschke and the Institute for the Study of World Politics in New York for enabling me to live and do research in Argentina for nearly a year. Emilio Cárdenas, Adrián Hope, and the lawyers of their firm taught me a great deal about Argentine law and Argentine hospitality. During my stay, I gathered innumerable books and documents and conducted hundreds of interviews. (Except where otherwise noted, all translations of written and oral sources are my own.) Many interviews were informal; I would ask Argentines I met from all walks of life about their views on democracy. I also spoke with politicians, soldiers, businessmen, unionists, priests, professors, judges, lawyers, economists, scientists, human rights activists, and government officials. Several cabinet ministers former and current, national senators and deputies, close advisors to the president and vice president, a former president, a secretary general of the General Labor Confederation, retired generals and admirals, and key party leaders, all graciously interrupted their busy schedules for interviews. Many others were kind enough to comment on portions of the manuscript. Although I did not accept all suggestions I benefited from every one. I owe a great debt to all of these people, but cannot thank them by name here, some because confidentiality was the price of frankness, others because it would be unfair to link them even implicitly to conclusions they may not share. Indeed, my only regret is that some close Argentine friends will be offended by various statements in the pages to follow. Yet it would ultimately be a disservice to those friendships were I to dissemble or bury my views in a cloud of "on-the-one-hand-on-the-other-hand" pseudo-objectivity. Any errors I have committed along the way are mine alone.

On a lighter note, it is a pleasure to thank Albert Carnesale, Paul Doty, Matthew Nimetz, Joseph Nye, David Smith, and Frederick Snyder for their early support of the project. My field research benefited from the guidance of Richard Kessler, Javier Zapiola, and Guillermo Zoccali. Julian Bach provided encouragement and much more. I am also grateful to Philip Bobbitt, Robert Litwak, Scott Sagan, and Gregory Treverton for reasons best known to them. In Argentina, Maria Laura Spirito and Andrea Ezcurra did a superb job in typing the draft of the manuscript. In the first-name tradition of record jackets, I would like to extend special thanks to Delores and Meyer, to Joan and Stuart. Above all, I would like to thank my wife, Susan. Her research, criticism, patience, and moral support made this project possible, and sometimes even fun. It is to her that the book is dedicated.

D.P.
Washington, D.C.

Preface

Argentina is an extraordinary country. Its people are open and spirited. Its vistas are breathtaking. In the north, the Iguazú Falls thunder in a jungle paradise of parrots and toucans, orchid-dripping trees, and a technicolored profusion of butterflies. In the south, the Perito Moreno glacier towers austerely as it edges across the milky blue Lake Argentina. Overhead, a soaring condor slowly disappears against a vast and cloudless sky. Buenos Aires conjures thoughts of the sugary aroma of the roasted peanuts sold on Florida Street at Christmastime, the summer relief brought by fruit-shakes called *licuados*, the two-inch-thick steaks grilled in the open air and washed down by sturdy Mendoza wines.

It would be delightful to dwell on these and other pleasures, but that is not the task of this book. Rather, the subject is the Argentine political system as it grapples with perhaps its greatest national challenge since independence—testing whether democracy in Argentina can long endure.

It is a noble experiment, one which never before has succeeded. As will become apparent in the following pages, there are those who would see it fail yet again. The many who wish it Godspeed are not fully armed to translate that wish into reality. These facts create serious difficulties for a writer who has great affection for Argentina yet knows that its democracy must overcome enormous obstacles. The problem is reminiscent of one once faced by the American realist painter, Thomas Eakins. A woman who had commissioned Eakins to paint her portrait refused payment on the grounds that she was not pleased with her appearance therein, to which the artist is said to have replied, "I am an artist, madam, not a magician." Here, too, an honest interpretation of Argentine political reality will not be adulterated by flattery. The problems that have undermined democracy must be frankly confronted, even at the risk of offending Argentine sensibilities.

Before venturing further, it is necessary to pause to inquire whether it is fair to analyze Argentine democracy as one would any other. After all, traditions vary drastically on either side of the Rio Grande. Democracy has not yet become a way of life in Argentina, and many Argentines may not desire it.

Nevertheless, three reasons justify analyzing Argentine democracy, as a general proposition, by standards similar to those applied to other democracies. First, the Argentine constitutional system is modeled on the U.S. version; both are based upon the separation of powers and respect for individual rights. In Argentina, the consent of the governed is manifested through the election of a president and two houses of Congress. An independent judiciary comprises the third branch of central government. The addition of provincial governments creates a system that is federal as well as democratic. If this set-up looks familiar to Americans, it should. When two systems are so closely cousined in origin and structure, it is useful to consider the experience of one in studying the evolution of the other.

Second, many Argentines have believed in the North Atlantic variant of democracy and have attempted unsuccessfully to establish it. President Domingo Sarmiento adopted Horace Mann's educational ideals. President Julio Roca encouraged European immigration and turned Argentina into the Western Hemisphere's second greatest melting pot. Notalio Botana, one of the most eminent political scientists in Argentina today, has directly applied the writings of Montesquieu, Adam Smith, de Tocqueville, and Madison to Argentine politics.[1] The Argentine Supreme Court gives precedential value to the decisions of the U.S. Supreme Court. Argentines today still stress their cultural and familial ties to Europe, where democracy is the norm. In Argentina, even democracy's enemies invoke its good name; every military coup in the past fifty years has called for genuine democracy.

Third, Argentines today are absorbed in a great and self-conscious effort to convert Argentina into a democratic nation and society. I did not choose democracy for Argentina or resort first to occidental values in analyzing it. Argentines did. It is their law, their history, and their people that have put democracy on trial. I merely bear witness to the attempt.

This book does not focus on the Malvinas, or Falklands, War. (I shall refer to the islands and the conflict by their Argentine name.) The reason is partly reluctance to retread ground already well covered in other books, and partly the belief that the war had no more to do with the fate of democracy than a starting pistol has with the outcome of a race. The war was a desperate gambit to arrest the deterioration of the popular and economic support for the military government, the noisy but useless braying of a broken mule stuck in the mire.[2]

Allow me one caveat. Much as I like Argentines, I am not one and cannot pretend to be one. I can only approach the country as an informed outsider.

That may not be a bad thing. Perspectives that are alien in source and method can bring freshness and insight to tired analytical conventions. How much poorer our understanding of ourselves and each other would be without the benefit of cross-cultural perspectives. Certainly it cannot be said that any existing analysis, Argentine or foreign, has so definitively analyzed democracy in Argentina that further discussion is pointless.

What is democracy? Clearly we are not talking here of the mere holding of elections and respect for the winners, though that in itself would be a signal accomplishment. Democracy must be a way of life. As a private citizen, Raúl Alfonsín once wrote that "there is no democracy without voting, but voting in and of itself is not sufficient. Democracy is a form of governing and of organizing society, derived from the fundamental premise of respect for the dignity of man. It is inconceivable without justice."[3]

For a working definition, let democracy be described as a political system based upon respect for the civil and political rights of the individual and governed through the consent of the citizenry. Democracy in this sense has been sorely wanting in Argentina for more than fifty years. The republican institutions of the Constitution have repeatedly been slapped aside, and in their stead has flourished an alternative set of institutions, powerful and undemocratic—the armed forces, the unions, and the Church.

Today an epic battle is being waged that will determine the future of Argentina. Democracy and its new champion, Raúl Alfonsín, are tilting against the Goliath-like institutions that have so dominated Argentina's recent past. It is a battle that engages all Argentines and will profoundly affect the political future of all Latin Americans. In 1960 Argentina, Bolivia, Brazil, Chile, Peru, and Uruguay all had elected governments. By 1973 all had been overthrown. Now the pendulum has swung back in favor of democracy. The military dictatorships of Chile and Paraguay have become the odd men out in the continent. While Central America boils with insurgency, changes of vital strategic importance to the United States are evolving unsteadily below Panama. This process warrants our attention.

Abbreviations

AAA	Argentine Anticommunist Action or Alliance
BIR	Bank of Regional Trade
CANDU	Canadian-Deuterium-Uranium reactor
CGT	General Confederation of Labor
CNEA	National Commission of Atomic Energy
ERP	People's Revolutionary Army
FAP	Peronist Armed Forces
FAR	Revolutionary Armed Forces
FM	General Directorate of Military Fabrications
GDP	Gross Domestic Product
IAEA	International Atomic Energy Agency
IMF	International Monetary Fund
MID	Movement for Integration and Development
MWe	Megawatts (electrical)
NPT	Treaty on the Non-Proliferation of Nuclear Weapons
OPEC	Organization of Petroleum Exporting Countries
PAN	National Food Program
PEN	National Executive Power (the presidential office)
UCD	Union of the Democratic Center
UCR	Radical Civic Union
UF_6	Uranium hexafluoride
YPF	State Oil Deposits [Company]

PART I

A GORDIAN KNOT

CHAPTER 1

Paradise Crossed

Argentina is a land of promise. The Constitution enshrines individual rights and democratic institutions. The people are the wealthiest and most literate of Latin America. The land is blessed by the pampas—perhaps the richest expanse of fertility in the world—and untapped mineral wealth. Industry manufactures goods ranging from textiles to tanks, from aircraft to automobiles. Before 1982 Argentines had not battled foreign military forces for over 100 years.

Yet somehow the plan, the people, the resources, and outward peace have brought neither prosperity nor democracy. The tragedy is that Argentina seemed well on the road. After seventy years of rapid growth, in 1930 Argentina's per capita income stood higher than Spain's and only slightly lower than Italy's. In beef and corn, its exports comprised 58 percent and 65 percent of the world export market.[1] Argentina in many ways resembled other democracies. Like Australia and Canada, it was a large, agricultural nation sparsely populated by well-educated European stock. (Argentina is the world's eighth largest nation.) Like the United States, waves of European immigrants swelled its shores in the decades spanning the turn of the twentieth century. And though the system had been challenged, sometimes violently, Argentines in 1930 could also look back upon a seventy year unbroken stretch of constitutional succession to the presidency, and eighteen years of participatory democracy.

Something went dreadfully wrong. In the early hours of 6 September 1930, the morning quiet was broken by a slender column of 900 soldiers and 600 teenaged cadets marching down the Avenida de Mayo toward the Casa Rosada, the seat of Argentine government. They met no resistance as they ousted the Radical Government, elected by a landslide two years before. The coup was led by retired General José F. Uriburu, who proclaimed himself president and declared his "respect for the Constitution and the basic laws in force."[2] This ironic defense of law and constitution would be ritualistically

3

incanted following military coups in 1943, 1955, 1962, 1966 and 1976. Notwithstanding these heartening words, no civilian elected as president in Argentina in the half century following 1930 ever served out his full term in office. Coups, on the other hand, have brought lengthening spans of military rule. In the eighteen years from 1966 to 1984, civilians ruled for less than three. That brief span, from 1973 to 1976, could hardly be called government, let alone democracy, bemired as it was in the terrorism and chaos of the final presidency of Juan and, after his death, Isabel Perón. Before Alfonsín, Argentines under thirty-five had no substantial experience with democratic government.

Economic stagnation goes hand in hand with political decay. By 1930 Argentina had become one of the top ten nations in per capita income. Exports of beef and wheat to Britain, reciprocated by extensive capital investment in Argentine railways and industry, had driven a powerful economic expansion. But growth skidded to a halt during World War I and the Great Depression. The Second World War brought economic recovery and left Argentina rich in international reserves. This chance for a fresh start was squandered; within four years the extravagance of President Perón converted Argentina's surplus into deficit. Periodic foreign exchange crises followed, culminating in the present $50 billion debt.

In the early postwar years, industries appeared in the urban sprawl encircling central Buenos Aires, but the much vaunted "take off" into industrialization never materialized. Beef exports stalled, then declined; export revenues have fallen from nearly $1 billion to under $300 million in the last five years alone. The Europeans, formerly consumers, have become beef exporters—and at subsidized prices. Now they have cut deeply into Argentina's best market: the Soviet Union. The saga of grain exports has been less dramatic, but deeply discouraging.

In the last decade, per capita income has fallen at an average annual rate of 1.2 percent.[3] Prosperity may not be indispensable to democracy. India proves that. But economic stagnation aggravates political discord and undermines the consensus necessary to protect the frail roots of a young democracy.

A ROGUES' GALLERY

Blame is liberally ladled out in Argentina, served up by different chefs but, in the end, covering all society. Were every ingredient included, the following recipe might emerge.

The oligarchy is reviled as the *patria financiera*, the "financial fatherland" that skims the nation's wealth to enrich itself ever more. The days have passed when 400 families ruled Argentina. The division of wealth, however, is still grossly uneven. Vast shanty towns—*villas miserias*—pepper the industrial belt that surrounds Buenos Aires. In this food-exporting nation, many people still go hungry. Infant mortality is four times higher than in the United States.[4] Meanwhile, gigantic *estancias* remain. In the humid pampa of Buenos Aires Province, 2,500-acre ranches are common. In the outlying provinces, they may be ten times larger. The *estanciero* may be an absentee landlord who leaves the cultivation to a foreman, lives in Buenos Aires to manage his assets, and travels abroad to spend them.

Twice the oligarchy openly ruled Argentina: from the time of the federalization of Buenos Aires in 1880 until the election of the first Radical president in 1916, and between the 1930 and 1943 military coups. Critics argue that it has *always* run the country, whether from within or without the government. For generations the upper classes have done business with foreign companies. Allegedly that makes them the servants of international capital and multinational enterprises, selling off Argentina's patrimony for a hefty commission. The critique goes on to say that agricultural production is suppressed because wealthy landowners, able to live luxuriously on a fraction of their vast acreages, choose leisure over profit, allowing rich lands to lie idle. Meanwhile, the oligarchy starves domestic industry of productive investment by investing its wealth in foreign currencies and assets. In every sector—land, capital, and labor—it is seen to be rapaciously exploiting the country as a fiefdom.

The last military government reinforced this image. Its most powerful civilian was the minister of economy, José Alfredo Martínez de Hoz—the quintessential oligarch, from one of the oldest and wealthiest *estanciero* families. Hailed abroad for his free market ideas, Martínez de Hoz presided over an enormous transfer of wealth to the already wealthy. From 1975 to 1980 salaried workers' share of national income declined from nearly one-half to one-third.[5] His policies led to the gross overvaluation of the peso, ushering in the era of "sweet money." As consumption soared, dollars became so cheap that people flew to Miami just to go shopping. When domestic producers could not compete with undervalued imports, thousands went bankrupt.

Speculators flourished. Taking advantage of high Argentine interest rates, they converted their dollars into peso investments and doubled their money within a year. This speculation was not only unproductive but also risk-free; a slow, fixed devaluation rate ensured investors that they could switch back and forth between pesos and dollars without endangering their huge profits.

When the party ended and massive devaluations began, that is exactly what they did. In this way it is estimated that over $20 billion left the country, while foreign debt shot up from under $10 billion in 1976 to $35.7 billion in 1981. The *patria financiera* profits, and the country suffers.

The middle class is seen to be as venal as the oligarchy, but less successful. Its crimes are mediocrity and collaborationism. The middle class emerged from the late nineteenth and early twentieth century waves of European immigration. The newcomers created the first mass party in Argentine history: the Radical Civic Union. By and large, though, successful merchants and industrialists of immigrant stock did not challenge the old order. Instead of trying to change the rules, they merely sought admission to the club. In the words of one historian, "wealth in trade and industry acquired respectability only when transferred into cattle or sheep ranches. The means of acquiring wealth had to be camouflaged."[6]

Even in its heyday, when its own Radical party occupied the Casa Rosada for fourteen years (1916–30), the middle class mounted no serious threat to landed class and privilege. In fact, during that period, Radicals introduced fifty-four of the ninety bills passed by Congress that favored the cattle interests. During the 1930s, when rural laborers flooded the cities in search of better opportunities, the Radicals did not earnestly seek the support of the new urban proletariat. That failure was exploited by Perón, who organized the working class into Argentina's most powerful political force.

Unlike the middle class, which has often appeared confused and aimless, at least the working class has had a strong identity and a true hero. Before World War II, the Argentine worker's struggle was largely frustrated. Then came Perón. He brought benefits and pride to the workers, along with increased demagoguery and authoritarianism to the government. These latter traits were grafted onto the working class movement, and constitute its chief insult to democracy. Anti-Peronists add mediocrity and corruption to their complaint, but these sins weigh on far more souls than comprise the Peronist movement. No, Perón's greatest sin was in delivering the lethal blows to political institutions already rotted by corruption. He sacked supreme court justices, purged universities, and jailed political opponents. He remolded the nascent trade union movement in his own image and filled its leadership with toadies. After his overthrow, during eighteen years of exile, Perón remained the *eminence grise* of Argentine politics. He encouraged the terrorists who killed and kidnaped in his name in the early 1970s. Though elected democratically, Perón systematically undermined democracy. He, like the Radical leaders of the 1920s, showed how democracy can sow the seed of its own destruction.

The Catholic Church is often blamed for promoting authoritarianism and not democracy. Although the Catholic hierarchy is no longer an exclusive preserve of the oligarchy, it remains powerful and politicized.[7] Roman Catholicism is the state religion, professed by over 90 percent of the population. The Constitution requires that the president be a baptized Roman Catholic. The army and air force have traditionally been bastions of Catholicism. The fall of Perón gives an idea of the political clout of the Church; for years he successfully suppressed opposition in the unions, newspapers, and political parties, but was ousted by the military only after directly assaulting the Church in 1954 and 1955.

The problem goes beyond mere acceptance of authoritarian government. Through lay organizations, Catholic interests have actively contributed to the failure of democracy. At one extreme, the Catholicism of the army has attracted significant clerical and lay support for its coups d'état. In 1976 the armed forces entered office with the promise to restore "Christian and moral values," before turning to industrial-scale torture and murder.[8] At the other extreme, the Montonero guerillas who plunged the country into chaos in the early 1970s were founded by extremists from the lay organization, *Acción Católica*, most notoriously Mario Firmenich. The Third World Priest movement of the late 1960s and early 1970s openly backed Peronism, led labor demonstrations, and was accused of aiding terrorist organizations.

The political eclecticism of militant Catholicism may seem paradoxical, but it is not. Though mortal enemies, the leadership of the army and the Montoneros were in many ways alike. Each held an absolutist vision of the world and messianic visions of its role in it. Each ordered the murder of those who might not share those visions, confidently presuming the right to decide who should live and who should die, refusing victims the opportunity to defend themselves, eschewing judicial safeguards to prevent killings by error or sheer caprice. From supposed worshipers of God, both sides became callous usurpers of His divine rights.

In the aftermath of the last military government, the Church seemed somewhat diminished in moral force. Its failure to take a firm stand against torture and forced disappearances could not be excused by its declared "render unto Caesar" neutrality before all forms of government. Throughout, priests had continued to attend military functions and to address officials such as General Albano Harguindeguy—interior minister and a principal architect of the repression—as "Excellency." A few priests were reported to have ministered to torturers without reproaching them and to torturees without defending them. Within a year of Alfonsín's election, at a mass held monthly to commemorate the deaths of those killed by subversion, and popular among retired and active duty officers, a priest called upon his listeners to "take up spiritual and material arms against this corrupt and pornographic democracy."[9]

The military rounds out the list. Start from a neutral perspective. That the armed forces uprooted civilian governments six times since 1930 does not prove them to be enemies of democracy. After all, the military juntas nearly always announce that their intention is to preserve or restore democracy. Arguably, the failures of the civilians (which are many) rather than the ambitions of the soldiers are the chief agents of coups d'état in Argentina. According to some scholars, the armed forces are not a pressure group, with fixed viewpoints and objectives that are contrary to democracy. Rather, it is argued, they are merely a *factor* of power, lobbied at one time or another by every civilian political interest group in order to act against an elected government. They are the instruments, not the architects, of political change.[10]

This view has some merit. Civilian politicians of every stripe—Radical, Peronist, Christian Democrat, Catholic Nationalist, and Socialist—have all supported military coups. At the same time, however, persistent resort to the generals has convinced them that they are, indeed, the principal guardians of the national interest. That conviction imbues the armed forces with arrogance and political ambition. Now many officers believe that it is their institutional right (or even God-given duty) to impose those views when the national interest is at stake (nearly always). In the last two military governments, the armed forces took power with drastic plans to reorder the Argentine political system, implemented them, and stayed for seven years each time. They rewarded their friends, persecuted their enemies, closed the Congress, ejected the provincial governments, fired the judges. Call the military what you will—"factor of power" or "pressure group"—with friends like that, democracy in Argentina needs no enemies.

THE NATIONAL PSYCHE

From the beginning, many Argentines have not cared much for democracy. The Spanish came in search of gold, not religious freedom. Wealthy landowners despised anything, including democracy, that threatened their status or wealth. They ruled like feudal lords and raised armies to stave off all comers. During the Great Immigration, hard-working new arrivals often wanted no more than to earn enough money to return to Europe and live in comfort. Many were called "swallows," because they migrated annually, taking advantage of the transequatorial reversal of seasons in order to work two autumn harvests. Neither rich nor poor grew either to know or love democracy.

Many immigrants themselves came from unstable parts of Europe—Northern Spain and Southern Italy. These regions share a violent undemocratic history, and local politics are of the old-style, buying protection and selling favors. Must Argentine politics naturally follow suit? That argument is difficult to prove and assumes that immigrants shape rather than conform to their new community. If this is true, it may reflect the absence of a sense of identity.

Argentina's early leaders unwittingly fueled this national incoherence. They promulgated laws to encourage immigration, liberally granting civil rights (to work, to buy property) to noncitizens, denying them only political rights (to vote, to hold office). "To govern is to populate," declared Juan Bautista Alberdi, the father of the Argentine Constitution.

This maxim was too simplistic; content to enjoy their civil rights and (after 1901) to avoid compulsory military service, many newcomers never bothered to become citizens. Former president Sarmiento wrote in 1881 that on their disembarking none of the 40,000 annual arrivals took out citizenship cards because of the expense, and that with the passing years they instead learned to disdain citizenship, "to savor the advantages of not being citizens and to pride themselves in knowing that across the Atlantic lies a country, whose name can serve to suspend, cloak, or extract the impulses of patriotism."

By 1914 less than 2 percent of foreign-born Argentine residents had been naturalized. Argentina became a country of inhabitants, not citizens. Even now many Argentines lament that "we have no national identity." This alienation discourages civic responsibility and encourages factional hatred. It helps explain how Argentines today can feel no remorse at the wicked treatment inflicted upon thousands of their compatriots. Sarmiento's century-old words still ring true: "The society has disappeared completely; there remains only the feudal family, isolated and inward-bound . . . in a word, there is no 'commonweal,' no *res publica*."[11]

Ask Argentines about democracy. Many support it in theory, in varying degrees, from "there's got to be democracy" to "well, at least we can talk now." But many are agnostic; if democracy works, fine. If not, try something else. Few devote their time, effort, or money to it. And many oppose it. A Peronist union official told me that "democracy is an alternative approach to our problems, not a solution. If not wedded to concrete proposals, it is not viable." For more than 100 years, a common refrain in elite circles has been that "the masses here are too ignorant to handle democracy."

What system do naysayers prefer? The same union leader, seated beneath portraits of Perón and the sanguinary nineteenth century dictator, Juan Manuel de Rosas, urged that if democracy fails, Argentina should find "a strong president to lead us—advised, of course, by a council of state." The elites would prefer to be governed by members of their own class, whose intelligence and intentions they trust. Many of those who expressed doubts about democracy, when pressed for a better alternative, offered none.

There is not even consensus over what democracy is. "You call this democracy?" asked one artist. "The oligarchs still run everything. I am afraid to open my mouth now because later when the military returns I will pay for it." The leadership of the General Confederation of Labor claims that "true" democracy is only achieved when the working classes have enough money to live decently. In Peronist doctrine, "social justice" is more important to democracy than freedom of speech and honest elections.

Why are undemocratic attitudes so common? Despite the stirring words of Rousseau, Locke, and Jefferson, democratic yearnings may not spring spontaneously from the human breast. Democracy requires acceptance of wrongheaded opinions, dangerous policies, and incompetent politicians. Such acceptance is not instinctive. Instinct may not lead one to submit to the rule of corrupt weaklings who could easily be ousted by force, or to prefer personal sacrifice to the breach of principle. But that is precisely what democracy demands.

These prerequisites can be justified by a recognition that one's long-term interests are best served by obeying the rules of the game even at considerable personal cost. Though justifiable, however, such dispassionate behavior is *not* innate. It must be learned through constant instruction at home and school. It must be a way of life. The alternatives to democracy should appear unthinkable or abhorrent. Otherwise they will appear seductive, because they offer easy shortcuts to wealth and power. Sadly, democracy is not yet a way of life in Argentina.

A final group of undemocratic traits can simply be called Latin American. Politics south of the Rio Grande have been dominated by soldiers. Since World War II, military coups d'état have succeeded in nineteen of the twenty Latin American nations. (Mexico is the sole exception.) The argument runs that in Latin America the sword is mightier than the pen. Power gravitates to the rich and ruthless, who preserve their advantages through corruption and repression. Dissenters and enemies risk unpleasant fates. The rest of the people resign themselves to the way of the world, getting by as best they can without making trouble. Participation is discouraged: *no se meta*, don't get involved. In Argentina, this Latino dictum is so taken for granted that it has been reduced to *yo, soy Argentino*—me, I am Argentine. If you see something, ignore it. If you know something, forget it. If you do not, you may suffer for your meddling.

Then there is the traditional Latin emotionalism, the affection for stirring speeches. Emotionalism and authoritarianism together promote *caudillismo*, the attachment to the leader on horseback. The *caudillo* (pronounced kow-dee-zho in Buenos Aires) has charisma. He may not be fair, but he is strong. He can lead people, and they will follow. President Franco of Spain was often simply called *El Caudillo*. Argentina has had two great *caudillos:* Perón and Rosas. Provincial *caudillos* are more common. Even today they continue to dominate some regions practically as satrapies.

Caudillismo is persistent. Peronists are still trying to exploit the charisma of their dead *caudillos*, Juan and Evita. *Caudillismo* helps to explain the continuing interest in the cryptic exile, Isabel Perón. Though she has not participated in Argentine politics for a decade and refused to see Peronist leaders who traveled to her current home in Spain just to visit her, after the 1983 restoration of civilian government she remained a rallying point for those hoping to cloak their ambitions with the mantle of her authority. She was a living link to a glorious past, the only surviving Perón. There is even talk that Alfonsín may become the next Argentine *caudillo*, which is dangerous because *caudillismo* and democracy do not mix.

UNLUCKY STARS

Some theories attribute the failure of Argentine democracy to foreign enemies or bad luck. Imperialism is a popular theme. Blaming foreigners feels good, because it obviates the need for soul-searching. It is easy, because often the imperialist powers and multinational corporations adeptly play their Simon Legree roles as rapacious exploiters of the economically vulnerable. And it is partly justified. The British owned cattle, the railroads that brought them to port, the plants where the meat was packed, the refrigerated ships that carried it to market, and the banks and insurance companies that kept the whole operation running smoothly. Unscrupulous behavior worsened the image; one company tried to smuggle out records (marked as "corned beef") that were subpoenaed by the Argentine Senate. Later, North American companies bought out many British-Argentine firms, and invested directly in power generation, transport, communications, and banking.[12] Investments in such key areas naturally increased foreign influence as well as profits.

Both as candidate and president, Raúl Alfonsín generously meted out responsibility for Argentina's dire economic straits to foreign capitalist powers. In a November 1984 soccer stadium rally, he lashed out at the "interests of the North" before a crowd of more than 60,000. "At every turn we are more discriminated against. At every turn we are paid less for our products and usurious interest rates increase more. At every turn the system that indebts us is more perfected, and . . . they lend us money on the condition that we do not develop ourselves."[13]

Alfonsín had a point. For every one percent increase in the U.S. prime rate, annual interest due on the Argentine external debt increased nearly $500 million. (Fortunately for Argentina, after 1984 interest rates declined substantially.) North American bankers had eagerly promoted loans to the developing countries in the first place as a way to recycle the huge petrodollar holdings deposited by Arab oil interests in the 1970s.

The United States also competes against Argentina in grain and meat exports, while European Common Market tariff barriers exclude Argentine produce, the more so now that Britain (which brings along Australian and New Zealand beef) and Spain (Argentina's traditional European outlet) are members. The Common Market boycotted all Argentine exports during the Malvinas conflict, and trade barriers have not yet descended to prewar levels. In late 1986, Great Britain extended its fishing zone around the islands from three to 150 miles.

Multinational companies are believed to suppress Argentine potential by soaking up natural resources for their own benefit and insidiously imposing their own tastes on a susceptible public through advertising and "cultural imperialism." Young Argentines, some say, have been mesmerized by Michael Jackson and Coca-Cola to the detriment of the tango and *yerba mate* tea. How can democracy survive in a country so economically repressed and stripped of its national identity?

Unfortunately, the imperialism argument is a dead end. In the first place, it cannot explain why Argentina's national income growth rate since 1930 (0.7 percent) is lower than Mexico's (3.9 percent), Brazil's (3.0 percent), and even Colombia's (1.7 percent), unless it establishes that the others suffered a milder form of imperialism. From a practical standpoint, most anti-imperialist proposals fall short. The most straightforward is to reject foreign investment. The problem is that foreign investment remains the richest (and, in the short term, the only) source of technology and capital available to Argentines. For years Argentine policy has swung back and forth between welcoming and shunning foreign capital. Consequently, there are few new foreign investments, imperialist or otherwise, to worry about today in Argentina.

Another proposed solution urges the wealthy countries to fulfill a moral duty to compensate those countries which they have exploited along the way. However just, these calls for a New International Economic Order have always been and will continue to be largely ignored. Nor can Buenos Aires politicians make this claim with clean hands, for they have done to Argentina's interior provinces as they complain the colonial powers have done to them. A final escape from dependence would be repudiation of the foreign debt. That would force Argentina into autarky, an incalculably high price to pay for a country so dependent on its foreign exports.

On the other hand, some say there is too little foreign influence, not too much. The Argentines are proud of their ethnic heritage; more than 90 percent of the inhabitants are of European birth or extraction. Of the over six million overseas immigrants who arrived in Argentina between 1857 and 1930, 46 percent were Italian, 32 percent Spanish, and most of the rest from other European countries. Apart from a few hundred thousand Indians from the Northwest provinces of Jujuy and Salta, the population is nearly all Caucasian. Times have changed since the 1930s, when many wealthy Argentines would live several months each year in Paris, but even now thousands travel abroad regularly, spending so much money that "export tourism" has become a serious balance of payments problem.

"They are so civilized, and we are not" is the complaint. "Earn in Argentina, spend in Europe" is the response. Before the Malvinas war, one Argentine acquaintance used to make a five-week pilgrimage to London each year to take in every West End theater offering. Now the United States has become the Argentine shopper's paradise, for goods ranging from suits and compact disks to toys and personal computers. "We are so far from everywhere that you cannot expect European and North American ideas of democracy to hold sway here," said another friend.

This xenophilic school of thought sees the traditional Latin America, instability—the violence and corruption—as incurably infecting the Argentine body politic. Yet anti-nationalism is a curiously incomplete doctrine that, in a way, tells more about its adherents than about their country. If Argentina is so European, why does it matter that it is not in Europe? Buenos Aires is far from Paris, but it is the lodestone of Argentina, a modern city of over 10 million inhabitants—called *porteños*, or port people—who lead lifestyles comparable to many Europeans. There are hundreds of theaters, cultural events, galleries, and libraries. Why should democracy there depend on events an ocean away? It should not, but the belief that it should betrays a telling lack of self-confidence.

Even Argentina's natural bounty comes in for a share of the blame. No one knows the extent of Argentina's minerals, because comprehensive surveys have never been done. The livestock is so plentiful that filet mignon still costs less than one dollar per pound in the market. All that, despite underutilization of livestock and government policies that discourage production. Jokes play on this theme: "I shall add one more country to South America," said the Lord. "It shall have a natural deep-water harbor, millions of acres of fertile black soil, powerful rivers, and mineral riches."

"But how will you prevent it from becoming so rich and powerful that it will dominate its neighbors and provoke bloody wars," asked the archangel Gabriel.

"I will populate it with Argentines," the Lord replied.

The implication is that where life is too easy, people have little incentive to cooperate and to develop sophisticated systems of compromise, such as democracy. By this logic, the antithesis of Argentina is Japan: a country thriving democratically despite scarce resources. V.S. Naipul argues that from the Spanish *conquistadores*, through the Europeans who came in the nineteenth century to make their fortunes and return home, to the present, the inhabitants of Argentina have been devoted to no more nor less than rapid exploitation of the country's economic offerings. In his words, "Argentina is a land of plunder, a new land, virtually peopled in this century. It remains a land to be plundered; and its politics can be nothing but the politics of plunder."[14]

The problem reflects the historic division into two Argentinas: Buenos Aires versus the provinces. For the first seventy years of the Republic, wars were fought to decide whether Buenos Aires would be a part of or separate from the rest of Argentina. Centered in the most fertile province in the land, pathway of all commerce moving into or out of the country, Buenos Aires threatened to enrich itself on customs duties at the expense of all other regions. When the railroads were built in the late 1800s, all routes from North to South were run through a hub at Buenos Aires, reinforcing this pattern.

Though the issue theoretically was settled after a brief war in 1880 in favor of separating the city from the surrounding province (much as Washington, D.C., was carved from Virginia and Maryland), the tension continues, with two drawbacks for democracy. First, Buenos Aires' continued superiority allows it to live somewhat beyond its means, literally enjoying the fruits of the provinces' labor. Its major interest groups can all get some of what they want without making the sacrifices required in democracy. Second, the relative political weakness of the provinces perpetuates their underdevelopment. Domination by Buenos Aires, and sometimes by powerful families, together reinforce the concentration of political power in a few hands.

The Constitution calls for a federal system, balancing central and provincial powers, but it also gives the president the right to replace provincial governors on his own authority. This so-called "right of intervention," combined with a centralized tax system and other laws, has impeded the diffusion of economic and political power to the provinces. Consequently, pluralistic political institutions have seldom developed, either to counter the power of the central government, or to provide an example of a working democracy.

Far more clearly than Argentina's natural bounty, economic stagnation undermines democracy. Democracy cannot function unless election losers respect the winners—at least enough to wait until the next election to try to displace them. Where the economy is stagnant, however, politics become a zero-sum game: if your opponent gains, you lose. One cannot take more of the pie without taking some of it from someone else. In a zero-sum game, if the stakes are high enough, the temptation becomes almost irresistable to carry the political battle out to every available front—including military conspiracy.

In Argentina the stakes are high. The economy is dominated by the state, which accounts for about half of the gross domestic product (GDP). The state is dominated by the president, whose constitutional powers are extensive and whose term is supposed to last for six years. And the game for half of the last fifteen years has dipped below the zero-sum to the negative-sum: per capita income—the pie—has been shrinking.[15] Merely to avoid losing what you *already have* you must take what another already has. You lose even if your opponent merely maintains his share (and electoral winners seldom do less). In Argentina, few people lose patiently for six straight years in the hopes of winning the next elections.

The final, and clearest, antidemocratic circumstance in Argentina is history. Argentina has never known stable democracy. Until 1810, it was ruled by the Spanish crown, which bequeathed it no viable democratic institutions. Itsearly years of independence were constantly disrupted by battles between the provinces. Rosas ruled Argentina as a ruthless despot from 1829 to 1852. The Constitution of 1853 brought elections, but not respect for the winners; national hero and president, Bartolomé Mitre fielded an army, first to keep Buenos Aires outside of the new constitution, and later to try to reverse his 1874 electoral defeat.

After the federalization of Buenos Aires in 1880, Argentina entered its phase of rapid economic growth. Anarchy, civil war, and the populism of Rosas had turned free-trade liberals against popular participation in politics, at least until the ignorant masses were adequately educated.[16] The economically liberal, politically conservative oligarchs surrendered the presidential baton, but only to each other. And for all of their purported enlightenment, the oligarchs gained office through fraud or favoritism and imperiously imposed their successors. President Julio A. Roca, the "Conqueror of the Desert" who opened millions of acres for settlement by routing the Tehuelches, Araucanos, and Mapuches Indians and initiated the era of economic growth, handed the presidency over to his brother-in-law, Miguel Juárez Celman. In its early days, the Radical party eschewed participation in this incestuous electoral system in favor of three armed rebellions against the government in 1890, 1893, and 1905. Its motto was "abstention and revolution."[17]

Prospects for democracy improved in 1912, when President Roque Sáenz Peña proposed the law that granted universal male suffrage and imposed mandatory voting. His effort to co-opt the moderate and middle class Radicals and so preempt more extreme challenges to the Conservatives ultimately backfired. The Radicals abandoned the script by actually defeating the Conservatives in the very next presidential election, four years later. Though many Radical policies continued to favor conservative economic interests, the new president, Hipolito Yrigoyen, alienated conservatives by turning the machine of state into a vehicle to reward his political allies and expand the Radical popular power base. He abused the president's power to intervene in the provinces by replacing elected conservative governors with Radical intervenors. Between 1860 and 1912, there had been sixty-two provincial interventions; in the first six years of Radical government, there were twenty.[18]

Popular politics had arrived, and spilled forth uncontrollably across a political landscape barren of checks and balances. When Yrigoyen was re-elected by a widened margin (57 percent) in 1928, he took his machine politics too far, establishing a proposition that Peron was later to prove to a fare-thee-well: democratic success in Argentina does not imply democratic belief or practices. Yrigoyen undermined army professionalism, granting promotions and back-salary to officers who had been punished for participating in the abortive Radical rebellions against the constitutional authorities. That alerted all would-be conspirators that, if successful, their persistence ultimately would be rewarded.

With the Radicals' increasing popularity, the Conservatives faced the prospect of losing their majority in the Senate, leaving them defenseless against the growing Radical majority in the Chamber of Deputies. At seventy-nine, Yrigoyen had become senile and increasingly capricious. Even many Radicals, including the only other Radical president (Marcelo T. de Alvear), did not object in 1930 when the military took over center stage. It has remained there ever since.

This brief historical excursion sounds a tocsin. Those who speak of the *return* of democracy in Argentina misstep. Democracy has never truly existed there. It must be *established*, which is vastly more difficult. The task is not merely to revive a familiar or respected system, but to reverse the long Argentine historical tradition against democracy and in favor of *caudillismo*, plotting, knavery, and violence. Reformation, not restoration, is needed.

Why has democracy failed in Argentina? At heart, it has failed because it is too little wanted. Perhaps most people hope and vote for it, but they are reluctant to rely only on democratic institutions when their self-interests are at stake. Instead, they resort to more effective, better established interest groups, which themselves are largely hostile to democratic government. No rules of the game are universally respected, so Argentine politics are conducted as a free-for-all of power plays and shifting alliances, with stability the biggest loser.

Stability can exist without democracy, but democracy cannot exist without stability. Stability eludes Argentine politics because political institutions are too weak to cope with the strong interests of different social groups—the wealthy, middle class, and working class; the Church, military, and universities. The "Argentine paradox"—how a nation so economically blessed can be so politically cursed—really is no paradox. In a country without effective and respected government, the very blessings themselves (natural resources, educated population, absence of external threats) create instability, by increasing the ability of interest groups to press their claims on society. The more sophisticated and better-off the people, the more unstable the system becomes, as more groups become more ambitious and better able to express their desires.

Argentina became a praetorian state, where social groups intervened in politics directly, rather than through formal institutions. Interest groups did not accept the government as the only forum to express their interests; they accepted no ground rules. In a praetorian society, as brilliantly analyzed by Samuel P. Huntington in *Political Order in Changing Societies,* each group's nature and capabilities determine its choice of weapons: "The wealthy bribe; students riot; workers strike; mobs demonstrate; and the military coup."[19] In Argentina today, each major social group is well organized. The wealthy have several agricultural associations, the Industrial Union, and a host of other groups. Students have played a major role through university politics (which makes national news), the youth branches of the major parties (especially the Young Peronists), and, unfortunately, terrorism. The workers are represented by the unions, in close cooperation with the Peronist party. The armed forces and Catholic Church are both enormously powerful.

These interests crowd out democracy. Though venerable and highly institutionalized, they are rarely democratic in form or objectives. The three most powerful interests—organized labor, the Church, and the military—are especially hierarchical and authoritarian. They have flourished in the vacuum of central political authority. While they can tolerate a strong *central* government that they may be able to control, a strong *democratic* government represents a mortal threat. True, voters are also workers, soldiers, and Catholics. But these institutions derive their power by monopolizing the representation of their constituents. The suffrage dilutes their political power.

Democracy's natural constituents are those unrepresented by special interest groups. These politically dispossessed can do little good for democracy precisely because they are poorly represented, poorly educated, and just plain poor. Parties that seldom govern lack incentives to behave as responsible oppositions which develop sound policy alternatives. (The Peronist party is different since it is linked to the powerful labor unions.) Idle legislatures atrophy; when Congress reopened in 1983 after a seven year hiatus it behaved chaotically and sometimes irresponsibly. Democratic institutions have just not been where the action is; the best people do not go there.

A vicious cycle results. Democratic institutions are weakened by their exclusion from power. When they are given the opportunity to govern, their weakness leads to silly policy and reckless behavior which, in turn, invites the next coup to displace them. With time, the democratic institutions grow weaker and weaker, their operation worse and worse, their replacement easier and easier. The cycle of disuse and misuse of power deepens.

Democracy cannot survive these circumstances. The politics of fragmentation sets in and cannot easily be dislodged. Neither the unions, the military, nor the Church wishes to yield any of its authority to the runt democratic institutions, their incompetent competitors. This would not be so bad, except that over the years the dominant interests have carved out ever-broadening roles for themselves. The unions claim guardianship of "social justice," the military of "the national interest," and the Church of "the soul"—that just about covers the lot.

Individual attitudes have evolved along the same lines. People may desire democracy, but most depend on interest groups. Though happy to vote for democracy when there happens to be an election, in the crunch they are powerfully tempted to side with the organizations that best promote their material interests. Buenos Aires evokes John le Carré's description of *A Small Town in Germany*: ". . . Bonn may be a democracy, but it's *frightfully* short of democrats."

Democracy never had a chance in Argentina. Politicians did not use the pre-1930 era of stability to incorporate emerging social groups into the constitutional system. The middle class had their moment but later were excluded from government by electoral fraud. The workers were suppressed until Perón reorganized them and won their support for his antidemocratic regime. Military coups punctuated the failure of civilian politics and government. While constitutional institutions stagnated, special interest groups proliferated and strengthened, winning loyal clienteles. Today's democratic government must carve out its niche among these competing institutions if it is to survive. It is an uphill battle.

The stereotypes described in this chapter, like all stereotypes, are crude and exaggerated and, like all stereotypes, are based in truth. No group has been blameless. No one is willing to sacrifice anything for a long-term that has never existed in Argentine politics. Take what is offered today because tomorrow's government may favor your enemy. Adam Smith's rational actor has run amok.[20]

Democracy requires a willingness to accept political defeat and wait for the next elections to recoup one's losses. In Argentina, however, impatience precludes compromise while intransigence destroys patience. Thus failure becomes self-perpetuating. Exit long-term perspective and, with it, investment and economic growth. Enter the hardball politics of the zero-sum game. The six-year presidential term is too long to wait for the loser's next turn at bat.

The myopia is pervasive. One cool spring evening in late 1984 I walked home with a friend. He mentioned that he expected Oscar Alende's Intransigent party to do well in the November 1985 congressional elections. "But Alende is seventy-six and lacks potential successors," I said. "What kind of future can his party have?" "Don't ask me," my friend replied. "Remember I am an Argentine. I never think beyond next year."

Only a sea change in attitudes will bring a long-term perspective to Argentina. People like Alfonsín, but speculation, strikes, violence, tax evasion, and other vices continue. The question is whether Alfonsín is charismatic and shrewd enough to break the cycle of exploitation and frustration, to slip a wedge of patience between ambition and action. Can he succeed as a *caudillo*? Was the system laid so low by the triple blow of the dirty war, the Malvinas debacle, and the debt crisis to allow a fresh start? Only time will tell.

CHAPTER 2

The Descent

At night, after taps, they knocked doors down with their rifle butts, hauled suspects out of their beds, and took them off on trips from which there was no return. The search for and extermination of the hoodlums, murderers, arsonists, and rebels of Decree No. 4 was still going on, but the military denied it even to the relatives of the victims who crowded the commandants' offices in search of news. "You must have been dreaming," the officers insisted. "Nothing has happened in Macondo, nothing has ever happened, and nothing ever will happen. This is a happy town." In that way they were finally able to wipe out the union leaders.

—GABRIEL GARCÍA MÁRQUEZ
One Hundred Years of Solitude

At last the old man was coming home to stay. Eighteen years earlier, President Juan Domingo Perón had boarded a small gunboat and ascended the muddy Paraguay River in quest of political asylum. After sojourns in Nicaragua, Panama, Venezuela, and the Dominican Republic, he had settled for a dozen years in Spain. Throughout his long exile, Perón's towering absence dominated Argentine politics. Perón's candidates won when permitted to run. Without his support, no other party could obtain a popular majority.

Now, at 2:10 P.M. on 20 June 1973, the chartered jet carrying the seventy-eight year-old ex-president approached Ezeiza International Airport. Perón was accompanied by his wife, María Estela Martínez de Perón, more popularly known as "Isabel," the name she had used as a cabaret dancer in Panama, where she had caught Perón's eye. The president of the republic, Dr. Héctor J. Cámpora, sat nearby. Three months earlier he had gained office as a surrogate for Perón (who had been barred from running himself) on the slogan, "Cámpora to Government, Perón to Power." The Peronist coalition garnered 49 percent of the popular vote, more than doubling the tally of its nearest competitor, longtime Radical leader, Ricardo Balbín.[1]

21

Perón's popularity was at a peak. In his absence, civilians and generals had all taken turns at the helm. All had failed. Now Argentina's problems seemed graver than ever. Wearied and sullied by seven years in government, by 1973 the military was ready to return to the barracks. To cap it all, terrorist organizations had sprung up and initiated a campaign of murders, kidnapings, and armed robberies.

No one but Perón appeared able to bring the situation under control. For one thing, many of the terrorists were his followers. For another, the passing years had shown that no one else had done much better and that Peronism remained the dominant popular force in Argentine politics. Nostalgia softened memories of his first two presidencies (1946–55), which appeared to many as a golden era, when new factories were built, and Evita lived and died for the betterment of the working class. The Peronist youth movement led the campaign to bring back Perón. Even the children of many staunch anti-Peronists became supporters of the former president.

Around the grandstand nailed together near the Ezeiza airport to accommodate the cabinet ministers, congressmen, and governors present, hundreds of thousands of young partisans had been gathering since the night before to greet Perón's return. They blocked the highway for miles. Huge banners bore aloft terrorist insignia—the Revolutionary Armed Forces, the People's Revolutionary Army, and the Montoneros. Official security arrangements were entrusted to members of the Peronist right, viscerally hostile to the young leftists gathered to claim Perón as their own. Hours before the scheduled landing, gunfire burst forth. Amidst the spreading panic youths appeared in combat positions firing rifles and pistols. Bodies fell from trees. Gruesome lynchings and mayhem were reported. To this day the details remain murky, but estimates of the toll range up to over 200 dead and 370 wounded.[2] To avoid this grisly scene, the presidential craft banked and touched down at the landing strip of the Seventh Air Brigade in Morón, eighteen kilometers northwest of Ezeiza. The day's events did not bode well for the three-week old democratic government.

CROSSING THE RUBICON

The chaos of 1973 was the culmination of more than forty years of decline, initiated by General Uriburu's 1930 coup.[3] Adopting fascism as the latest European vogue, Uriburu wanted to convert Argentina into a corporativist state —one that eschewed democratic institutions in favor of a strongman who would govern in consultation with leaders of the most powerful interest groups. These corporate sectors (in the non-business sense) included the military, the Church, industrialists, and rural interests. Uriburu, however, lacked the political support to implement his scheme, and was forced to call for elections in 1931. The winner was another general and Uriburu's chief rival, Agustín P. Justo. The disappointed Uriburu died two months after Justo's inauguration.

The portly, jovial-looking President Justo presided over a coalition of Conservatives and anti-Yrigoyen Radicals. Justo was the only president since 1930 besides Perón to serve out a full six-year term (both were military officers when elected). Though Justo feigned respect for the republican form of government despised by Uriburu, in practice he abused that system by guaranteeing the election of his supporters through wholesale fraud and corruption. The 1930s became known as the "Infamous Decade" or, euphemistically, the era of "Patriotic Fraud."

Justo's hand-picked successor, Roberto M. Ortiz, surprised and dismayed his backers by trying to clean up the electoral system. But illness and blindness cut short his reforms and left the reins of government in the hands of Vice President Ramón Castillo, who quickly revived governmental fraud. The rot, though, by now had compromised the government's authority. So when Castillo, like Justo before him, sought to put *his* hand-picked successor in the Casa Rosada, the army preempted the planned elections and threw him out of office.

The 1943 coup led to the ascendance of a secret officers' lodge known as the G.O.U., whose origins were so obscure that historians have disputed even the meaning of the acronym.[4] (Group of United Officers is the prevailing interpretation.) A leading figure of the fascist, pro-Axis G.O.U. was Colonel Juan Domingo Perón. Perón converted his post in the military government as secretary of labor and welfare into a power base, through which he secured control over the unions and support of the workers. He instituted collective bargaining, secured large wage increases for unions that were loyal to him, and harried uncooperative unions. A change in government, provoked by Argentina's eleventh-hour (January 1945) declaration of war against Germany, brought Perón the posts of war minister and vice president.

Meanwhile, political opposition to the ambitious colonel mounted within the army, aggravated by Perón's flagrant affair with a second-rate and (in military eyes) impudent actress, Eva Duarte. The crisis came with the appointment of one of Eva's friends over the favored army candidate to a high post in the interior ministry.[5] A power struggle apparently ended on 12 October 1945 with Perón's resignation from all posts, arrest, and confinement on the island Martín García, in the Rio de la Plata.

Perón, however, outmatched his enemies in cunning and drive. First, Perón's friends managed to get him back into Buenos Aires on the pretext that the colonel needed hospital treatment there. (No doctor's note was requested or provided.) Then, on 17 October 1945 his supporters arranged an enormous rally in the Plaza de Mayo and chanted for Perón's release. For hours Perón allowed the crowd to whip itself into a frenzy. When finally he emerged on the balcony of the Casa Rosada and spoke to his countrymen, *el pueblo argentino*, it was clear that he had carried the day.

Perón's opponents wilted before this massive show of popular support. Perón was released, and easily went on to win the presidential elections of February 1946. Ham-handed U.S. "diplomacy" backfired in Perón's favor; two weeks before the election the State Department released the "Blue Book," a report supervised by the recent ambassador to Argentina, Spruille Braden, which tried to discredit Perón by publishing the sins and Nazi tendencies of the 1943–46 military government. Perón cannily picked up the gauntlet of U.S. interference in internal Argentine affairs and made political hay on a new nationalistic slogan: Braden or Perón. Perón won 56 percent of the popular vote.

This first presidency was the Golden Age of Perónism. With gold and hard currency reserves of $1.6 billion ($20 billion in current terms), Perón pursued his twin goals of economic independence and social justice. He bought out the British-owned national railroads, an effective but expensive way to promote the image of independence from the imperialists. He increased the salaried workers' share of national income from 35 to 50 percent. Politically, he gagged dissent and promulgated constitutional reforms that ratified worker rights and allowed the president to succeed himself.

Not surprisingly, Perón was the first beneficiary of the new constitutional arrangement. In 1951, he won a second term with 62.4 percent of the vote, compared to the Radicals' 31.8 percent. Perón's monopoly over access to national communications media made the elections less fair than those of 1945, but probably did not alter the fundamental result.

Perón's second term started badly and ended worse. In the inaugural motorcade of 4 June 1952, Eva Perón made her last public appearance—a wasted, cancer-ridden figure, pathetically propped up by a brace under her fur coat as she stood alongside Perón in an open car. She died in July. The economy had begun to go sour during the first term, when Argentine reserves had run out, but 1952 brought severe recession. Workers were reduced to eating unpalatable black bread. Many recent worker gains were lost. Perón himself cut a less impressive figure; he established a sports camp for teenaged girls on the grounds of the presidential residence at Olivos. The president would disport himself for hours in this nubile atmosphere, and in 1953 welcomed one of his charges, thirteen-year-old Nelly Rivas, as his live-in companion. Rumors of orgies quickly fanned the capital. All this deeply offended Argentina's Catholic sensibilities. To top it off, Perón in late 1954 launched a prolonged attack on the Catholic Church.

Finally, the armed forces moved. A failed navy uprising of 16 June 1955 is historically notable as the only aerial bombing of Buenos Aires in history. Some navy pilots raked the crowded Plaza de Mayo with machine-gun bursts while others dropped their loads over fleeing pedestrians. Perón was tipped off and left the Casa Rosada in time, but 355 less fortunate civilians lay dead after the assault.[6] The day's events showed a criminal disregard for innocent life that would tragically resurface twenty years later.

A combined army-navy rebellion that September succeeded in ending Perón's presidency and sending the *caudillo* off into exile. The "Liberating Revolution," as it called itself, was led by General Eduardo Lonardi. The new president's motto, "neither victors nor vanquished," signified his determination to reincorporate the Peronist masses into the political mainstream. Lonardi tried to wean moderate, younger union leaders away from Perón and to convince them to cooperate with the new government.

This moderate approach aggravated the hard-line anti-Peronists, who shoved Lonardi aside after two months. The new president, General Pedro Aramburu, dissolved the Peronist Party, suppressed the unions, limited wage increases, and banned the public mention of Perón's name. The perfectly preserved body of Eva Perón, feared as a potential rallying point for the opposition, was stolen and secretly buried in an Italian cemetery, where it remained for fifteen years. One fateful action of "The Revenge," as Peronists called the Liberating Revolution, would come back to haunt Aramburu. In June 1956 General José Valle led an attempted coup agains the government. He and twenty-six others were quickly executed by firing squad.

Though harsh, the Liberating Revolution had its principles. One was that the military should remain in government only long enough to establish the stability required for the return to constitutional government. Elections were called for 1958. The leading candidate, Popular Radical Ricardo Balbín, enjoyed the support of the military government. His rival and former associate, Arturo Frondizi, led the Intransigent Radicals. The Popular Radicals had outpolled the Intransigents in a 1957 poll on constitutional reforms, but the blank ballots voted by the Peronists outnumbered even Balbín's faction. Frondizi secretly struck a deal with the exiled Perón, agreeing to legalize Peronism if elected.[7] Perón instructed his faithful to vote for Frondizi, and the Intransigent Radical easily defeated Balbín.

Frondizi was a shrewd pragmatist. His political watchword was "developmentalism" (desarrollismo), an economic doctrine that gives the state a leading role in the development of basic industries, which in turn will spur the further industrialization and modernization of the economy.[8] Frondizi shocked friends and foes alike when he broke his campaign promise to reserve oil for strictly national development, by inviting foreign oil companies to contract for production of Argentine oil. This action enraged nationalists (both Peronists and Popular Radicals), but it plugged the oil import drain on Argentine foreign currency reserves by tripling Argentine oil production in five years.

From the moment Peronist votes assured Frondizi's election, the military mistrusted him.[9] Generals launched dozens of plots and demands against the president, who managed to hang on to office in a tightrope act of consummate political skill. Eventually Frondizi's luck ran out. He angered many generals by secretly meeting with the Argentine-turned-Cuban-revolutionary, Che Guevara, and in resisting U.S. pressure to break relations with Cuba in February 1962. In March, the first elections in which Peronists were allowed to participate since 1955 provided the last straw. Frondizi had hoped to prove that Peronism was a spent political force, but the indomitable Peronists won eleven out of eighteen gubernatorial races, including the all-important Buenos Aires province. Frondizi neutralized the elections by intervening several provinces, and tried once more to restore his balance over the political abyss, but to no avail. On 29 March the military forced him to resign and confined him on Martín García, where Yrigoyen and Perón had gone before.

The fall of Frondizi initiated a period of internecine struggle within the army. The azules (blues) were "legalists," who believed that the military should be subordinated to constitutional authority. The rival colorados (reds) were hard-line "gorillas"—believers in the obliteration of Peronism—prepared to displace the Constitution and civilian government for as long as necessary to achieve their aim. The colorados had led the 1962 coup against the Intransigent Radical, Arturo Frondizi, and dominated the civilian government of his provisional successor, former senate president José María Guido. By September 1963 they were preparing to install a general in the Casa Rosada.

From his post as commander of the Campo de Mayo garrison on the outskirts of Buenos Aires the azul leader, General Juan Carlos Onganía, defended the civilian government. Tanks advanced on the capital and, in a brief confrontation, the azules defeated the colorados. Ten months later, Arturo Illia, a little known country doctor from Córdoba province, with a mere quarter of the popular vote led the Popular Radicals to electoral victory over a divided opposition. The Intransigent Radicals had had their chance with Frondizi. Now the Popular Radicals would have theirs with Illia.

In Argentina, the best way to maintain popularity is to stay out of government. It is far easier to score points either by criticizing the incumbent's shortcomings or simply by avoiding the inevitable taint governments suffer when they try to manage a society polarized into powerful competing interests. The Argentines are notoriously impatient, even amnesiac, when it comes to politics. Government popularity quickly erodes, and Illia accelerated the decline by his forthright but politically foolish refusal to bargain with other political forces. After all, he had ascended to the presidency with only a narrow plurality. His party had no congressional majority. But in fulfilling the Radical tradition of intransigence—the noble but sanctimonious refusal to compromise on principles, "to break but not bend"—Illia hastened his own demise.

One of the many erstwhile supporters he alienated was General Onganía, who had been promoted to the post of army commander-in-chief. Over Onganía's objections, Illia had appointed an active service general, junior to the army commander, to be secretary of war. This double insult provoked Onganía's retirement which, not so incidentally, liberated him from the professional soldier's commitment to uphold the constitutional government. So it came to pass that the savior of constitutional government in 1963 became the destroyer of constitutional government in 1966, in a military coup that aimed not to restore civilian rule as soon as possible but to stay as long as necessary to reshape the political order.

GREAT EXPECTATIONS

Coups in Argentina have always emerged from a murky amalgam of dissatisfaction and conspiracy, but the 28 June 1966 overthrow of President Arturo Illia is the least explicable of all. Illia was neither engaged in the senile abuse of power, like Yrigoyen, nor intent on subjugating Argentina to his personality, like Perón. He was not poised to impose a successor by electoral fraud, like Castillo in 1943, nor had his party just been defeated by the Peronists, like Frondizi's in 1962. Chaos and terror did not grip the country, as in 1976. Economic growth averaged 9.7 percent per year in 1964 and 1965. Yes, there were problems: an annual inflation rate of over 20 percent (a rate that would later appear rather quaint) and an organized labor "battle plan" of strikes and factory occupations. But here was no subversion, no rampant corruption, no perilous threat to the fatherland or its constitutional order. The nation's problems were not those that beg for military solutions at the sacrifice of constitutional norms. For these reasons the military takeover of 1966 is sometimes called the frivolous coup.

Despite its lightweight justification, basically the "drift and inefficiency" of the Illia administration, the 1966 coup was not resisted. To the contrary, it was popular. The people did not protest or take to the streets; they fondly remembered Onganía as the hero of the battle between the *azules* and the *colorados*. The officer corps, bitterly divided in that conflict, now closed ranks behind Onganía. Organized labor had actively opposed Illia from the start and expected to participate in the new military government. Catholic lay organizations also rallied around Onganía and supplied many high officials early in the general's administration.

Freshly installed in the Casa Rosada, President Onganía seemed to embody ideal leadership qualities: integrity, rectitude, and strength. Business, Catholic, and union leaders attended his inauguration, showing significant consensus among the powerful. The new revolutionary junta called itself the "Argentine Revolution," in the ill-fated optimistic vein of other 1960s' modernization slogans, such as British Prime Minister Harold Wilson's "White Heat of Technology" and the Shah of Iran's "White Revolution." Onganía admired the modern approach to governing through technocracies adopted by Franco and de Gaulle.

In seizing power, the junta declared its intention to "reestablish an authentic representative democracy in which order reigns within law, justice, and the interest of the commonwealth." To drive home its commitment to authentic democracy, the junta then dissolved the Congress, provincial legislatures, and all political parties, ousted all provincial governments, and replaced the entire Supreme Court.

The junta justified this destroy-democracy-in-order-to-save-it approach in a vague "Message to the People," which complained of the lack of "authentic authority," a "scene of anarchy," inflation, and a lamentable image abroad.[10] That is a pretty weak broth to impel a revolution. Most obscure and ominous was the charge of "vitiated electoralism," an implicit reference to Illia's low percentage victory and the continuing prospects of a Peronist resurgence. "Vitiated electoralism" sounds like what one might more honestly call "electoral defeat." All in all, stripped of its high-flown rhetoric, the "Argentine Revolution" comes across as the naked power grab it was.

Displaying a hubris that would be laughable were it not so tragically ironic, the junta huffed out its "fundamental objective":

Today, as in all the decisive steps of our history, the Armed Forces, interpreting the highest common interest, assumes the irrenounceable responsibility to safeguard the national union and promote its general welfare, incorporating in the country the modern elements of culture, science, and technology, which will work a substantial transformation, situating it in its rightful place based on the intelligence and human valor of its inhabitants and the riches that Providence placed in its territory.[11]

The supposed objectives of the revolution were scarcely more enlightening than the "Message to the People," comprising a laundry list of platitudes ranging from "consolidate spiritual and moral values" to "eliminate the profound causes of its present economic stagnation."[12] Many people contentedly awaited improvements under Onganía's strong and vital leadership.

Economically, Onganía achieved some positive results. The inflation rate fell from 32 percent annually in 1966 to 7.6 percent in 1969, in which year GDP grew 6.8 percent in real terms. An alliance with important CGT leaders contributed to relative tranquility on the labor front, at least for the first couple of years. Foreign investment capital flowed in.[13]

Politically, Onganía imposed a harsh regime. Apart from abolishing all democratic institutions, the most draconian of all was the intervention in the universities, feared to be a breeding ground for subversion. Student resistance in the University of Buenos Aires was violently put down by police in "the night of the long sticks." Professors were barred from making "political declarations," and those thought to be subversive were physically ejected from their classrooms. A new law barred students from all political activities, discarded the traditional tripartite (student-faculty-alumni) decisionmaking in universities, and strengthened the powers of the university rector and deans.[14] Of course, these measures served to radicalize student politics rather than to neutralize them, and contributed directly to the bloody chapter of the 1970s' subversion and suppression.

With time, Onganía's sterling virtues began to tarnish; rectitude and strength came to appear as rigidity and despotism. He favored the fascist ideal of the corporativist state, where policy would emerge from direct negotiations between the president and leaders of the major interest groups—the Church, labor leaders, the armed forces, businessmen, and *estancieros*. Even these privileged groups, however, gradually became exasperated with Onganía, who was as impervious to compromise as Illia had been.

The crisis came in 1969. As in Europe and America, in Argentina the student movements of the late 1960s fundamentally challenged the political status quo. In May, students and workers joined together for a major protest in Argentina's third city, the provincial capital of Córdoba. Police and soldiers eventually moved in to stop the rioting, and when the smoke cleared fourteen people lay dead in the streets. The *cordobazo* (Argentina watersheds often became -*azos*) began Onganía's end. Violence increased. Onganía's principal union interlocutor, metalworker leader Augusto Vandor, was assassinated, presumably for collaborating with the military regime. Former president Arturo Frondizi had supported the 1966 coup. (After all, Illia's Popular Radicals were the Intransigent Radicals' archenemies and had plotted with the military to disrupt *his* presidency.) Now Frondizi declared that the Argentine Revolution had failed.

The military commanders tried to convince Onganía to call elections, but the embattled president refused, saying that the Argentine Revolution would continue several more years. A few days later he relented, not to the extent of permitting elections, but at least agreeing to discuss political solutions with political leaders. His arrogance and detachment from reality unabated, Onganía delivered a document containing 163 conditions to negotiation. He did not understand that his day to issue demands had passed. Three days later, on 8 June 1970, Onganía was overthrown by his own military commanders, led by the army commander General Alejandro Agustín Lanusse.

Thus commenced a three-year political exit for the military. When Onganía's replacement, General Roberto Marcelo Levingston, sought to prolong military rule, he too was ejected by Lanusse, who took over the presidential baton in March 1971. Lanusse initiated discussions with Perón in Madrid, intending to allow the exiled leader to return to Argentina and politics. He publicly stated that Perón could return at any moment and lent a hand by dismissing over two dozen lawsuits pending against the former president.

Perón's political capital was appreciating, and he knew it. He believed that soon the government would fall into his hands like a ripe fruit. He felt sure enough of his position that he refused to cooperate with Lanusse's plan for a Grand National Accord. Meanwhile, the terror increased, much of it authored by radical Peronists. Leading terrorist organizations included the Trotskyite Revolutionary Army of the People (ERP), the Revolutionary Armed Forces (FAR), and the Peronist Armed Forces (FAP). The principal Peronist terrorist group was the Montoneros, who took their name from the roughhewn cavalry units from the mountainous provinces who fought against the domination of Buenos Aires in the nineteenth century.[15]

Though other terrorist actions had gone before, the Montoneros came to the fore through the kidnaping and execution of a former president, retired General Pedro Aramburu. Aramburu had commanded the "Liberating Revolution" that overthrew Perón in 1955 and was particularly loathed for the executions following the Valle rebellion of 1956. At the time of his kidnaping, moreover, he was involved in discussions to replace President Onganía. These negotiations threatened to bring a smooth transition from Onganía to moderate rule, a prospect which was anathema to young revolutionaries who saw greater opportunity for their cause in the continuation of Onganía's authoritarianism.

Dressed as soldiers, two young Montoneros were admitted to Aramburu's apartment by Mrs. Aramburu, who served the young visitors coffee. After she withdrew, they forced her husband to leave with them. In hiding, the Montoneros "tried" and "convicted" Aramburu on a host of charges: responsibility for the Valle executions and other repressive actions, publicly discrediting Juan and Eva Perón, delivering the national patrimony to foreign interests, and aiding the oligarchy's revenge against Christian justice. Denying Aramburu's last request for a priest to deliver the final sacraments, Montonero leader Mario Firmenich and his accomplices marched the general down to the basement of their hideaway, and dispatched him with bullets to the heart and brain.

Perón wrote to his "dear compañeros" to express his "full agreement and praise" for all their actions, condoning Aramburu's killing as "an action desired by all Peronists."[16]

During the next three years, over fifty people were murdered by revolutionary organizations. The terrorists also conducted operations to "recover" weapons and to raise money through robberies and kidnapings. They robbed Aramburu's grave, holding the corpse of their most prominent victim as hostage until the remains of Eva Perón were returned. (This corpse for a corpse scheme was ghoulishly elegant. It had been Aramburu who, in 1956, had ordered the sequestration of Evita's body.)

Physically and politically frightened, leading politicians did not openly repudiate the terrorists during Lanusse's government. But their timidity was soon dwarfed by an enormous wrong that ushered in Peronism's 1973 return; in his first official act as president, Perón's stand-in Héctor Cámpora proposed and the Congress in two days approved an amnesty for all acts "perpetrated for political, social, labor- or student-related motives."[17] Under mob pressure, jailers had already released some 370 convicted terrorists the very night of Cámpora's inauguration. Many of the released prisoners had committed such political acts as murder and kidnaping, and soon were at it again. Since terrorists often killed soldiers and policemen, one can understand, if not condone, the reluctance of many officers to continue to turn over suspected terrorists to the craven civilian authorities who had betrayed them. Next time the security forces would finish the job; an amnesty would not help a suspected terrorist who had disappeared.

PERÓN'S FINAL DAYS

After the bloody events surrounding Perón's return to Argentina in June 1973, Cámpora's days were numbered. Perón no longer needed a surrogate, so soon Cámpora was unceremoniously forced to resign. New elections were called for September 1973. For a running mate, Perón chose his utterly unqualified wife.[18] Strangely, few protested this grotesque insult to the country. The issue was of some importance, as Perón's seventy-eight years suggested and Isabel's disastrous succession subsequently confirmed. But only the rapturous presence of Perón mattered, and he walked away with 62 percent of the popular vote. He had nine months left to live.

Things got off to a rocky start because the Peronist movement itself was deeply divided. Students and unionists both viewed Perón with admiration, but each other with loathing. The old-time, conservative labor leaders despised the young, socialist radicals, who felt that their vanguard actions had paved the way for Perón's triumphant return. Had Perón not praised and encouraged them from his exile in Madrid? Was he not the First Worker of Argentina, the hero and protector of the working class? So thought the Third World Priests, the FAP and the FAR. Montonero manifestos bore the legend "Evita Montonera."

These groups were in for a surprise. Perón had been happy to use them to unsettle the military regime and facilitate his return to power, but he was unwilling to give them a significant role in his government. Instead, he surrounded himself with traditional Peronist politicians and union leaders of the political right. Terrorist attacks continued, but now they were on Perón's watch, an insult to this authority. This he would not tolerate.

May Day of 1974 opened the breach. The Plaza de Mayo filled with thousands who came to hear the president commemorate the Worker's Day of National Unity. The Montoneros came, too, to air their grievances with the First Worker. When he began to speak, they began to shout, accusing Perón of filling his government with right-wingers, damning the "syndicalist bureaucracy" of the old-guard unionists. "*Si Evita viviera, sería montonera.* If Evita were alive she would be a Montonera." Perhaps. But Perón had had enough. He called them "shouting idiots," scorning these "beardless ones who pretend to have greater merits than those who have struggled for twenty years." He promised to liberate the country not only from imperialism, "but also from these infiltrators who work from within, and who treacherously are more dangerous than those who work from abroad, apart from which the majority of them are mercenaries in the service of foreign money."[19] The Montoneros retreated from the Plaza, reverted from overt to underground operations, and stepped up the pace of their deadly assaults.

When Perón died two months later, Isabel ascended to the presidency. Her administration was a fiasco. Important documents sent to her for signature simply disappeared. Ministers held their portfolios on average for about four months each. Her principal advisor and perhaps the most powerful man in the country was José López Rega, minister of social welfare. An ex-police corporal who initially served as valet to the Peróns, López Rega became a Rasputin-like advisor to both Juan and Isabel Perón. He wrote books on witchcraft, which he practiced. The Warlock, as he was known, allegedly had Isabel Perón lie on Evita's coffin while he implored the spirits to transfer the *caudilla* essence from the dead to the living.[20]

López Rega was also a member of Italy's infamous Propaganda-2, the fascist lodge whose members included generals and ministers; the revelation of this secret lodge in 1981 brought down the Fanfani government and led to the $790 million collapse of the Banco Ambrosiano. Through López Rega's good offices, the leader of the P-2, Licio Gelli, received a medal and the blue-and-white Argentine sash from President Perón. López Rega himself reportedly directed the infamous Triple A (Argentine Anticommunist Action), a right wing death squad that from 1973 on took matters into its own hands, and whose victims included a priest, the brother of ex-president Frondizi, and a four-month old boy. Sometimes corpses would bear placards, reading "I was a Montonero."

During the days of Isabel, the leftist terrorists reached their peak. From knocking over restaurants and jewelry stores they had graduated to far more sophisticated operations, seizing prominent businessmen and freeing them for enormous ransoms. Biggest of all was the Born brothers kidnaping. Bunge and Born, which the brothers control, is a grain-exporting multinational and one of Argentina's largest companies. At 7:30 A.M. one bright September morning in 1974, in an affluent section of suburban Buenos Aires, more than a dozen Montonero men and women used two autos and two pickup trucks with clocklike precision to cut off the car carrying Juan and Jorge Born from their bodyguards' vehicle. They seized the two brothers and murdered their chauffeur and the general manager of one of their companies. The Montoneros reportedly netted a ransom of $60 million in the operation.

Killings continued. Labor leaders, businessmen, a former minister, a senator, two successive chiefs of the Federal Police of Buenos Aires, an army corps commander, an American consul, and a host of other military officers of all ranks, were but some of the more notorious among the 1,358 terrorist murder victims in the three years following the return to civilian rule.[21] The terrorists adopted military ranks and sometimes operated in uniform. They attacked police stations and army regiments.

Unlike the Montoneros, the Revolutionary Army of the People (ERP) was Trotskyite, not Peronist. In an effort to win the countryside, the ERP sought to "liberate" Tucumán, the poor, densely populated sugar-growing province in the northwest of Argentina. The ERP recruited guerillas, exacted tribute from "the masses," and briefly took over a few villages. President Isabel Perón declared a national state of siege in November 1974. The next February, with full ministerial concurrence, she signed the fateful "Operation Independence" decree, which authorized the army to "neutralize and/or annihilate the action" of the subversive elements operating in Tucumán.[22] Seven months later, a second decree extended the annihilation mandate throughout the whole national territory. Whether "to annihilate" authorized the widespread torture, killing, and "disappearing" of subversives continues to be debated. During their 1985 trial, the ex-military junta members seized upon these decrees to justify such methods to suppress subversion, much as the U.S. Administration seized upon the Gulf of Tonkin resolution passed by the U.S. Congress to justify the escalation of American involvement in Vietnam twenty years earlier.

By late 1975, the tide had turned against the terrorists. More right-wing death squads cropped up and took their toll. On the military front, two major defeats mark a watershed. On 6 October 1975 the Montoneros unsuccessfully attacked a garrison and an airport in the frontier province of Formosa, leaving twenty-six dead behind as they fled in a hijacked Boeing 737. On 23 December some 200 members of the ERP attacked the 601st Army Battalion barracks and arsenal at Monte Chingolo, south of Buenos Aires. Nine defenders were killed, but more than 100 attackers perished. Monte Chingolo was the last major military operation mounted by Argentine terrorists, though killings, bombings, and kidnapings continued.

Meanwhile, the economy spun out of control. Perón had pursued a middle-of-the-road stabilization program, based on a "social pact" among economic sectors. His death released pent-up demands, and under Isabel Perón government economic policy shifted to the extreme right. The unions rebelled, nearly brought down the government, and won enormous wage increases that set off an inflationary spiral. From March 1975 to March 1976 the value of the peso against the dollar plummeted more than tenfold, and prices rose 731 percent. The price mechanism became "the principal battleground for the distribution of income."[23] By March 1976 Argentina was on the verge of international default, its reserves whittled down to a mere $2 million.

THE PROCESS TO PERDITION

It is now convenient to forget how enthusiastically the people welcomed the military when it took over in March 1976. Official ineptitude, an insidious terrorism from both right and left, and rampant inflation left the government of Isabel Perón with few friends. Some political party leaders, including longtime Radical Ricardo Balbín, half-heartedly entered last minute negotiations to try to form a multiparty coalition that could save civilian rule. But it was too late. Order had to be restored; the military seemed the natural candidate for the job. The faded scruples against military intervention in civilian politics seemed trivial in that dire hour. The coup brought a collective sigh of relief, and was supported by such notable civilians as former president Arturo Frondizi and newspaper editor Jacobo Timerman.

The junta was well prepared. It had drawn up lists of people to appoint and people to eliminate. Eighteen decrees were issued in the first week; forty laws in the first month. By now the procedure had become routine. The Congress was dissolved, supreme court justices dismissed, provincial governments intervened, and political parties banned. To deal with the unions, the junta appointed intervenors, froze bank accounts, and prohibited strikes.

The framework for these changes appeared in the "Act Fixing the Purpose and Basic Objectives for the Process of National Reorganization" (hence this military government became known as "the Process").[24] A self-righteous document phrased in typically prolix militarese, the act called for the restoration of essential values, "emphasizing the sense of morality, suitability and efficiency, indispensable to rebuild and promote the economic development of national life, based on the equilibrium and responsible participation of the different sectors, with the aim to assure the future installation of a republican, representative, and federal democracy, adequate for the realities and requirements of a solution and progress for the Argentine people." The act aimed to "eradicate subversion," as well as to promote "Christian morality" and "the full operation of legal and social order."

It certainly eradicated subversion. Major terrorist attacks continued into 1979, punctuated by one explosion in the defense ministry and another in the home of the naval chief of staff, Admiral Armando Lambruschini (later convicted for human rights abuses), that wounded ten and killed three, including the admiral's fifteen year-old daughter, Paula. But the security forces and paramilitary death squads wrested the initiative. They adopted their adversary's tactics, organizing themselves into autonomous cells. One retired general told me "the only way to defeat the terrorism was to retaliate with an even fiercer terrorism." This was the time of the infamous Ford Falcons, symbol of midnight kidnapings. Ransom no longer was the motive. Bodies would show up at a morgue, or on the beach in Uruguay, or not at all. A new word—*desaparecidos*, the disappeared ones—was coined to describe the thousands of victims who never reappeared, dead or alive.

In one of his first official acts President Alfonsín ordered a full investigation of the *desapericidos*. In September 1984 the National Commission on the Disappearance of Persons, chaired by writer Ernesto Sábato, delivered its final report.[25] The commission found a recurrent pattern throughout the width and breadth of Argentina in the conduct of the so-called "struggle against subversion." Most commonly, an armed gang would kidnap the suspect at night in his or her home, usually in the presence of family. The kidnap victim would be hooded and taken to one of the 340 clandestine detention centers discovered by the commission. Then the torture began. Physical methods included electric shocks to the genitalia, beating, flaying the soles of the feet with a razor, hanging the trussed victim from a beam, and more. Psychological torture included mock executions and forcing the victim to listen to the screams of family members being tortured.

The Sábato Commission also encountered thousands of deaths, from "torture, electric shock, immersion, suffocation and also . . . by throwing in the sea, by shooting."[26] At the Chacarita Cemetery, the number of cremations increased from 13,120 in 1974 to over 30,000 per year from 1978 through 1979. In 1980 the number fell back to 21,381.[27] Mass graves were found, filled with skeletons, many of which bore single bullet entrance wounds in the back of the skull, a curious feature in light of military claims that most of the subversives had died in armed confrontations.

Apart from the liquidation of the victims, the security forces sometimes looted their homes and adopted their children. Elderly people and cripples were taken. Eighty-four journalists and 107 lawyers disappeared, an effective deterrent to the reporting and defense of *desapericidos*.

"The armed forces decided to do their killing clandestinely. They were determined not to make the same mistake as Pinochet and Franco, because if they had held open executions even the Pope would protest. Besides, Martínez de Hoz wanted the killing to be clandestine so that there would be no stop in the influx of foreign capital," said Emilio Mignone, director of the Center for Legal and Social Studies. The center, which takes human rights cases to court, itself was raided and Dr. Mignone detained in 1981. His daughter had disappeared five years earlier. "Fifteen men armed with machine guns took my daughter from the very room where we are now sitting," he told me in a conversation at his home. "For forty minutes they were here. We never saw her again." Later he added, "If there's a body, you must accept the death. But without a body, you cannot. The human psyche resists it. So she's neither alive nor dead." Dr. Mignone's torment is sadly common; the Sábato Commission chronicled 8,960 disappearances, admitting that there could be errors, but emphasizing that many disappearances had not been reported due to the victim's lack of family or to the survivor's desire for anonymity.

Life went on in other areas. In the economic sphere, efficiency and modernization were the watchwords. The economic minister, José Alfredo Martínez de Hoz, a lawyer by training, took inspiration from the Chicago school of economics, calling for the opening of the economy to the salutary winds of free competition and for the reduction of the extensive state intervention in the economy. Initial signs were encouraging. Foreign currency reserves in Argentine coffers climbed to $10.5 billion by 1980. Inflation began to decline, finally dipping into double-figures (87.6 percent) in 1980.

Soon, however, the reforms launched by Martínez de Hoz hurled Argentina into a tailspin from which it has yet to recover. The last chapter showed how the overvalued peso led to rampant speculation at the expense of productive investment. In addition, grandiose military projects and arms purchases inflated the fiscal deficit, financed by foreign loans. Companies that could not stand up to undervalued imports or that took out too many loans went bankrupt. Crisis in the overgrown financial sector, triggered by the bankruptcy of Argentina's largest private bank—the Regional Trade Bank, or BIR—forced the Central Bank to bail out a number of enterprises, costing the nation some $4.5 billion.

One day I spent three hours talking with Martínez de Hoz, a slight and mild-mannered man. I was surprised and impressed that someone of his class, let alone one with so many enemies, should answer the door himself. The former minister (by then a constant butt of political derision) seemed eager to be understood. He patiently explained his strategy for opening the Argentine economy to competition, his successes in promoting the modernization of its industry, his frustration in trying to obtain military approval for the privatization of state enterprises.[28] The salient similarity between his convictions and those of the military commanders under whom he served was a cataclysmic view of the 1970s' subversion. (Without that belief, he could not possibly have justified his five-year collaboration with them.) Martínez de Hoz told me that once a guerilla hospital was discovered—fully-supplied and literally underground. He insisted that the economic situation only became hopeless after his departure from government. I left wondering whether I had just encountered the banality of evil or simply ill-fated amorality.

Economic crisis became the military government's millstone in the 1980s. Lieutenant General Roberto Viola succeeded President Videla in March 1981 for a brief and unlucky tenure. Lorenzo Sigaut, who replaced Martínez de Hoz as economy minister, said that "those who bet on the dollar will lose;" the next day the peso was devalued by 30 percent against the dollar. Bankruptcies continued. President Viola wanted to manage a transition to democracy; Army Chief Leopoldo Galtieri wanted military government to continue. In December 1981 Galtieri ousted Viola in a palace coup.

The economic mess sapped the military government of the support it needed to govern. On 30 March 1982 thousands of demonstrators took to the streets in a general strike. The government ruthlessly suppressed the crowd, arresting and injuring hundreds. The desire to divert criticism and rally public support led President Galtieri to bring forward a fateful date: the seizure of the Malvinas Islands, carried out three days after the tumultuous events in the Plaza de Mayo. That the invasion flowed from rash miscalculations (e.g., that the British would not fight, that the Americans would not support them) did not matter. Now the Plaza de Mayo was filled with cheering multitudes. This artificial high was maintained through wildly inaccurate news reports of the thumping the British were receiving. On the day of surrender, 14 June 1982, the shame and outrage of ignominious defeat were heightened by the shock of having been utterly deceived by the Argentine government.[29]

That was the last straw. The armed forces had arrogated to themselves the role of protector of the national interest, but when it came down to their *raison d'être*—defense of the national territory—they had failed miserably. They could not successfully wage war or produce prosperity. Military prestige was at a nadir. Terrorism had been extinguished—their one major "accomplishment"—but even if the armed forces were not roundly condemned for the heinous methods they employed, they simply were no longer needed for that unsavory task. General Galtieri was sacked, and a new president-general, Reynaldo Bignone, called elections for 30 October 1983.

Compression exaggerates history. The Argentine drama described in these few pages in fact stretched out over a half century. It appeared as remote as a dime-store novel to many Argentines, who continued along their quotidian ways untouched by the violence though not by the decline. The terrorists' targets were generally security forces or prominent figures, so the man in the street was not greatly threatened. The disappearances touched many more, but a shroud of silence allowed people to fool themselves into thinking that the terror was an illusion or a minor excess above a dirty but necessary task.

Nevertheless, the selectivity and exaggeration of human memory justifies concentration on the center court. Perón, subversion, suppression, and speculation are imbedded in the national consciousness. They continue to shape popular opinion. One cannot understand Alfonsín, the unions, the military—in short, contemporary Argentina—outside of these dramatic circumstances.

On the other hand, historical context cannot justify abject immorality. When I asked about the brutal repression of the Process, people from all walks—including lawyers, priests, and members of the Alfonsin government—would reply, "Ah, but you must understand what went on before. I do not justify the excesses, mind you, but the terrorism was *bravísimo*." That reply is bankrupt, an apology masquerading asa justification. For although it is true that the terrorism was atrocious and helps explain people's brutalized perceptions, it cannot excuse the abdication of all responsibility to decide who shall live and who shall die to an uncontrolled group of soldiers and marauders beholden only to themselves. It cannot excuse torture and murder even of the guilty, without benefit of legal procedures.

And what of the innocent? "Well, if someone disappeared, he must have been involved in *something*. If he wasn't a terrorist, he was very close to them." Since when is the penalty for being involved in "something" or being "close" to terrorists torture and peremptory execution by some faceless lieutenant? Where are due process and individual rights?

In these fractious years, violence erupted everywhere. Apart from the physical existed the economic and institutional violence. Those already wealthy enough to speculate prospered most when inflation afflicted wage-earners worst. Unions and the military trumped democracy with force. Civilian politicians either collaborated in this constitutional affront or encouraged it by their incompetence. Discredit touches all.

Simple, left-right, civil-military distinctions fail. Perón first sought power through the Radicals. The Radicals later sought power through Perón. Perón was willing to incorporate the strangest bedfellows to widen his political base: socialists and capitalists, workers and industrialists, soldiers and civilians. Perón, in the words of one analyst,

> was fascist and communist, anticommunist and antifascist, conservative and radical, a Christian burner of churches and a repentant pagan, hurried capitalist and disguised unionist. He didn't give two hoots about the Constitution.[30]

Civilians sought power through military coups. Soldiers (Perón and Lanusse) sought power through civilian elections. Opportunism was the only constant.

Institutions cannot be built on sand; the foundations just slip away. The institutional vacuum at the center of Argentine politics undermined every Argentine president. The tissue of alliances among the military, unions, Church, and businessmen sooner or later weakened and broke under the pressure of competing claims and insufficient resources to satisfy them. All except Illia compromised the Constitution in order to maintain office. Each constitutional abuse became a precedent for further abuses, leaving a constitutional abyss so deep that, during the Process, even the most basic right—the right to life—lacked effective protection from either the courts, the bar, the parties, or popular opinion.

With such constitutional debility, how could constitutional democracy reappear in 1983? By default. Alfonsín's victory was not arduously won against tyrannical forces. The armed forces, discredited by the debacles in the Malvinas and the economy, retreated to the barracks and left the government behind them like a spent shell.[31] (The struggle against subversion did not fatally compromise the military's public support; but for its other failures the military might still be in power.) Elections were the only alternative; everything else had failed. Into this political wasteland moved Raúl Alfonsín, seeking the presidency and the vitalization of Argentina's supine democracy.

CHAPTER 3

The Challenge

It would be naive to think that the same regime that destroyed the citizens' liberties, submerged the national economy in catastrophe, and demolished the institutions of the Republic has the capacity—on its own—to prepare an adequate transition for democracy.

—RAÚL ALFONSÍN

Chascomús is a two-storied pueblo in the low-lying plains of the humid pampa, sixty-five miles south of Buenos Aires. Like so many other old towns, it has a traditional central square, sided by a church, a bank, and the town hall. On the fourth side, an old mansion has been converted into a cultural center. In the middle stands an equestrian bronze, commanding the palm and jacaranda trees of the surrounding green. Alongside a freshwater lagoon, campers pitch tents and fish. Rich aromas rise from their sizzling *parillas*, Argentine barbecues of spiced sausages and steaks.

It is a pleasant, provincial town. The old neighborhoods are filled with squat rows of attached houses, shuttered against the midday sun. Raúl Alfonsín grew up near the plaza in one of these sun-bleached neighborhoods. His family is well represented by the Alfonsín Pharmacy and the Alfonsín General Store, where one can buy anything from nails to tractors. His paternal grandfather was Gallician, and his father supported the republicans against Franco in the Spanish Civil War. His mother's English blood made the family Allied partisans during the Second World War. One hundred years earlier, the people of Chascomús battled against the dictator, Juan Manuel de Rosas. "For this series of reasons," says Alfonsín, "there was no choice but to be a fighter for democracy."[1]

Since there were no college preparatory schools in Chascomús, Alfonsín went to Buenos Aires to attend a military secondary school, after which "the only thing I knew was that I was not going to be a soldier."[2] He studied law,

41

returned to Chascomús in 1951, and entered municipal politics. Like his father, Raúl Alfonsín was a Radical, which led to brief jailings under Perón. When the Radical party split between Frondizi's Intransigent and Balbín's Popular branches, Alfonsín opted for the latter. He became a representative in the provincial legislature, president of the Chascomús Committee and, during Illia's presidency, finally arrived at the National Congress as a deputy.[3] In those days he was known as one of Balbín's young turks.

In 1972 Alfonsín founded a new line within Radicalism, the Movement for Renovation and Change. He broke with his former mentor, Ricardo Balbín, whom he unsuccessfully challenged for the presidential nomination in 1973. Renovation and Change became known as the most antimilitary, social democratic wing of the Radical party. In 1976 Alfonsín cofounded the Permanent Assembly for Human Rights—a courageous act amidst the widespread disappearances of the first year of the Process. Later he published *The Argentine Question,* a thoughtful book that explored the reasons for Argentina's half-century decline and openly criticized the existing military government. Before discussing Alfonsín's political thought in detail, though, it should be put in the context of Radical party traditions.

RADICALISM

The Radical Civil Union (UCR) was founded by Leandro Alem in 1890. Its principal demands were free suffrage and honest elections. In opposing the conservative elite that ruled the government, the Radicals relied on revolutionary tactics, since fraud and the limited franchise prevented them from defeating the oligarchy at the polls. Conspiracy was the chosen method; the Radicals mounted unsuccessful rebellions in alliance with discontented army officers in 1890, 1893, and 1905. Despite their violent tactics, early Radical leaders insisted that their mission was to reform Argentine morality. To this day, Radical leaders continue to speak of Radicalism as an ethic more than a party.[4]

The years of exclusion from power congealed in the party's first historical trait: intransigence. The Radicals would not compromise with Argentina's venal rulers but would hew unwaveringly to their own principles. The early Radical leader, Hipólito Yrigoyen, refused several offers of cabinet positions from the ruling party. He wanted all or nothing. This intransigence persists today, notably in the philistine variant of Radical nationalism. Until his final years, after decades of party leadership, Ricardo Balbín used to boast that he had never left Argentina, except for one trip to Uruguay.

Ignorant chauvinism entertains the belief that the United States is out to get Argentina, spending vast amounts of time and energy to lay and bait snares of dependence. If U.S. companies are willing to sign contracts for exploration and production of Argentine oil, it must be a trap. How dare they siphon off the nation's natural wealth! No matter that the Argentine state oil company, YPF, lacks the capital and ability to do the job, or that Argentina can earn handsome revenues under the contract. It would be better to leave that oil under Argentine soil until, well, later. How much later is anyone's guess. Let us hope it is not until YPF can perform economically. By that time, the age of oil may be past.

Another aspect of Radical intransigence was the early refusal to participate in elections, on grounds that they merely served to legitimate the corrupt rule of the oligarchy. The year 1912 represented a watershed. Generations of European immigration had swollen the ranks of the middle classes, the natural Radical constituency. In order to bring these large and growing ranks into the system, President Roque Sáenz Peña decided to make a strategic concession in order to dilute the revolutionary ardor of the working classes. He sponsored a 1912 electoral reform that legislated universal and obligatory male suffrage.

Four years later, Hipólito Yrigoyen captured the Casa Rosada with more votes than were won by the three opposition parties combined. Yrigoyen symbolized a second historic trait of the UCR: personalism. Yrigoyen governed not through institutions, but through individuals. One-on-one he was enormously persuasive. He avoided large gatherings, shied from cameras, and spoke in a convoluted jargon, high-flown and impenetrable. He ignored army rules and regulations, rewarding insubordinate officers whose careers had suffered for supporting the earlier, unsuccessful Radical uprisings. Thus he compromised army professionalism and paved the way for his own removal at military hands.

Personalism has a family side. Yrigoyen himself was the nephew of UCR founder, Leandro Alem, though it is sometimes said that Alem's suicide was instigated by Yrigoyen's withdrawal of support within the party. Individual connections, unfortunately, remain important to this day. Two sons of Alfonsín's first secretary of energy are national deputies. Another minister's son-in-law was named foreign commerce secretary. Perhaps these scions are qualified, and it cannot be denied that after so long in the cold it is not easy for the Radicals to find competent candidates for all major posts, or that other administrations have shown no aversion to nepotism. For a party that prides itself on being ethical, though, the UCR's continued reliance on know-who rather than know-how raises serious questions.

Personalism can be costly, too. Perhaps the most egregious example was Bernardo Grinspun, long a close friend of Alfonsín. After a year-long tenure as economy minister, in which his grating, bullying style alienated foreign creditors and local businessmen with equal dispatch, Grinspun finally went too far. On a visit to Mar del Plata, he managed to be photographed playing the card game, *truco*, in the Gold Room casino of the Hermitage Hotel, with an ace of spades stuck to his forehead. Moments later he nearly got into a fight.[5] Only after this episode was Alfonsín able to face the necessity of replacing Grinspun. (The next minister, Juan Sourouille, proved far abler.)

Intransigence and personalism are contentious issues that have bred a series of party splits from the 1920s down to the present, between factions more and less faithful to these seminal principles. By 1982 there were several important factions: the mainstream, Balbinista National Line; the breakaway, Alfonsinista Movement for Renovation and Change; and the traditional Radical bastion, the Córdoba Line. Alfonsín forged an alliance with the Córdobans and surprisingly defeated the National Line candidate, former senator and 1973 vice-presidential candidate, Fernando de la Rúa. So the man from Chascomús would carry the party colors into electoral battle.

ALFONSÍN'S PHILOSOPHY

Argentine politics are so fluid that familiar labels—right, left; liberal, conservative—do not accurately describe parties and politicians. Though the Peronist amalgam is the most notoriously confusing, Alfonsín's Radicalism is not easy. An artist told me that Alfonsín is "just another puppet of the oligarchy." A retired army colonel said, "He's not a Radical; he's a leftist." *Newsweek* called him a "Kennedy-style Democrat."

Alfonsín is none of these things. Leftists and rightists loathe heterodoxy; Alfonsín fits neither category perfectly, so leftists call him rightist and rightists call him leftist. Those too sophisticated to resort to simplistic name-calling point to Alfonsín's populist rhetoric and call him a demagogue. These misnomers obscure Alfonsín's true creed: social democracy.[6] For this reason it is important to set the record straight.

Alfonsín himself set forth a clear typology of regimes that helps to place him on the political spectrum. In an essay entitled "Neofascism and Political Parties," he described four states of government.[7] The first arose from the French Revolution, the cornerstone of the "liberal state of law," which promoted the separation of powers and judicial guarantees of individual rights and liberties. Not a bad start, in Alfonsín's view, but insufficient because the high bourgeoisie tends to help itself while suppressing the hopes of the great majority of the people. That defect has provoked illiberal and liberal responses. The illiberal response is fascism. Fascism rejects liberalism and limited government as obstacles to the full flowering of capitalism, and replaces the rule of law by "the will of the dictator," who exalts violence and uses terror to cut off dissent. This elitist and messianic doctrine, most familiar from the German and Italian experiences of the 1930s, subjugates the good of the individual to the good of the state.

The liberal response to the injustices of capitalism is "neocapitalism," the welfare state, which permits private property and the capitalist system of production but seeks to remedy its discriminatory effects by equalizing access to health care, education, leisure, and aesthetic enjoyments. Unfortunately, neocapitalism tends to bring on the bureaucratic state, wherein a dominant executive power invades all facets of the individual's life, with consequent Big Brother-type threats to civil liberties.

Finally, as fascism responds to liberalism, according to Alfonsín, so neofascism responds to the welfare state. Neofacism seizes the strong executive and democratic rhetoric of the welfare state and welds it to the elitism and harsh realities of fascist capitalism. The people descend to the poverty that is endemic in classical capitalism, but now are stripped of the protection of representative government and civil liberties. Meanwhile, clothed in the legitimating rhetoric of democracy, privilege prospers. Democracy here has ceased to be a way of life, converting itself into no more than a method to elect governments, an aim "which becomes easy to manage through the manipulation of opinion."[8]

In Alfonsín's schematic, the major villains are elitism and unrestained capitalism. The major goals are judicially-protected individual rights and liberties. Though he does not say so explicitly, he implies that in this scheme he stands behind the welfare state, stripped of its dangerous bureaucratization.

The villains are personified by the oligarchy. Argentina, according to Alfonsín, in essence is socially democratic, but the oligarchy has suppressed this essence. But the very word, "oligarchy," reeks of oversimplification and demagoguery. Does a ruling class truly exist? Can all Argentines of great wealth or social rank stand united against democracy? The idea seems implausible, but Alfonsín has defended his use of the term:

> Here it is not a matter of elaborate conspiratorial explanations of history. There is no General Convention of the Oligarchy that meets periodically to decide with perverse inspiration the destiny of the country.

But there is indeed a coincidence of behavior that defines traits of a social group, and circles in which the oligarchy is recognized and organized. . . . Some remain from yesterday, others are being incorporated. . . . More than by their surnames they are defined by what they do and what they are prepared to do. Economically, to take advantage of the speculative opportunity before thinking of production. Politically, to exclude those that annoy and to monopolize power, using the State to create opportunities to speculate.[9]

The oligarchy prefers speculation to productive investments because speculation is more profitable. The prospect of large and quick gains encourages the wealthy to keep their assets highly liquid rather than to tie them up in long-term investments. Without such investments the economy does not develop. When world recession hit in 1930 and dried up speculative opportunities along with international trade, control of the government became decisive as to who would bear how much of the cost of recession. In democracy, however, since by definition the oligarchy is a minority, it could not possibly obtain control of the government. So the oligarchy cultivated some soldiers and overthrew Yrigoyen.

According to Alfonsín, during the 1930s the Radicals failed to understand that the massive rural immigration to the cities and especially Buenos Aires had created a new political power base: urban workers. Perón organized these workers, won over the military, rejected democracy, and established an authoritarian movement and government. The Radicals, the only major political player that supported democracy, lost their natural majority. As the Peronists and oligarchy battled it out for support of the armed forces, democracy quietly faded from the picture.

Based on that diagnosis, Alfonsín's prescription is simple: democracy. He repeats it over and over. Within democracy, Alfonsín insists that Radicalism has been historically united in the struggle for liberty, justice and human rights. To those who urge that economic recovery is a prerequisite to democracy, he replies that democracy is a prerequisite to recovery. "It is through democracy that we will be able to resolve national issues. There is no other way. All else was tried, all was tested, and all failed."[10] Democracy, then, still offers the most practical solution for the country's major problems. The confrontation of ideas promotes the best solutions. An authoritarian government can act more quickly, but less ably, and is unlikely even to confess, much less remedy, its own mistakes.

By democracy, Alfonsín means not merely the vote, but also a method to organize and govern society. As a *social* democrat, he insists that the national income should be increasingly shared by all Argentines. To people accustomed to living in well-established, working democracies, Alfonsín's conclusions may seem to be obvious. That misses the point. In Argentina democracy cannot be taken for granted. It has to be discussed in basic terms because it remains absent at the basic level of national consciousness.

In varying degrees, Argentine presidents have all subordinated democracy to another goal—be it consolidation or maintenance of authority, economic development or spiritual rejuvenation, national reorganization or revolution. Some objectives were laudable and idealistic, others cynical and pragmatic. But all in some way undermined democracy. Alfonsín tried to reverse that trend. His politics did not revolve around pasting together a package to try to satisfy the secular interests of all the country's leading interest groups. They revolved around the idea of democracy. However venerable, however praised, that idea in 1983 came forth naked to the field of electoral battle. If it won, it would win not by union street action, not by military coercion, but by its own persuasive force, as embodied in Raúl Alfonsín.

THE STRATEGY

One election does not a democracy make, and in many ways the situation Alfonsín faced after his inauguration on 10 December 1983 looked decidedly bleak. Seven years of rampant military power had begun in hubris and ended in humiliation. The armed forces had presented themselves as saviors, brandishing their supposed efficiency, legality, and morality, only to bring waste, lawlessness, and depravity. For nourishment in their vanguard task, they amply helped themselves to weaponry and salaries. Their signal achievement was the annihilation of subversion, but at what a cost—mass murder, state terror, and international shame.

People were afraid to speak, to walk the streets, to petition the government, to report crimes to the police. Add to this fear the abject surrender in the Malvinas Islands, the corruption from seven years of unmonitored power, the demoralization of 400% inflation and a $45 billion debt with little to show for it. The people had had enough of the "military-syndical pact" and so had voted for Alfonsín. But the spoor of the military government was everywhere, weakening the popular confidence necessary to a working democracy.

Alfonsín represented hope. But how could that image be used to build popular confidence in democracy? How could he mobilize the atrophied civilian institutions to hold their own in confrontations with the unions, businessmen, military (still strong though weakened), and the Church? He lacked the hardware of the military and the rank-and-file loyalty of the unions. His principal tangible asset was the state apparatus. That gave him substantial control of the economy, as the employer of roughly one-fifth of the national workforce, the arbiter of prices, source of credit and economic regulation, master of the national and provincial budgets. It also gave him virtually unlimited access to the press. Unfortunately, this asset was also a liability; the overgrown state sector of the economy, accounting for roughly half of the national product, threatened to choke off the private sector and any hope for economic recovery.

Alfonsín also had two important, intangible assets. The first was charisma. People liked his decency and openness. They trusted him. Here was a politician who was not wealthy, who had turned down the pension from his stint in Congress. He campaigned for the presidency in a borrowed car and, when in Buenos Aires, slept in a borrowed apartment. Alfonsín managed a rare feat in Argentine politics; he made democracy look feasible as well as desirable, without appearing hypocritical in the process.

Alfonsín's second asset was the popular mood. Argentines were tired of the old days. After seventeen years of military government, Peronist chaos, and violence, they were ready for a change, a new approach. Alfonsín offered one.

With such a debilitated system, goals must be modest. First and foremost, Alfonsín's main objective had to be to hold his office for the constitutionally prescribed six years—an eternity in Argentine politics—and deliver the presidential baton to an elected, civilian successor. The task was as simple to conceive as it was difficult to fulfill. It required Alfonsín to keep entrenched interest groups satisfied (or at least at bay), to instill a greater commitment to democracy among Argentines, to reverse a deteriorating, half-century trend in political history. It also seemed imperative to generate economic recovery.

In confronting the armed forces, Alfonsín's strategy was to decapitate and reduce. By presidential decree, he immediately initiated legal proceedings against the nine members of the first three juntas of the Process for homicide, illegal imprisonment, and torture, on the grounds that "the existence of plans and orders makes the members of the Military Junta on active duty during the Process . . . directly responsible for the crimes that were perpetrated within the framework of the plans that were drafted and supervised by superior officers."[11] The last of these juntas, led by General Leopoldo Galtieri, would also stand accused before the Armed Forces Supreme Council for its conduct of the Malvinas war.

Alfonsín did not want to destroy the armed forces. More to the point, he did not want the armed forces to destroy him. But public outrage had to be vented. By longstanding Argentine military tradition, from the days of Cortez in the sixteenth century to the Prussian model of the twentieth, commanders and vice-regents stood to account for their actions once their writs terminated. Alfonsín hoped that the armed forces might be willing to sacrifice their retired, former chiefs, if that would close the chapter. In contrast, he knew that prosecution of active duty officers and their subordinates could ignite an explosive reaction.

The armed forces saw themselves as national saviors. Though there was substantial criticism from within the armed forces over the way in which the military government managed the economy and the Malvinas campaign, there was virtual unanimity in favor of the manner in which it crushed subversion. Many officers had died in the process. Their comrades viscerally rejected the possibility of allowing civilians to punish them for their conduct.

Alfonsín tread gingerly, keenly aware of the strong emotions on both sides of the question. He distinguished three levels of official responsibility in the struggle against subversion: those who gave the orders, those who merely followed orders, and those who tortured or killed people for profit or sport. Only the first and last groups would be punishable. He permitted military courts to try human rights abuse cases in the first instance, but provided for appeal to civilian courts. He charged members of the first three juntas, but not of the last junta, which had handed over the government to the civilians.[11] He appointed a commission of civilians to report on the fate of the *desaparecidos*, but did not give it the right to initiate legal proceedings against those responsible.

In a companion decree to that charging the first three juntas, Alfonsín also called for the prosecution of Montonero leaders (including Mario Firmenich, the Montonero leader who opened the guerilla campaign by engineering the Aramburu abduction) for terrorist acts "perpetrated after 25 May 1973," the date of the Cámpora amnesty.[12] The indictment included charges of homicide, illegal association, rebellion, and instigating criminal activity.

By making concessions to both sides, Alfonsín hoped to defuse a potentially explosive situation. He knew neither side would be fully satisfied. Many officers loathed *any* prospect of receiving condemnation instead of the medals they thought they deserved. Meanwhile, the Mothers of the Plaza de Mayo continued chanting "judgment and punishment to the guilty." The Mothers had not marched in front of the Casa Rosada every Thursday during the Process, demanding to know the fate of their missing children, only to give up the search during a civilian government and condone the exoneration of their children's tormentors. Three founding mothers *themselves* had disappeared. And as for those who "merely" followed orders, the Mothers' president, Hebe de Bonafini, had this to say: "Armed men from the intelligence services knocked on the door of a pregnant woman in my neighborhood, and when she answered they shot and killed her in cold blood. . . . The man who pulled the trigger is guilty, too, isn't he?"[13]

Regarding the second critical military issue—reorganization—Alfonsín acted more boldly. In his inaugural message to Congress, he declared:

> The Argentine Armed Forces were created and organized to defend the country under the rules, principles, and technical regulations in force in the civilized countries of the world. What both military and civilians forgot, to the detriment of the country and the military organizations themselves, is the golden rule applied in all civilized nations of the world, regardless of their political systems or ideologies, which determines that the Armed Forces must take orders from the civilian authority that has been institutionally installed. Due to the lack of strict compliance with this rule, we have suffered innumerable hardships, painful distortions, and real decadence. In the democratic Argentina that we are again founding, such a deviation will never again occur. Those who attempt to do so, if there were a chance to think of this possibility, will assume the most serious responsibility and the corresponding punishment. There will be no more coups d'état or military "demands" in the Argentina of the future.

Money and men are power, and the armed forces had lots of both: $4.5 billion and 153,000 in 1983. Alfonsín swiftly cashiered two-thirds of the army generals and one-half of the navy admirals. The posts of commander-in-chief of each service were eliminated. He pledged to cut drastically both military spending, by as much as 50 percent, and conscription, with the aim of eliminating it entirely. For the first time, civilians were appointed to head the National War College and the General Directorate of Military Factories (*Dirección General de Fabricaciones Militares*), the army's industrial fiefdom. Alfonsín intended to democratize military instruction, to replace the long-standing military self-perception as the guardian of the national interest with the more modest but still essential role as servant of the constitutional authorities. This change in attitudes could only occur slowly.

Not surprisingly, military officers did not take these changes kindly. They felt that they had been made the butt of official scorn. Their former commanders were in jail, and their budget had been halved. The Sábato Commission had condemned the "struggle against subversion" as the darkest chapter in all of Argentine history, while the Supreme Council of the armed forces labeled their conduct "unobjectionable." The irony reflected deep tension. Fugitive Montoneros brazenly took out a newspaper advertisement threatening violence to Alfonsín's government should their leader, Mario Firmenich, be condemned. Military officers earnestly, if incredibly, averred that the subversives were already reorganizing themsleves in the country, and ghoulishly hinted that continued concern for the "NNs"—the "no-name" corpses recently unearthed—could lead to "MMs"—many more, *mucho más.*

Alfonsín approached the unions differently. Many workers had disappeared and general strikes had been called against the Process. Though some union leaders collaborated with the military government and others had contributed to the chaos that brought on the 1976 coup, as a group they claimed credit for the restoration of democracy. Although their candidate, Italo Argentino Luder, had lost to Alfonsín, he had won 40 percent of the vote, and the Peronists had won more provincial elections than the Radicals.

Alfonsín pursued two related goals: to break the old-guard Peronist stranglehold on the unions, and to win as much labor support as any Radical could. For the first objective, "democratize the unions" was the motto. The Radical electoral platform had called for a new law to assure democratic union structures and increasing worker participation in union decisions. This purportedly neutral effort to "depoliticize" the unions in fact represented a direct assault on Peronism, whose "vertebral column" had always been organized labor. The demand that worker representation be isolated from partisan politics directly threatened the Peronists' thirty-five-year domination of the unions. The vast majority of union leaders soon to stand for reelection for the first time in over seven years were Peronists. Many of these incumbents had achieved and maintained power over the years through anything but democratic methods. "Democratization" meant government-monitored elections to ensure that challengers and dissident factions would have a fair chance in running against the old-guard.

Alfonsín overplayed his hand. It was a strong one, supported by his fresh electoral victory, and union leaders were prepared to give Alfonsín much of what he wanted. But the president's bill went too far, demanding minority representation on union boards of directors and facilitating the election of union dissidents to leadership positions. In opposition, old-line unionists were able to exploit businessmen's aversion to the prospect of Marxist unions. The bill was handled clumsily. It passed the Chamber of Deputies, where the Radicals enjoyed an absolute majority. At 5:00 A.M. on 15 March 1984, however, the bill was forced to the floor of the Senate, where the president lost key votes from the independent parties. The defeat of the union election reform bill signaled the end of Alfonsín's political honeymoon and the beginning of renewed union assertiveness. Alfonsín knew he would now have to compromise. Ultimately, union elections were held and the Peronists retained control of nearly all major unions, while the Radicals made scant gains.

Having failed to beat the unions, Alfonsín sought to join them—his second union goal. After all, Alfonsín had long spoken as a friend of the workers. Often he sounded like Perón: "The worker must have a privileged destiny because he is, at the same time, the central protagonist of the constant progress of humanity and the inspiration of the expansion of society's frontiers."[14] Like Perón, Alfonsín railed against dependence upon the imperialism of England and the United States, in permanent collusion with the national oligarchy.

As one Peronist leader recalled, "I remember a Radical rally for Frondizi twenty-odd years ago. Everyone was dressed well, quietly standing and listening. During Alfonsín's campaign, Radical rallies looked like the Peronists of the forties—mass demonstrations and *bombos*." (*Bombos* are drums, beaten atavistically with meter-long plumbing hoses.) The sunrise following electoral defeat, a dejected Italo Luder and his advisors went out for a coffee on the deserted Ninth of July Avenue, the world's widest boulevard, which bisects downtown Buenos Aires. "*Mozo*," one called out to the waiter, "what did you think of the elections?"

"I think Alfonsín learned more from Perón than the Peronists did themselves," the young man replied.

Alfonsín's first step in his co-optation strategy was to convoke a *concertación*, where business and labor leaders met with government representatives to reach a joint social-economic policy. The *concertación* served to channel union energies in a harmless direction. "Why did Alfonsín convoke the *concertación* through the Interior Ministry?" asked one participant. "That is where they monitor security risks, not economic policy. It looks like he is trying to bring the traditionally destabilizing political elements inside the tent, where they won't do any harm."

More aggressively, the Radical government sought to undercut a key element of the unions' power base—the exclusive control of the "social works" funds, the hundreds of millions of dollars worth of annual salary deductions appropriated by unions for health clinics, day care centers, vacation hotels, and other recreational programs. Control of the social works meant the power to punish and reward workers, to command their loyalty or, at least, their obedience.

At the same time, Alfonsín sought to go over the heads of the union leaders, by appealing directly to the people. He began the National Food Program (the acronym, PAN, means "bread" in Spanish), giving away free food in poverty-stricken areas. The Peronists were enraged. "We don't want giveaways. We want work!" one told me. What truly bothered them, though, was that Alfonsín's plan trespassed on their "social justice" turf. It was exactly the type of program that the Eva Peron Foundation had run thirty-five years earlier to win the hearts of the people. Now it was Alfonsín seeking popular support by promoting social justice and broader income distribution.

To consolidate his position, Alfonsín traveled everywhere to speak. In his first year in office, he visited forty-three Argentine cities (some more than once), delivered sixty messages to the country, and made nine nationwide addresses.[15] Charisma buoyed the president's popularity—his greatest political asset. Despite the deteriorating economy, Alfonsín remained extremely popular during his first year, his approval ratings remaining strong at 53 percent.[16]

People began speaking of Alfonsín as the leader of Argentina's Third Historic Movement (after Yrigoyen's and Perón's), which could join together all of the nation's popular sectors to carry Argentina forward. Alfonsín seemed an excellent *caudillo* prospect—*un gran tipo*, a great fellow—a good and honest man, valiant and decent, unaffected and intelligent, if no genius. "The masses want a leader," it was said. Cooler heads urged that this temptation be resisted; movements of the whole tend to become authoritarian in order to maintain internal cohesion, while the absence of a viable opposition party leaves the military as the only alternative once the historic movement loses its charm. The best thing that could be said about the Third Historic Movement proposal is that its prospect catalyzed Peronist efforts to bridge their differences and create the image of a viable political party instead of a circus.

On balance, Alfonsín's labor strategy bore mixed results. He enjoyed some worker support and union cooperation, especially during the first year when workers' real wages increased, despite declining productivity. In 1984 consumption increased 6 percent; even then, on average there were two strikes per day. The General Confederation of Labor (CGT) called its first general strike to protest wage policies nine months into the civilian government. It had waited three years to take that step against the military. By mid-1986, austerity measures had reduced real wages by more than one-quarter and general strikes were common. The diminishing response to strike calls, though, indicated that the rank-and-file was less hostile to Alfonsín than was the CGT leadership. To that extent, the president had made some headway. Still, he could not hope to woo many unionists away from the Peronist ranks.

Turning to the business sector, one presidential advisor said privately, "There is no choice but to attack it. It is oversized and will never profit as much under civilian rule as it does under the military." On the other hand, this same official urged caution; the Radical government wished to promote investment, and for that market stability and accepted rules of the game were essential. He might have added that the first thing foreign investors look at is the local investment climate which, if unsettled or inhospitable, can be a powerful deterrent. Moreover, despite Radical desires, the local financial community could continue to prosper even with a hostile government, so long as the underground economy continued to flourish.

Even though prominent Radicals joined in condemnation of the "financial fatherland," Peronists remained skeptical, because the tough talk did not lead to tough action. If there was no choice but to attack the *financistas*, then why had the Radicals not done so already? Personal income and wealth taxes remained insignificant, while regressive taxes increased. Speculation and black-market lending continued unabated.

Though treated gently, businessmen still managed to be displeased. They grumbled that the new government lacked any coherent economic policy and was infiltrated by incompetents, leftists, and incompetent leftists. The abrasive economic minister Bernardo Grinspun was their *bête noire*. Economists asserted that the government had failed to establish clear game-rules that would create a climate of confidence and encourage productive investment.

Many businessmen loudly complained that the government was blocking the operation of market forces. In practice, most Argentine businessmen avoid free competition like the plague. One young commerce ministry official told me that "no one will ever make a serious investment in this country without special government dispensations, like tax relief or high tariff protection." In April 1985, when the government finally implemented financial and tax reforms, business complaints turned into a howl.

Relations with the Church were awkward. The Radicals by tradition were anticlerical, opposed to active priestly involvement in government. Alfonsín favored legalization of divorce, equal rights for women in the family, and reduced censorship—positions which were anathema to the Church. The new government sought to democratize education. In 1985 the Congress passed a law granting equal rights to mothers (vis-à-vis fathers) in family decision-making and to illegitimate (vis-à-vis legitimate) offspring in matters of inheritance. In 1986 the Lower House passed a bill legalizing divorce. These proposals smacked of libertinage to many clerics.

Despite his personal views, Alfonsín had little desire to cross swords with the Catholic hierarchy. The Church remained powerful, and Alfonsín had enough trouble in confronting the armed forces and the Peronists, without throwing angry churchmen into the picture. One official at the episcopate told me that Alfonsín had soothed the bishops by telling them, "I am a bad Catholic, but a Catholic, and I trust that when I err you will call it to my notice." Yet given the yawning gulf that separated Radical and clerical views, strained relations seemed inevitable.

THE AUSTRAL PLAN

Economic distress complicated the political equation. Inflation and the debt destroyed prospects for productive investment. Foreign exchange reserves were low. No one saved. Confidence in the Argentine economy was nil; available assets poured into speculation and black market lending, or out of the country. Alfonsín's election inspired little more, since the Radicals were traditionally illiterate in economics and the new president excoriated the business community, while urging it to invest.

Alfonsín presented three basic economic objectives: to reduce inflation, renew economic growth, and raise real wages. In his first months, though, no strategy emerged to attain these conflicting aims simultaneously. Real wages increased but fired inflation. The first time price controls were imposed, they discouraged the investment needed to renew economic growth. When these price controls ultimately failed, inflation went through the roof. Alfonsín had promised in one year to reduce by half the 400 percent inflation he inherited; instead he virtually doubled it.

Much of the difficulty in reviving the economy stemmed from the Sword of Damocles hung over Argentina by its enormous debt burden. Interest payments alone amounted to 60 percent of Argentina's total export earnings, and total debt equaled 75 percent of gross domestic product. During his campaign Alfonsín had sounded a nationalistic, defiant note on the debt issue, reflecting resentment toward the economic burdens imposed by the North. He promised to analyze the debt to distinguish how much of it was "legitimate," in other words, funds that actually entered the country and were applied to a purpose other than fraud or graft. The "legitimate" debt would be paid, though not with the hunger of the Argentine people. Alfonsín promised that Argentina would not submit to recessive policies imposed from abroad.

In the showdown that ensued with the international banking community, Alfonsín blinked first. Bridging loans arranged at the brink of the first two quarterly deadlines of 1984 allowed creditor banks to keep Argentine loans out of the non-performing category, a move that would have required the banks to write off millions of dollars in earnings. The double September shocks of 27.5 percent monthly inflation and the imminent prospect of having Argentine loans classified substandard finally convinced the government to abandon its defiant posture and accept the conventional International

Monetary Fund (IMF) prerequisite for the granting of fresh money: austerity. At least for the moment, the legitimate debt card would not be played. That month, agreement for $1.7 billion in IMF facilities was reached, paving the way for the negotiation of $4.2 billion from commercial banks, $2 billion from official creditors, and the rescheduling of $18 billion of existing debt.

The 1984 IMF agreement, however, could not halt the rapidly accelerating deterioration of the Argentine economy. Inflation paralyzed all hope for recovery. By June 1985 the annual rate had reached 30 percent per month, or over 1,000 percent per year. President Alfonsín decided that only a major shock could salvage the situation.

Thus was born the Austral Plan, named after the new currency which would replace the peso and signify a fresh start. (*Austral* means "south," so the name also aimed to encourage support through nationalistic appeal.) One austral would equal 100 pesos and would be pegged at a fixed rate against the dollar. Prices would be frozen, and citizens were encouraged to assist the authorities by reporting any merchant who tried to increase them. The government, for its part, pledged to reduce its budget deficit and to stop financing it by printing more currency unbacked by reserves.

It worked. Inflation fell immediately to a monthly rate of 2 to 3 percent. The government deficit fell from 12 percent to .25 percent of GDP between the first and second halves of 1985 and was financed completely through foreign loans.[17] The long-mooted privatization of state enterprises finally seemed about to begin. National spirits lifted.

Like any shock treatment, the effects of the Austral Plan could not be expected to last indefinitely. The plan was a lifesaver; it spared the economy from sinking but was not designed to propel it anywhere. And it entailed inevitable costs. Salaries declined by an estimated 30 percent, and GDP for the year declined 4.4 percent. Everyone knew that when summer vacations ended at the end of January 1986, the old pressures for economic expansion would revive.

On February 7 Alfonsín launched the second stage of the Austral Plan. It aimed to manage the transition from a shock strategy to a growth strategy. The government granted export credits to companies that increased their exports by at least $2 million for two years or more. It would reduce export duties on agricultural products. The Central Bank would promote the use of credit for growth through exports and investments. The government would sell shares in steel and petrochemical state enterprises to the private sector and use the revenues generated by privatization as a fund for industrial modernization and development.[18]

The second stage of the Austral Plan initially failed to stimulate production. In order to stir investment, the old-style Radical leaders of the Central Bank eased up on the money supply. By August loose money brought inflation back to a triple-digit annual level, along with the replacement of the Central Bank president by a new team committed to tight money. Meanwhile, fraudulent misuse of industrial and export promotion funds was discovered in the provinces and in Buenos Aires banks.

It would be a hard row to hoe.

FOREIGN POLICY

In foreign policy, Alfonsín initially placed Argentina's interests squarely within the Third World, affiliating Argentina with the Non-Aligned Movement and the New International Economic Order. The president promoted integration with the sister republics of Latin America, beginning with a debtors club to try to force a "political" treatment in the North for the debt crisis in the South. Some twenty-one oil exploration and production contracts with foreign companies were renegotiated. The Soviet Union and its allies were important customers for Argentine exports. The Alfonsín government opened a $65 million credit line to the Sandinista regime in Nicaragua. In a speech before a joint session of the U.S. Congress, he implicitly condemned the Reagan Administration's aid to the *contras* in Nicaragua.

Alfonsín's nationalistic approach descended from Yrigoyen and Perón, standing in stark contrast to the internationalist outlook of the economic liberals of Argentina's financial community. Alfonsín also stressed pacifism, promising to accept the papal proposal to settle the century-old Beagle Channel dispute and to press the Malvinas claims exclusively through diplomatic channels. He realized that a Beagle treaty with Chile would remove Argentina's only serious prospect for armed conflict, thereby strengthening his hand against the armed forces and their budgets.

Argentina's dire economic straits, however, made Alfonsín think again. The United States may be an imperialist giant, but Argentina sorely needed investments, and they sure were not coming on the home front. So Alfonsín ordered the conclusion of the oil contract renegotiations, and in a Houston meeting with oil executives promised favorable terms for U.S. oil companies that invested in Argentina. (Shortly thereafter, the oil market collapsed.)

Perhaps the most fundamental foreign policy task was to restore Argentina to respectability in the eyes of the world community. Though few leaders had reacted as harshly against Argentine abuses of human rights as had U.S.

president Jimmy Carter, recent events on the political, military, and economic fronts had badly sullied the national image. Alfonsín, simply by being a democratically-minded and elected leader, did much to restore Argentina's good name. Soon he did more, traveling to twelve nations in his first year in office to improve links with other governments. If Alfonsín built up enough credit in enough capitals, he might prevent a coup on that fateful day when his problems outweighed his popularity. At such a moment, the president's international prestige and quiet pressure from Europe and North America could help deter the would-be usurpers. Surely the president recalled that when President Illia's advisors were desperately trying to avert Onganía's coup, they were unable to round up the diplomatic support that could have saved Argentina's democratic government.

THE THREE-YEAR ITCH

Inevitably, the euphoria of the return to civilian rule wore off. Many problems remained unresolved, and new ones appeared. On the credit side of the ledger, Argentines enjoyed more personal freedom than they could ever remember. Countless books and articles on formerly taboo subjects—Marxism, the repression, and sex—appeared in kiosks and bookstores everywhere. Every evening at the downtown pedestrian intersection of Florida and Lavalle, groups of people gathered to argue and discuss politics or just to watch the debate, while mimes and street musicians performed nearby.

On Sundays the parks filled with local artists and craftsmen plying their creations. Naturally, this surge of self-expression struck many as licentious, subversive, and just plain annoying. "The streets are so clogged by these musicians you can hardly walk by. The military never would have allowed this," lamented one. But the restoration of free expression was the first and biggest step toward democracy. Many people told me that, despite the wretched state of the economy, they felt better than they ever had as Argentines. "For the first time I felt proud to show my passport at Kennedy Airport," commented one former defense minister.

In Argentina, however, popularity can be fleeting. Another former minister under military governments said that Argentine politics are like a marriage, only the seven-year itch sets in after three years. Disillusioned comments were often heard in the streets during the first year of democracy: "He promised everything and has done nothing. *Todo anda mal.* Everything is going poorly." The principal complaint was the economy, which indeed was going poorly. The initial economic policy brought the economy to the brink of hyperinflation and collapse. The emergency economic measures of 1985 stopped inflation—at least for a while—but at the cost of a steep drop in the real wages of most workers. Prosperity seemed beyond reach.

Alfonsín also faced rough sailing in dealing with the traditional power bastions. Business and union leaders, churchmen and military officers, all were unhappy with the president.

Crime was on the increase, and the police seemed to vacillate between ignoring it and suppressing it by shooting first, asking questions later. By 1985 daily newspapers reported frequent "delinquent" deaths in shootouts. No one expected a military coup, and most expected Alfonsín to serve out the six years of his constitutional mandate. Still, Argentina's problems were grave. Whether Alfonsín would be recalled as an aberration or the father of democracy would not depend on him alone. It would depend on the Argentine people and their ability to adapt to democratic customs both new and strange to them. It would also depend on whether Argentina's powerful institutions would become democratic, and whether Argentina's democratic institutions would become powerful. To these institutions we now turn.

PART II

THE CHAMPIONS

CHAPTER 4

The Peronists

Perón! Perón! How great you are!
My general! How worthy you are!
Perón! Perón! Great leader!
You are the First Worker!

—THE PERONIST MARCH

Juan Domingo Perón was the most successful politician in Argentine history, running three presidential campaigns and winning all decisively. His political career spanned three decades. Paradoxically, however, once the votes were counted, Perón sought to destroy democratic institutions. He jailed or exiled opponents, including those in the Congress. He sacked the Supreme Court and trammeled the press. He subjugated all labor activity to the General Confederation of Labor, which in turn he subjugated to himself. He orchestrated the apotheosis of himself and his second wife, Evita.

Perón has been gone for a decade. Now his third wife and widow, Isabel, is gone, too. Her own presidency had been swamped in terrorism and incompetence, which led directly to the military takeover of 1976. One stultifying summer day in February 1985 her handwritten resignation as titular president of the party appeared in Buenos Aires' dailies. After five years of house arrest and three of expatriation, Isabel concluded that "my cycle is through." That left Peronism without a Perón at its head for the first time in forty years. In reality, Isabel had not led the Peronists in opposition, and in Alfonsín's first year in office she did not even communicate with most party leaders. She was useful at best as a figurehead, at worst as a mascot bearing the only name that could convoke all of the many warring factions of Peronism.

The electoral magic is gone, too. The Peronists cruised confidently into the 1983 presidential election campaign. They were stunned by their defeat.[1] (Many leading Radicals were equally surprised.) Peronism could no longer

63

complacently consider itself the "natural majority" party. Fissures appeared and deepened within the party, between right and left, unions and politicians, reformers and traditionalists. Though powerful, the grip of the CGT had weakened.

Leaderless, defeated, and divided, Peronism confronts the gravest crisis in its history. For Peronists, the key question is whether Peronism can survive Perón. If it can, a key question arises for Argentina: can democracy survive Peronism? To answer this question requires a close look at Peronism, Perón and the Peronists.

PERONISM

What is Peronism? Politically, it has been the most powerful electoral force in postwar Argentina. Philosophically, the question is more difficult to answer. "Can't you ask me something simpler?" replied one instructor of Peronist doctrine. The party is officially called the Justicialist party, but Justicialism itself is an elusive doctrine. Perón's extensive writings on the subject are often woolly and obscure.

This vagueness, as the Russians might say, is no accident. Perón sought to lead all Argentines. He liked to speak not of a party, but of a movement; not to the membership, but to the People, *el pueblo*. It is easier to agree on generalities than on specifics. So Perón stuck to generalities. "If I define, I exclude," he said.[2] If he proposed a specific policy, he might alienate those who disagreed with that policy, or create a split among his loyalists.

Although Perón's political stronghold was organized labor, he never fundamentally attacked businessmen and major landholders. He may have redirected the national income, but he did not confiscate existing assets or property and transfer them to the workers. The wealthy *estancias* were not expropriated.

Though a cynical power-seeker, Perón also had a doctrine. He saw a perfect coincidence between the People and Justicialism; both were national, social, and Christian.[3] These traits translated into a slogan: "Political Sovereignty; Economic Nationalism; Social Justice." This combination constituted the Third Position, the golden mean between heartless capitalism and godless Marxism. In foreign policy, the Third Position dictated close identification with the Third World Movement, which rejected fealty to both "empires," the United States and the Soviet Union.

Now we are getting somewhere. For one thing, it is clear that the description of the People and Justicialism would appeal to Argentina's most power-

ful interest groups. A doctrine national, social, and Christian offers something
to each of the military, the unions, and the Church. Perón built his political
machine on the basis of the powers that be. He rose to command the armed
forces and gave them a leading role in national development on the grounds
of their strong organization and nationwide presence. He purged the labor
movement of its European antecedents—anarchism, syndicalism, and socialism—and appealed to the creoles from the interior who flooded into Buenos
Aires.

Perón could not command the Church, so he tried to pacify it. The Church
had stood staunchly beside the oligarchy Perón helped overthrow in 1943.
The colonel won it over in a straightforward appeal. He adopted the name
"Justicialism" from a papal encyclical of 1931, restored religious teaching in
public schools after a sixty-year ban (thus satisfying the leading political demand of the Church), and stressed the integral importance of the family to
his political doctrine.

The military, postwar unions, and Church all had centralized authorities
and hierarchical structures. That suited Perón just fine. Despite his democratic success, Perón preferred authoritarian methods. He clearly explained
this in his 1951 book, *Political Leadership*. "I always say what I learned
when very young: I should be obeyed and I should be respected. And in this I
cannot complain. Fortunately, I have always been obeyed, and I have always
been respected."[4] He had little patience for pluralism: "Sectarianism is the
first enemy of leadership, because leadership has a universal meaning, it is
ample, and where there is sectarianism it dies because leadership does not
have enough oxygen to live."[5]

Perón believed it necessary to "win the street" at decisive historic moments. He recalled how successfully he had dealt with students and other opponents who took to the streets to oppose him in 1944: "I called the wood-
workers and told them, 'Boys, make me some big clubs.' Then we called the
meat union and said to them, 'Boys, are you game to go out on the street with
500 truncheons?' We gave them 500 sticks, they went out, won the street and
the others did not return to recover it again. . . . When you have the tool in
your hand, strike hard and well."[6] Perón's defenders say he mellowed with
the years, but more than a quarter century later, he actively supported the
"boys"—and girls now, too—who had graduated from sticks and stones to
machine guns and bombs.

So in Perón we find an authoritarian leader, democratically elected, culti-
vating undemocratic institutions. Where does it all fit together? In the "Organized Community," argued Perón in 1949. The Organized Community is
one of Perón's fuzziest concepts. Indeed, he never said exactly what it was.

He said its ultimate object is "Man and his Truth" and implied that it will "reestablish harmony between material progress and spiritual values."[7] In 1974, just before he died, he wrote that to build the Organized Community (apparently it was still in the works), it was necessary "to establish an inalienable principle of objectivity." Perón does not say what an "objective" organization would be, though he says that its only criterion would be the "will of the people" and helpfully suggests that subjectivity should be avoided, remembering that "reality is the only truth."[8]

Since it is undefined, the Organized Community must be found in the eye of the beholder. Perón's abstruse rhetoric allowed him to try to be all things to all people. Some may see the Organized Community as the corporativist state, akin to that desired by Onganía. As a military attaché in Rome at the outset of World War II, Perón had a close look at the corporativist states organized by Franco in Spain and Mussolini in Italy. (Remember that Spanish and Italian immigrants comprise Argentina's largest ethnic groups.) Perón admired Mussolini and is reported to have said, "I will act as did Mussolini, but without Mussolini's mistakes."

The Organized Community can also be given a democratic interpretation. In *The National Plan*, Perón insisted that social democratic government must be consolidated, in a form "Representative, Republican, Federal and Social." The citizen should express himself through political parties with "explicit ideological bases," and thence through the National Congress.[9] Popular politics and representation can be placed in parallel to non-governmental power groups, to complete the outline of the Organized Community. (See Figure 4-1).

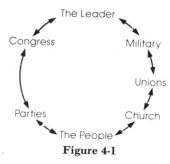

Figure 4-1

Note that this system is headed by "The Leader." A mere president will not do, because he will be unable to cope with the groups on the right side of the figure. Nominally, the president is the commander-in-chief of the armed forces, but far more often the armed forces have been the commander-in-chief of the president. The unions and Church lie entirely outside of the president's constitutional authority (though naturally he has some influence over them, since both depend heavily on government funds and programs). So the Organized Community needs a Leader.

This need reflects what could be called the "democrat's dilemma" in the Organized Community. It needs a leader more than a president, because it integrates the military, the unions, and the Church as independent *political* actors, stretching beyond their constitutional roles. As political actors, though, these institutions are undemocratic, in structure and in purpose. The dilemma follows. The Leader either does or does not dominate these undemocratic institutions. If he does, then his power must exceed those of a democratic president. If he does not, then he will be overpowered by the undemocratic institutions that surround him. Either way, democracy loses.

History confirms this theoretical dilemma. Perón and the military governments were powerful and undemocratic. The community got organized, all right, under the authoritarian thumb of the Leader, his henchmen, and their thugs. Their ample power proved irresistible to abuse. The civilian governments of Frondizi and Illia were relatively (though not completely) democratic, and succumbed to the depradations of soldiers and unionists.

Apart from this "democrat's dilemma," the Organized Community was doomed from the start. It was designed by Perón for Perón. Leaders less charismatic or shrewd could not hope to carry it off as well as he did. Even Perón could not maintain himself as Leader forever. He tried to find a place for everyone—under his wise tutelage, of course. Trouble was, many people were unhappy with their assigned places and rejected Perón's leadership. In particular, most of the upper class and parts of the middle class held internationalist and economically liberal views, eschewing Perón's nationalism and statism. Intellectuals were repelled by his authoritarianism and demagoguery.

Anti-Peronism went beyond policy disputes, right to the bone. Perón's opponents thought him a charlatan and Evita a harlot. They despised the *descamisados*, their shirtless followers, reeking of the hickdom of Argentina's vast interior. The very name, Perón, became an obscenity to many. Was that right?

PERÓN: HERO OR SCOUNDREL?

Many others see Perón as a hero and Evita as a saint. Peronists are viscerally loyal, and they are many. Indeed, Peronists have played decisive roles in every major postwar election, even when their party was banned. Perón's support gave Frondizi the presidency in 1958. In 1962, when Frondizi allowed Peronist candidates to run in gubernatorial elections, Peronist victories in Buenos Aires and ten other provinces provoked a military coup. The two presidential elections Peronism won over unconstrained opposition—1946 and 1973—were scrupulously clean.

Most Argentines are vehement partisans because both sides play for keeps. Perón jailed and exiled opponents. Peronists were protagonists of the terror of the early 1970s with Perón's blessing. In the late 1950s anti-Peronists proscribed the mere utterance or printing of Perón's name and banned his party from political participation. They also broke longstanding Argentine tradition by executing Peronist rebels who sought to overthrow the Liberating Revolution. During the Process, more *desaparecidos* (30 percent) came from the ranks of the workers—Perón's natural constituency—than from any other category.[10]

So was Perón a hero or a scoundrel? He was both. He was a hero to the working class. Workers had been excluded from effective political representation. Perón included them. The Conservatives opposed worker interests; Radicals ignored them; Perón exploited them. But in so doing, Perón gave the worker riches previously unknown.

For the record, we should note that Perón did not *create* the Argentine labor movement. Working class organization and strikes began in the late nineteenth century. Violence occasionally erupted; hundreds of workers were killed or jailed in the Tragic Week of January 1919 alone. (A young lieutenant, Juan D. Perón, was said to have commanded troops in this brutal repression.) The General Labor Confederation was founded in 1930.

Before Perón, however, the unions had enjoyed only limited success. Their leaders were European in outlook. That was fine so long as the workers themselves remained European immigrants. In 1914 three out of every four Buenos Aires adults were foreign-born. Second-generation Argentines, though, could not easily relate to dated European "isms" of which they may not even have heard.

Meanwhile, creoles from the interior provinces converged on the cities, especially Buenos Aires. One million rural immigrants flooded into the national capital between 1937 and 1947, as jobs decreased on the farms and increased in the factories. These newcomers, scornfully called *cabecitas negras*, "little blackheads," would carry Perón to power.[11]

Perón mobilized the workers politically. He gave them pride and a sense of dignity. When vilified as "shirtless ones," the workers took the pejorative, *descamisados*, as a badge of honor, which Eva Perón invoked to great effect.

Perón brought the workers more tangible benefits, too. "In 1941, when I started working," recalled Miguel Agostini, secretary-general of the 18,000-member papermakers' union, "the workers wore torn trousers and couldn't afford leather shoes. Perón changed all that." From 1943, the year Perón became the secretary of labor and welfare, until his overthrow in 1955, the share of national income that went to salaried workers increased from 30 percent to 50 percent. Real wages for unskilled workers rose by a third between 1943 and 1949, before economic crisis forced a partial retrenchment.[12]

Perón also promoted women's rights. It is a shame that this virtue had to be mixed with nepotism, that Eva was an unelected demagogue, and that Isabel was an incompetent. For the elevation of Perón's wives to the apex of Argentine politics opened a door to women that before was slammed and locked. The Peronist Congress in 1949 gave women the right to vote. Women comprised one of the four official branches of Peronism, beside youths, workers, and politicians. That mattered in a society where, to this day, many Argentine women seem frozen at the "I Love Lucy" stage of liberation.

Even Perón's enemies must concede that he kept Argentina out of war—including civil war. Perón's regime was repressive, and sometimes bloody, but the scale of repression would later be dwarfed. In 1951 the news that a communist student had been tortured by the police raised a hue and cry.[13] Twenty-five years later, the screams, gunfire, and dull thuds of the torture, murder, and forced disappearance of some 10,000 Argentines echoed hollowly through a ghastly public silence. At least Perón did not have the 1951 army officers who rebelled against him put up against a wall and shot, as Aramburu did to General Valle and twenty-six others in 1956. At least he did not use secret detention centers and kill on an industrial scale without *any* legal proceedings, however compromised.

Perón's enemies must also concede that Peronism preempted the growth of Marxism in Argentina. Indeed, Peronist leaders have often tried to win business support by presenting themselves as bulwarks against Marxism and communism in the Argentine labor movement. Argentine workers have a native hero, Perón. Pictures of Perón and Evita appear on every union office wall, alongside the crucifix. Who needs Marx?

So much for Perón's virtues. Now for his defects. Politically, Perón did grievous harm to the possibility of democracy in Argentina. He destroyed anyone in his path, including supporters who did not bow low enough. For instance, he won the February 1946 presidential election as the candidate of a coalition led by the brand new Labor Party. After the election, he sought to assure his control over the Labor party, but party leaders insisted on its independence. Not to be thwarted, Perón dissolved all parties of the winning coa-

lition and established the Official Party of the Revolution. After a few bootless flailings, the Labor party wilted.[14]

A similar fate befell CGT leaders' hopes to maintain a measure of independence. President Perón's candidate lost the election for CGT leadership in
November 1946 to Luis Gay, the former president of the Labor party, who
continued to resist government control. Perón exploited the visit of a tactless
U.S. delegation from the American Federation of Labor to accuse Gay of be-
traying the movement to foreign interests and forcing him to resign. He was
replaced by the aptly-named José Espejo (the surname means "mirror") who
carried out the Peróns' wishes, and whose chief qualification seems to have
been his experience as doorman in Juan and Eva's Posadas Street apartment
building. In the words of Perón's biographer, Joseph Page, the CGT then
shifted from promotion of worker interests before the government to the promotion of government interests before the worker.[15]

Within Peronist ranks, this authoritarianism was justified by the concept of
"verticalism." Verticalism means unquestioned rule from the top by the
Leader—a military hierarchy in mufti. This "digitocracy," where decisions
were made at the wave of Perón's hand, created a regimental mentality ill-
disposed to the free exercise of democracy. For the forgetful, bullyboys were
happy to provide physical reminders that obedience was prudent. Those who
disliked the system could leave . . . if they got to the door.

Harsher treatment awaited Perón's political enemies. The Supreme Court
had long been a thorn in his side, holding unconstitutional many proposals he
made as minister. He instigated the impeachment of the three anti-Peronist
justices, who were duly convicted by the Senate. In addition to their "illegal"
(i.e. anti-Peronist) decisions of 1943 to 1946, the justices stood accused of mal-
feasance for recognizing the military governments that had taken power
through the 1930 and 1943 coups (in both of which Perón participated). The
next year Perón purged the judges of all lower tribunals. Unlike his successors, Perón did act through the constitutional mechanics of impeachment.
Nevertheless, Perón set a precedent for judicial purges that accelerated the
decay of the Argentine Constitution.

The Peronist-controlled Congress passed laws that further restricted dissent. The crime of disrespect against public officials was amended to exclude
the truthfulness of the challenged comments as a defense. Under this law,
several Radical deputies lost their seats and the Radical leader, Ricardo Balbín, went to jail. So much for freedom of speech. Perón denied his opponents
access to radio broadcasting and dominated Buenos Aires newspapers. In
1951 he expropriated the independently-owned, anti-Peronist daily, *La
Prensa*. After that, the two remaining independent newspapers, *Clarín* and
La Nación, toed the official line. So much for freedom of the press.

Meanwhile, an unelected, unofficial figure became second only to Perón in political power. The province of La Pampa and the capital city of Buenos Aires Province, La Plata, were renamed Eva Perón. (Chaco Province was renamed General Juan Perón.) Eva and Juan Perón whipped up popular emotions in massive street rallies. In moments of political crisis, these rallies incited violence. After a bomb exploded at a 1953 rally, Perón egged on his militant followers, who proceeded to burn the exclusive Jockey Club, bastion of the Buenos Aires elite. In Perón's last major speech before his September 1955 ouster, he told the throngs in the Plaza de Mayo, "We must respond to violence with a greater violence. . . . When one of our people falls, five of theirs will fall."

Perón is also blamed for having ruined Argentina's economy. He squandered the country's enormous postwar gold and currency reserves so that by 1949 Argentina had become a net debtor. His profligacy succeeded in buying the affection of the workers and armed forces, but this high-tariff, import-substitution strategy led to the proliferation of small and inefficient light industries. Capital investment was diverted from industries that could manufacture the machinery to produce final goods and so spur further industrialization.

To liberate the economy from foreign dominance, he bought out the British-owned railroads and American-owned telephone system. In these and other basic industries, he created state enterprises, whose notorious inefficiency and overstaffing led to a yawning government deficit, financed through the inflationary measure of printing pesos. Perón got the ball rolling, increasing the annual inflation rate from 14 to over 30 percent, between 1946 and 1952. His detractors say that Perón caused Argentina's miserable economic failure: stunting industrialization, stifling free market forces, and promoting inflation. Unproved allegations that Juan and Eva Perón enriched themselves through corruption adds piquancy to this charge.

On balance, Perón lovers and haters both have ample grist for their mill. In fairness, it should be noted that Perón never could have arisen in a stable, legitimate political system. The Conservatives' abuse of power and use of electoral fraud to secure a monopoly of government showed the way. The Radicals, too, had failed to challenge the bases of this exclusive system, and had themselves ignored the changing facts of life in Argentine demography.

Long suppressed demands burst forth with Perón. Excesses were inevitable, however regrettable. Perón did not introduce authoritarianism and corruption to Argentine politics. But he carried these unfortunate traditions to new heights and put them to the music of Justicialist doctrine. He flaunted power in the face of the classes who had traditionally monopolized it. He had charisma. Though Perón condemned the *caudillo*, he was one. A *caudillo* destroys democratic values, but was exactly what many Argentines wanted.[16]

Perón was not an absolute dictator. He did respect legal forms, even though he bent many of them to suit his convenience. He did not entirely reduce political institutions to his thrall, because he was not sufficiently ruthless. He was not a true revolutionary, because he did not dispossess the rich of either their wealth or their land. He just redirected national income to his favored constituents.

Dissent was muted, but not obliterated. Opposition was able to grow in the military, the Church, and the unions. Deeds prove the point. The military staged three coups against Perón, the last successful. The president's attack on the Church led directly to his downfall. When the downfall came, the unions did not step in to protect their patron. Some of Perón's successors would much more effectively extinguish dissent.

THE PERONISTS

Peronism is a workers' movement. But Peronism could not be so successful in elections unless it reached out to gain the support of other groups, since the working and lower-middle classes comprise no more than 35 to 40 percent of the voting population. The two other important Peronist groups are the middle classes of the interior provinces and the postwar industrialists, whose enterprises were born and survived thanks to Perón's import-substitution strategy. Surprisingly, at least to the foreigner, there are also Peronist bankers, lawyers, businessmen, and doctors. The leaders of the political branch of the Peronist movement come from these ranks.

Today, though there are few card-carrying Peronists in the Church and armed forces, the movement has maintained links with both institutions, despite many ups and downs over the years. The links with the Church go back to the foundations of Peronism. Perón's 1946 campaign benefited from Church support. Relations soured, though, when Perón began to advocate devotion to himself and Evita more than to the Holy Trinity. After Evita's death, the church was further repelled by Perón's installation of the girls camp at Olivos.

Soon the Church would have greater reason for complaint. In 1954, for reasons that remain unclear, Perón launched an anticlerical campaign. In addition to verbal abuse, Perón terminated religious education in the schools, legalized divorce and prostitution, and granted rights to illegitimate children. Catholics rallied in the streets; Perón deported two bishops; the Vatican excommunicated Perón. The night following the failed June 1955 coup several churches in downtown Buenos Aires were torched by gangs, while policemen, soldiers, and firefighters stood by idly.

From these ashes, relations revived a dozen years later between leftist Peronists and leftist priests. The Third World Priest movement believed in the necessity of class struggle and saw Perón as "the inexorable road to Socialism." The Montoneros, who emerged from Catholic Action, terrorized Argentina to secure Perón's return. "Perón or Death" was one of their cheery mottos. During the military government, other priests acted as intermediaries between the Peronist unions and the military government. Unionists are still respectful: "The Church is humble," one told me, "and every day with the people." A Peronist leader went further, ascribing his politics to religious belief. "I'm a Catholic," he said, "and there is nothing closer to Catholicism than Justicialism."

The military connection was more direct. Perón rose to power through the army and wore his uniform proudly. Anti-Peronism, however, grew in the ranks, fed first by distaste for Evita and finally by Perón's attack on the Church. An attempted army coup failed in 1951. The navy never had been as "Peronized" as the army, and played key roles in both uprisings of 1955. After 1955, the many "gorilla" officers were willing to sacrifice democracy in order to rid Argentina of what they saw as the weevil of Peronism.

Here, too, Peronism proved resilient. The military, however grudgingly, did permit Perón's return to Argentina. They restored the leader's rank of lieutenant general (the highest army grade), stripped in 1956 by a military honor tribunal. During the 1983 election campaign, Peronists and military officers quietly negotiated to trade pre-election military support for a post-election presidential amnesty for crimes committed in the dirty war.

Most important are the unions, the "vertebral column" of the movement. During Perón's presidency, total union membership rose from 500,000 to 2.5 million. Workers' wages and fringe benefits rose substantially during the same period. More than material benefits, Perón gave the workers pride and a sense of identity. And Eva Perón won their hearts.

María Eva Duarte was born in poverty and illegitimacy. An ambitious but untalented actress when she met Colonel Perón in 1944, Evita became a savior to the working classes, "my dear shirtless ones, *mis queridos descamisados.*" Her Eva Perón Foundation, generously funded from voluntary (but prudent) contributions, a cut from union dues and salary increases, and the national lottery, dispensed enormous sums for the benefit of the less advantaged. As Page describes:

The organization built homes for orphans, unwed mothers, and the elderly; shelters for working women; lunch facilities for school children; children's hospitals; vacation colonies for workers; low-cost housing; schools for nurses. Many of these projects were located far from the capital and brought social welfare to the interior for the first time.[17]

Even if Evita siphoned huge sums off into wardrobe, jewelry, and bank accounts, her Foundation performed a great service and instilled lasting loyalty. When asked what political views he supported, one forty-five-year old artist confided: "I'm still an *Evitista*." In a simplistic expression of political faith, he explained, "When I was a child, she gave me a lunch box. I adored her."

Eva Perón exuded hate as well as love. "*Mis queridos descamisados*," she exhorted in her final speech before the masses in the Plaza de Mayo, "we will never again let ourselves be kicked around by the traitorous and corrupt oligarchy and their foreign masters. Woe be to them the day they lift a hand against Perón."[18] Reportedly she purchased pistols and machine guns with which to arm CGT workers, but Perón wisely intercepted their delivery.

In 1952, after a long decline, Evita died of cancer, three weeks into Perón's second term. She was thirty-three, and her image will be forever frozen in youth and beauty. She became a martyr to the cause. The shanty walls of *villas miserias* often bore two pasted-up likenesses: the Virgin of Lujan and Eva Perón. While her name was banned, people surreptitiously built small shrines to her in their homes. The union of food-workers cabled Pope Pius XII to nominate Eva for canonization, noting that "many sick are now well, many sorrowful are happy because of her."[19] The Vatican gently demurred.

The military successors to Perón sought to de-Peronize organized labor. They failed. Aramburu cut short Lonardi's brief attempt to wean workers gradually away from Perón. Instead, Aramburu resorted to blunt repression. Peronists remember his tenure as "the Revenge." He jailed, prosecuted, and exiled hundreds of union leaders and replaced them with military delegates. All references to Perón—including his home—were obliterated.

Meanwhile, workers' salaries fell sharply as a percentage of GDP. Aramburu's efforts were put to the test in 1957 when Argentines voted for delegates to a convention to reform the Constitution. (A 1949 Peronist constitutional reform had established broad rights for workers and allowed the president to succeed himself.) The Peronists voted in blank, outpolling both branches of the Radical party.

Still, Perón's exile took its toll. Even a great leader cannot exercise perfect control from thousands of miles away. In the 1960s loyalty to Perón began to yield to the more pragmatic concerns of labor under the new political regime. The leader of this "Peronism without Perón" movement was Augusto Vandor, leader of the powerful metallurgical union. Vandor was prepared to deal with the governments in office, even if they refused to grant full political rights to the Peronist party. Vandor was attacked for straying from Perón by union rival, José Alonso. The CGT split down the middle. Vandor attended Onganía's inauguration, and his branch of the CGT cooperated initially with the Onganía regime. Before Perón's return, both Vandor and Alonso would die in hails of assassins' bullets.

Alonso's successor as CGT president, José Rucci, was loyally devoted to Perón. He joined the delegation that brought Perón home from Spain. He stood beside Perón on the balcony of the Casa Rosada before the cheering thousands on the night of Perón's election. Three weeks later, he too was fatally ambushed, as he stepped out of a house.

Rucci was unlucky. He died on the eve of a unionist resurgence. Lorenzo Miguel, head of the metalworkers and the "62 Organizations" (the union branch of Peronism), became one of the country's most influential leaders. (He still is.) After the death of Perón, the old-time Peronist union leaders held sway for nearly two years, until the March 1976 coup. Wherever Isabel Perón appeared, they stood beside her.

The Process signaled the return of proscription. The CGT was intervened and its funds blocked. The government took over the huge social works funds of the unions. The 62 Organizations was banned. So was union activity, especially strikes. Many union activists were jailed. Others disappeared, including light and power workers' leader, Oscar Smith, who dared to stage a strike in January 1977. In four years, the salaried sector dropped from 46 to 34 percent of national income.

Some union leaders did collaborate and prosper under the Process. The Process feared unemployment and labor protests and, therefore, sought the support of some union leaders. But overall, 1976 to 1983 were dark years for organized labor.

POWER AND PURPOSE

Whether Peronism can survive under democracy depends on what it has and what it wants. What it has is near total control of the unions. That influence is highly concentrated since, pursuant to early Peronist legislation, the government recognizes only one union per industry. Thus each union has become a fiefdom, run from the top. The mightiest unions have been those with most members—metallurgical, construction, railroads, textiles, and govern-ment employees. The centralization of power within each union and, in turn, within the confederation of unions (the CGT), helped insure the collective ability to win the streets.

Street power has been a crucial element to political success in Argentine history, often more important than winning elections. The mass demonstra-tion of 17 October 1945 converted Perón from prisoner to president. The "Battle Plan" of the 1960s underlined Illia's inability to govern. The enor-mous antimilitary demonstration of 30 March 1982 reportedly led General Galtieri to move up the Malvinas invasion date to 2 April. (Initially, the junta intended to launch the invasion later, during the harsh Argentine winter, to discourage British attempts to recover the islands.) Alfonsín demonstrated his viability as a candidate during the 1983 campaign by winning the streets with mass rallies the likes of which Radicals had not managed since the days of Yrigoyen.

Money is the second key Peronist asset. The unions collect 1 percent of each worker's wages as mandatory union dues. When social works are in union hands, they collect another 3.5 percent. That adds up to hundreds of millions of dollars per year.

In one typical, 35,000-member union headquarters I visited, each floor is devoted to a different service for workers. The medical clinics have facilities for general practitioners, dentists, orthodontists, gynecologists, and psychia-trists. Down the hall is a medical laboratory and pharmacy. Upstairs is a travel agency. On the walls are photographs of the union's five hotels and eight campgrounds. On the top floor is a nursery. The 90,000 dependents of union members also enjoy the benefits of the social works.

Unions have as many of these facilities as their size permits. Favorite hotel spots are the beach near Mar del Plata, the mountains and lakes of Bariloche, and the Córdoba hills. The light and power union has fourteen hotels, three at Bariloche alone. The cost for staying at one of these vacation spots may be only $2 per day.

Through these social works, Perón gave employees benefits they had never been able to afford. Workers depend on the unions for access to these facili-ties. Availability can be a problem; in unions where members outstrip facili-ties, the worker must often play ball with the union hierarchy to get a medi-cal appointment or hotel room.

Spend one day in a major headquarters, and the reason for the unions' enormous ability to mobilize and control their members becomes clear. Maybe the leaders are corrupt, but at least they serve their constituents. A weaker union means fewer social benefits. No one else is going to make up the difference, especially in Argentina, where times are hard and social enmities harsh.

It is easier to describe what the Peronists have than what they want; the party is badly split. Nevertheless, there is some consensus on the basics. The first and foremost desire is to recover their share of national income. They want Argentina's economic recovery to be led, naturally, by consumption. For that, wages should increase, rather than fall, as they have in real terms since 1980. Increased buying power will spur demand for increased production which, in turn, will require the hiring of more workers.

No longer should wages be "the variable of adjustment," the first expense to be reduced whenever economic austerity is required. Instead, the government should attack the *patria financiera*, the financial fatherland, which robs the country through speculation and the stashing of Argentine riches in foreign banks. Peronists resent foreign banks and the International Monetary Fund, and many say that Argentina should stand up more firmly against foreign imperialists. The threat of default hangs in the air.

The Peronists also want to retain the dignity Perón gave them. This is intangible but essential. President Alfonsín has tried to win labor support by advocating worker interests, verbally attacking the local financiers, and sometimes using the same rhetoric as Perón. Yet Peronists have not flocked to his banner. Partly this is because his actions for the worker and against the *patria financiera* have not matched his words. "It is better to act than to speak," said Perón. Many Peronists also see Alfonsín as a representative of middle class interests who does not make workers feel like protagonists. Unlike Perón, he did not call them the "vertebral column" in a "New Argentina." Peronists miss their leader, but he will never return. Can Peronism survive without him?

PERONISM WITHOUT PERÓN

Perón himself did not provide for Peronism without Perón. In his last speech from the balcony of the Casa Rosada, he said, "My only heir is the People." During Perón's life, it made good tactical sense to name no successor; had he tapped the leader of any one sector, the movement could have split into battling factions. Moreover, Perón had always cut off any heirs apparent of sufficient stature to threaten his absolute supremacy of the movement.[20]

When forced to show his hand by choosing his vice-presidential running mate in 1973, he eschewed all serious contenders and chose his wife, Isabel.

Perhaps she was such a cipher that she was the candidate least likely to divide the party while Perón lived. Certainly she was such an incompetent that she was the leader least likely to unite the party after Perón died. When she ascended to the presidency, she meekly submitted to the right-leaning domination of José López Rega and Lorenzo Miguel.

During the Process, when party activity was prohibited, Isabel Perón remained the titular head of the party, as Perón's de facto heir. She never played the part. (She had never really played the part while president, either.) Even after the Alfonsín administration obtained her immunity against pending lawsuits, she still refused to participate. Her final resignation stripped the movement of its only figleaf of unity.

Meanwhile, the movement had been slowly drifting apart. The split between Peronist right and left opened before Perón's death and quickly widened thereafter. During the Process, the CGT split between those willing to negotiate with the military government and those opposed. Other groups emerged. By the end of military rule, the CGT had broken up into six factions. Jockeying for power among CGT factions continued for more than a year after Alfonsín's inauguration, before the selection of a single secretary general nominally united the confederation under one head. The new union chief was Saúl Ubaldini, the beer-brewer hero from the antimilitary strikes of 1982. Even then, the internal power struggle within the labor movement continued.

The political branch of Peronism was also divided. Buenos Aires party chief and losing gubernatorial candidate, Herminio Iglesias, was a tough party leader in the traditional mold, reputed to be involved in several shady dealings. Moderate Peronists find Iglesias repulsive and embarrassing. His disastrous 1983 campaign for governor of Buenos Aires Province, highlighted when he set fire to an effigy of Alfonsín, may have cost the Peronist candidate, Italo Luder, the presidency. His faction did miserably in the 1985 midterm elections.

Despite all that, and despite violent attacks from within the party, Iglesias keeps bouncing back. His power base is strong because he is constantly "with the people"—a cardinal virtue in the Peronist idiom. The Peronist political movement has broken into two large chunks, orthodox and reformist, with other splinters in the Congress and the provinces.[21]

The centrifugal forces are powerful. No one since Perón has been able to hold together Peronism's divergent strains, so groups are going their own way. Old leaders want to hang on to power; young ones want to wrest it from them. Bad blood runs among many.

1.   Perón speaks to the people during his first presidency, with his wife Eva
at his side.

2. Eva Perón strikes her trademark pose on the balcony of the Casa Rosada. The caption to this photograph, taken from a Peronist publication, explained that "her arms were always raised, encouragingly, in a gesture of love."

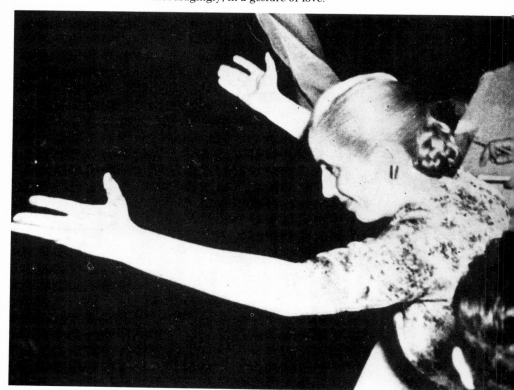

3.   President Pedro Aramburu, leader of the Liberating Revolution that
overthrew Perón in 1955, whose kidnaping and assassination fifteen years later
inaugurated the phase of greatest guerilla ascendance in Argentina.

4.   President Arturo Frondizi, shown here during President Eisenhower's visit to Argentina, ultimately lost his balancing act between the Peronists and the military.

5.   Although its timing was off, the photographer's note to his editor regarding this 1963 inaugural parade shot of (from left to right), President Arturo Illia, Admiral Eladio Vasquez, and General Juan Carlos Onganía says it all: "Save this neg. as it will become of actuality [Spanglish for "current"] when Onganía will organize a revolution against Illia in about six months—after the vacations." (*Associated Press*)

6.   President Isabel Perón speaks before the watchful (some would say evil) eye of her powerful minister, José Lopez Rega. (*Alain Nogues/Sygma Photo News*)

7.   The 1976 junta, from left to right: Admiral
Emilio Massera, General Jorge Rafael Videla, and
Air Force Brigadier Orlando Agosti. All were later
convicted for human rights abuses during their
tenure.

8. President Videla addresses the nation.

Still, an obituary would be premature. The magic of the name has not been entirely lost. The iconography continues. Perón's speeches blare from cassette-players at street-corner stands where Perón badges, books, photographs, and calendars are on sale. Many Argentines automatically vote Peronist, without even knowing who is running. Peronist leaders know this and, despite their wrangling, would like to preserve and exploit their bedrock constituency. Those from the reformist wing of the party may succeed.

Peronists know that if they do not put their house in order it will collapse. They still have the strong party and union structures in place, and a large natural constituency to mobilize. Radical Party efforts to move in on traditional Peronist turf have been largely rebuffed. The Peronists swamped the Radicals in the 1984 union elections, maintaining control of all major unions except the bank clerks and railroad workers.

Whether centrifugal or centripetal forces will prevail remains unclear. Perón himself said, "Only the idea wins over time." But what is the idea? Peronist leaders do not know, or have not told. Loyalty to the dead is not an idea and, when carried to extremes, becomes a fetish. "Enough of this necrophilia," complained one Peronist reformer. Old Peronists still vote Peronist automatically, despite the party's disarray. But their wives and children do not, which is why Raúl Alfonsín won in 1983.

AND DEMOCRACY?

Can Peronism be democratic? Yes, under certain circumstances. It will depend upon where political power lies. If it gravitates toward Argentina's democratic institutions, political coherence will become necessary for any party to control the presidency and the Congress. That would provide an incentive for Peronism to settle its internal accounts and revive itself as a viable party. Fortified democratic institutions would also help the political branch of Peronism to escape from the shadow of the union branch. When democratic institutions are weak and organized labor strong, union leaders look down on "the boys," *los muchachos*, they send to Congress. Many union leaders themselves have taken congressional seats, including the leaders of the oil, grain, construction, and paper workers.

If democratic institutions remain weak, however, Peronism may well remain undemocratic, for the unions will remain the foci of political power. For unions, winning the street and other forms of pressure matter more than what goes on in Congress. Serious labor unrest could accelerate the drift toward a military solution. The crocodile tears shed by some Radicals over the demise of Peronism could become real enough should they find themselves in the unenviable position of being the only credible political party, attacked from all sides, with no graceful constitutional exit. A one-party Argentina is a ticket to military rule.

It is too early to tell whether nascent political institutions will make enough headway against the well-entrenched social institutions to allow the Peronist Party to become more than an appendage of the union leadership. The question will not be resolved within Peronism itself, but in the overall context of Argentine politics and society. If congressional legislation becomes more important, then the Peronist politicians will obtain a real power base, independent of organized labor. They lack that now. Specific legislation could weaken organized labor as a political monolith. Its object should not be to deny the worker just compensation or adequate union representation. Rather it should be to rein in a traditionally authoritarian union movement grown too large and powerful to coexist easily with democratic institutions.

Peronism, by design, is amorphous. Its malleability allows it to be all things to all people. It can become democratic. The Organized Community can be defined to support democracy. Peronism has the potential to be a winner under democracy, so the prospect should not be frightening. It is not inherently minoritarian, like the Conservatives in the 1930s, so it need not rely on fraud and force to obtain power. The reformists rebelled especially against the thuggery and verticalism of Iglesias and Miguel. The new leaders have begun to democratize the internal structure of Peronism, albeit slowly.

There must also be a consensus as to what democracy is. When I asked Manuel Diz Rey, a union leader closely linked to Miguel, whether Peronism could support democracy, he replied, "Do not confuse democracy with hypocrisy. Democracy is not simply the right to criticize and dissent, but also requires preservation of the workers' rights, social justice, education, health, and nutrition."

Traditional Peronists see democracy as a social as well as political goal. As Secretary-General Ubaldini declared at a Peronist Unity Day rally, "We are never going to be able to understand how democracy can exist with hunger and without social justice."[22] These sentiments are genuine—and convenient for traditionally autocratic union leaders, loath to change their style after rising to the top of a verticalist hierarchy. These sentiments are also dangerous, for in the name of human welfare they help justify the repression of free expression of political will.

So Peronism's naturally large constituency does not guarantee its transformation into a democratic political party. There must also be the will to change, to leave verticalism and Perón's fascist notions of leadership behind.

Military conspiracies must be forsaken. Only a fundamental change in attitude will lead Peronism to trade in battle plans for ballot boxes, to respect the democratic rules of the game. This change is not only necessary for Peronist leaders and rank and file, but also for the rest of Argentine society.

CHAPTER 5

The Military

Give armies to countries that do not have enemies or the need to make war and you create a cottage industry that will occupy itself with making and unmaking governments, or with making civil war in the absence of foreign wars. The army will degenerate into a governing class and the people into a governed or conquered class.

—JUAN BAUTISTA ALBERDI

Will they come back? That is the question. For more than half a century, the armed forces have dominated Argentine politics. They have had their entrances and exits, sometimes well orchestrated, sometimes not. But they never stray far from center stage. Their last exit was perhaps the least graceful of all. The economy tottered on international default. The junta had started a war with a distant, declining colonial power, only to run up the white flag of unconditional surrender within three months. Though most Argentines welcomed the military defeat of subversion, they shifted uneasily under the international opprobrium meted out to one of the world's worst offenders of human rights.

Even in Argentina the armed forces do not rule forever in opposition to overwhelming popular sentiment. By 1983 the military had lost its mandate. Its seven years in power had already exceeded all prior military regimes in duration. *Ya basta*, enough already.

From a democratic viewpoint, the good news is that as governors the armed forces are thoroughly discredited. The bad news is that the armed forces are thoroughly unrepentant. In their eyes, they fought and won a dirty war that needed fighting. They thwarted the advance of international communism. Officers felt proud of their victory, which in their view was the *sine qua non* for the return to democracy. An oft-repeated sentiment was that "Alfonsín would not be sitting in the Casa Rosada today had we not defeated the subversives." If army officers could take credit for Alfonsín's arrival, they might also feel able to take the responsibility for his departure.

As for the Malvinas and economic debacles, the armed forces could hope for grace via the notoriously short political memory of the Argentines. The Malvinas War was a costly blunder, but the citizenry closed ranks around the fervent belief that the islands rightfully belonged to Argentina. Civilians proved equally unable to achieve prosperity. Economic discontent could eventually ripen into another coup.

Talk of a military return to government began within a year of Alfonsín's inauguration. People were not proposing such a thing, and perhaps such talk could be dismissed as the idle chatter of those who had grown so used to military involvement in politics that they simply could not stop thinking and talking about it. Nevertheless, the armed forces still maintained their hardware. They lay prostrate, a sea-tossed Gulliver tied down by Lilliputian laws, yet strong enough to tear free from these civilian-imposed bonds when they had recovered their consciousness, resolve, and popular support. So the talk continued, quietly, at times dismissively, but persistently. "There are three stages in a coup," according retired Colonel José Garcia, of the Center of Military Officers for Democracy. "Raising consciousness, planning, and execution. We are in the first stage."

There is disturbing precedent for a phoenix-like revival of military government. After the *cordobazo* in 1969, the armed forces took four years to extract themselves from the Casa Rosada. Then, too, the armed forces seemed discredited as viable governors. On the riotous Independence Day of 1973, when Dr. Cámpora assumed the presidency, his young supporters chanted, "*Se van, se van, y nunca volverán.* They're going, they're going, and never will return."[1] But they did return. Terrorism and near-default on the foreign debt brought them back in less than three years.

Indeed, those three years seemed interminably long; the press was predicting a coup for months before it actually occurred. Even the *Buenos Aires Herald*, later celebrated (and justly so) for its courage in reporting disappearances despite the repeated death threats against editor Robert Cox and family, seemed eager for a coup to stop the violence. A week beforehand, an editorial praised General Videla's "wise, cool head and restraining hand," adding that "the tolerance of the armed forces is almost saintly, their capacity to accept sacrifice quite Trojan. . . . This is the armed forces' finest hour."[2] Rather than offering a civilian alternative to the Peronist chaos, Radical leader Ricardo Balbín held desultory last-minute talks with other party leaders and gurgled over the "most meritorious" armed forces he had ever known. It is said that the military wanted to wait to be *begged* to return, to see their failed policies of the Argentine Revolution expunged from the national memory.

No one could compare the mid-eighties to the mid-seventies, when Argentina's social fabric, already frayed by terror, threatened to unravel completely. On the other hand, by 1985 rumors of a revival of subversion were rife. Street crime rose alarmingly. Many Argentines worried more about threats to order than to democracy. As interior minister Antonio Troccoli said in an interview at that time, with characteristic circumspection, "The temperature in the streets is not good."

The Argentine liberator and national hero, General José de San Martin, said that "the army is a lion that must be kept in a cage and not let out until the day of battle."[3] To do that, Alfonsín had to take firm civilian control of the military, reduce its sheer power, somehow manage the dirty war issue, and keep outside threats at bay. But how?

Before answering that question, it must be noted that it is unfair to speak of the armed forces as a monolithic whole. Interservice jealousies among the army, navy, and air force are intense, and each service has been divided into warring factions on many occasions. The bottom line *democratically*, though, is that coup proponents have held the day often enough to destroy the continuity of Argentina's republican institutions. So at the risk of oversimplification, this chapter will leave aside internal divisions in order to treat the fundamental military issues at play in the effort to establish Argentine democracy.

MILITARY REORGANIZATION

During the Process, the military flourished. Now, to reduce the military's political influence, it would be essential to reduce its physical power. As Alexis de Tocqueville noted, "A large army in the midst of a democratic people will always be a source of great danger. The most effectual way of diminishing that danger would be to reduce the army, but this is a remedy that all nations are not able to apply." He explained further:

It is then no matter of surprise that democratic armies are often restless, ill-tempered, and dissatisfied with their lot, although their physical condition is commonly far better and their discipline less strict than in other countries. The soldier feels that he occupies an inferior position, and his wounded pride either stimulates his taste for hostilities that would render his services necessary or gives him a desire for revolution, during which he may hope to win by force of arms the political influence and personal importance now denied him.[4]

Upon assuming office, Alfonsín cashiered one-half of the generals and one-third of the admirals. (Within two years, fifty-one of the fifty-three generals on active duty when Alfonsín took office would retire.) He sent three-quarters of the one-year conscripts home. He reduced the budget by half, to about 3.1 percent of gross domestic product.[5]

Alfonsín also tried to redesign the force structure to reduce future coup possibilities. He dissolved the First Army Corps, headquartered in Buenos Aires and at the nearby Campo de Mayo base. The First Corps had played a pivotal political role, for it had provided the troops that took over the Casa Rosada and other government buildings. The new civilian government would feel a little more secure knowing that the Tenth Infantry Brigade was not breathing down its neck from the barracks in the Palermo district of Buenos Aires, a mere three miles from the Casa Rosada.

The Ministry of the Interior also initiated a series of police reforms. Police torture was not new, but had scaled new heights during the Process, when cops cruised without license plates and patrolled without badges. Now all police officers would be obliged to take a course in law before qualifying for senior positions, and each police station was assigned an attorney to monitor observance of defendants' rights. A senior interior ministry official, Raúl Galván, hyperbolically told a television reporter that with the new requirements, senior police officers would be nearly as well-trained in the law as criminal lawyers.[6]

In an interview in his large, ground-floor office in the Casa Rosada, Minister Troccoli spoke of the police reforms. His low, gravelly voice barely rose above the thumping tom-toms and blaring brass of the day's Plaza de Mayo protest, just outside his windows. "As for me," he said, "what I declare with legitimate pride is that in one year, nearly a year and a half, there has not been one single report of illegal compulsion in any police station in any province. In the days when the methodology constantly employed was torture, they would grab a delinquent and instead of using the rules of evidence they used the *picana*, the electric prod, to force him to confess anything, even that he killed his own mother."[7]

Military intelligence also required reform. Each branch of the armed forces had its own intelligence service, which kept its own files on Argentine citizens considered to be subversive. Short of criminal acts, subversion lies in the eyes of the beholder, and these unpoliced police agencies beheld it whenever they encountered a Communist party member, an antigovernment demonstrator, or a civil rights defender. According to the magazine, *Military Voice*, "Those who from within or without seek to question the violence or drastic nature of the conduct of the antisubversive operations begin to be our 'enemies' a little."[8]

Alfonsín intended to confine the military to "specifically military" intelligence gathering, but some evidence suggests that this reform fell short. Both active duty and retired military officers told me that they continued to receive intelligence reports on subversive activities. One young lieutenant told me that when "leftist" congressional deputies planned to raid military intelligence files, the unit in question was tipped off and dispatched the desired files in a truck to another intelligence service until after the raid. "We have files and photos on lots of subversives. The Montoneros are coming back. We defeated them militarily, but not here," he said, tapping his temple. "Now they are reorganizing into cells." He added, "The services are not supposed to do that type of intelligence any more. But we still get our weekly reports. Now we just tear them up after we read them." A senior defense ministry official conceded that this insubordination continues.

The deep budget cuts were hard for the military to swallow. Now there would be fewer raises, fewer weapons, fewer exercises. Civilian suppliers of military provisions frequently suspended deliveries because they were not receiving payments. Conscripts were sent home because the army could not afford to feed them. Rumors circulated that irate soldiers planned to stage a demonstration against their poor living conditions, but were talked out of it. Officers were concerned that they would be unable to support their families in the style their wives had come to expect. "The next revolution will be started by the colonels' wives," was one refrain.

The Alfonsín approach appeared to be to rein in the armed forces gradually, forcing retirements, reducing funds, all in order to weaken them as a threat to civilian government. If done slowly, this plan could be implemented without provoking a military backlash. To be successful, however, that approach had to be articulated in a coherent strategy. If the government appeared to be indiscriminately hacking away at the military, even friendly officers would be unable to defend the civilian government from coup-prone colleagues.

Clear strategic guidelines were not quick in coming, although the government's attitude was clear enough. Alfonsín did speak of "depachydermizing" the military in order to create a lean, efficient, and modern fighting force. He also sought to reduce the justifications for a large defense commitment by removing external threats. Alfonsín immediately forswore military methods to recover the Malvinas Islands and concluded a treaty with the Chileans to resolve the century-old dispute over three islands in the Beagle Channel, at the tip of Tierra del Fuego.

Fundamental military reform, however, proved elusive. This was not surprising. Few new faces appeared in the defense ministry in December 1983.

The five top positions were filled by civilians. Minister Raúl Borrás and his deputy and ultimate successor José Horacio Jaunarena were lawyers from the town of Pergamino, in Buenos Aires province. Both were bright and politically astute, but neither had substantial experience in military matters. Bad luck also interfered; Alfonsín's first two defense ministers, Borrás and Roque Carranza, both died in office and his third, Germán López, resigned within four months of assuming office.

The new defense chiefs eschewed the appointment of civilian secretaries to head each service. They reasoned that these secretaries too often were captured by the services and represented parochial interests to the minister, rather than ministerial interests to the services. Instead of adding a layer of bureaucracy which could impede communications, top ministry officials preferred to speak directly to the military commanders themselves. This scheme fell in line with the Radical tradition of *personalismo*, of manipulating events from the top, through personal contact, rather than through clearly defined lines of authority. Anyway, there were few civilians willing and able to take on the job of controlling the services.

The Radical government may have bitten off more than it could chew. In the United States, where civilian authority over the military is unquestioned, even the ablest politician of our time found it damnably difficult to impose his will on his military subordinates. Recalling his experience as Secretary of the Navy during World War I, Franklin D. Roosevelt commented that "[t]o change anything in the Na-a-vy is like punching a feather bed. You punch it with your right and you punch it with your left until finally you are exhausted, and then you find the damn bed just as it was before you started punching."[9] In Argentina, a half dozen civilians are matched against 20,000 officers who are largely hostile, less passive than a feather bed, and long accustomed to obeying only each other.

To guarantee their control, the new civilian authorities sought to repeal the so-called Doctrine of National Security. (Military officers deny that this doctrine ever existed.) Under this doctrine, the greatest national security threat is communism, not foreign attack. Since communism strikes from within the body politic, troops must be dispersed throughout the country, not concentrated on the frontier.

The Doctrine of National Security turns arms against democracy, directly and indirectly. First, the concentration of troops in key cities of the interior comprise an ever ready coup force, within easy reach of key government facilities. Historically, Argentina's three largest cities—Buenos Aires, Rosario, and Córdoba—have been implicit hostages to the First, Second, and Third Army Corps, respectively. Second, a strategy that disperses troops also disperses resources, so instead of small but well-equipped units to repel foreign attack at the borders, units are overmanned and undersupplied. Shortages weaken the armed forces enough to embitter them but not to disable them vis-à-vis civilian government. It is the worst of both worlds.

Some campaign advisors had urged Alfonsín to force all officers of higher rank into retirement, to purge all the bad blood and start afresh. The president chose a less provocative course. Perhaps he feared that abruptly decimating the officer corps would unite the military even more strongly against him and sow the seeds for later rebellion. Total depletion of the higher ranks would also bring to the leadership of the armed forces yesterday's colonels and majors, the guys who *ran* the dirty war on the ground. Their superiors could affect a remote aspect—they may have merely given oral orders or even more subtly communicated their wishes. The junior officers, however, were steeped in the gore: not ideal candidates to lead the newly democratized armed forces. Alfonsín could also call on hundreds of retired officers, unconnected with the Process, but would they have the authority to run the show? Early retirees usually are those whose careers have aborted. They would have to shake their losers' image to command respect.

Call it timidity or prudence, Alfonsín's gradualism in dealing with the armed forces meant that instead of one great donnybrook at the outset of his term, the government had to thrust and parry through a series of minicrises. Less than a fortnight after his inauguration, the first two presidents of the Process, Jorge R. Videla and Roberto Viola, were invited to attend the swearing-in of the new army commander, Jorge Arguindegui. Alfonsín reproved Minister Borrás for their presence.

Incidents continued, coming to a head in June 1984 when the commander of the Third Corps, General Pedro Mansilla, denied the Sábato Commission access to army installations in Córdoba where human rights abuses were alleged, and supported junior officers who were urging a federal judge to transfer a case dealing with two captains charged with torture to military courts. Mansilla refused Arguindegui's order to resign. Borrás sacked both: Mansilla for insubordination, Arguindegui for weakness. Eight months later, yet another military crisis sent the commanders of the army, the joint chiefs of staff, and several other seniors officers into peremptory retirement. To the horror of the army and navy, an air force officer now headed the armed forces for the first time in history. For an institution theoretically subordinated to civilian rule, the military spent a lot of time on the front pages of Buenos Aires dailies.

What did this continuous rumbling signify? Government supporters hailed these minicrises as a series of minivictories. The president lacked the political clout to depoliticize the armed forces at one blow, so he was muddling through, gradually sapping their independence while avoiding a confrontation with the men who held the guns.

Cynics saw weakness, not cunning, in Alfonsín's approach. The president, according to this view, had no strategic sense, dallied when he should have decisively decapitated the officer corps, and thus lost the initiative. Each minicrisis advertised the Radicals' tenuous hold on government, undermined civilian rule, and alienated more and more officers.

Whether Alfonsín's policy was shrewd or bumbling, a couple of fundamentals are clear. First, notwithstanding its recent disgrace, the Argentine officer corps is still prepared to challenge civilian authority when its vital interests are at stake. The bonds of honor and loyalty instilled in every cadet still run far more strongly among soldiers than between soldiers and their civilian superiors. This fraternal loyalty has a darker side, in the pact of blood secrecy that binds the many officers who waged the dirty war and know who did what to whom.

Second, despite profound discontent, the military was too much out of favor for the first half of Alfonsín's term to do much about it. The disgruntled can retire; the retired can fulminate; the worst can plant bombs. But the time is not ripe to strike down constitutional rule yet again. Unfortunately, if the situation deteriorates, the armed forces' role as ultimate defender of the national interest remains legitimate in their own eyes. In late 1986, when I asked an Argentine what his military friends were up to, he replied, "Biding their time." Nor has the military been denied the wherewithal to act decisively when the balloon goes up.

The Argentine military is here to stay. How can it be permanently excluded from the political arena? There are two necessary conditions. First, military education must instill allegiance to the constitutional authorities. That requires a ground-up revamping of this system. Each year officers simply declare "I swear" to the flag, instead of pledging to defend the Constitution. Argentine military training has been guided by the autocratic Prussian example. Before 1984 the officer training curriculum taught nothing about the virtues of democracy. A generation ago, General Luis Rodolfo González criticized military classroom "attacks against our democratic development," noting that the professors

teach civil history by accusing the most representative men of having tolerated all the evil we suffer and of not giving us all the good we need. This excites the impatient soul of the cadet, and his patriotism predisposes him against our system of constitutional government; at the same time he loses faith in parties and ends up denying the virtues of the majority of our public men. Simultaneously the professor of military history awakens enthusiasm in an adverse sense by showing the great works and the expeditions and shining victories of successful dictators from the most remote times to the present.

As a result, the general concluded, Argentine officers became phobic of the free discussion of ideas, depreciative of those interested in public affairs, and barren of faith in the citizenry.[10] The new government began to reform military education and appointed the first civilian ever to head the National Defense College. Still, officers weaned on the supremacist model will occupy key command positions for many years to come.

The second essential to military reform is civilian reform. Soldiers are not the only ones who lack allegiance to democracy. Every military coup has been egged on by civilians. Military conspiracy has become a standard political tool. The Conservatives backed the military overthrow of the Radicals in 1930. The Radicals backed the overthrow of the Conservatives in 1943 and of Perón in 1955. The Popular Radicals backed the ouster of the Intransigent Radicals in 1962; the Intransigents returned the disfavor when the Popular Radicals were deposed with their help in 1966. Civilians must stop knocking on the barracks doors. The fault stretches beyond the political elite. Never have the people protested or resisted a military coup. Often they have gathered in the Plaza de Mayo to salute the new pretender.

MILITARY JUSTICE

This is a raw nerve, as well it should be. In the 1970s, some 9,000 Argentines or more were kidnaped, tortured, and murdered. Their homes were ransacked, their sisters raped. An indeterminate number, as even President Videla and his colleagues admit, were innocent. In the euphemism of warspeak, these poor souls were victims of "excesses." A warped perception may consider these excesses a surfeit of zeal in the patriotic exercise of duty. Common sense tells us that these excesses revealed a surfeit of greed, sadism, and personal score-settling. In sum, it was an excess of unregulated power, the megalomania of those who kill with impunity . . . and authority.

In 1982 some 1,000 Argentine soldiers died in a disastrous war. The exact toll is unknown, since the army never released an official figure. After the sinking of the *Belgrano*, the navy's combat ships remained bottled-up in port, ceding the all-important control of the island seas to the British. The army leaders reportedly sent raw recruits into combat, inadequately fed and armed. Only the air force, the service most reluctant to enter the war, distinguished itself in battle.

How did the armed forces deal with these two national disgraces?

The Supreme Council of the Armed Forces began its Malvinas inquiry soon after Argentina's surrender. It appointed a commission, chaired by retired General Benjamin Rattenbach, to investigate the conduct of the war. The Rattenbach Report concluded that the occupation was disastrously planned, timed, and organized, and was undertaken in ignorance of the war potential of Britain and her allies.[11] Sixteen officers were charged with responsibility for the defeat. Two of the three ruling junta members, General Leopoldo Galtieri and Admiral Jorge Anaya, faced maximum sentences of death.[12] The case went to the Supreme Council, which held hearings, and stalled. After the 1983 elections interrupted the proceedings, the Supreme Council was flooded by hundreds of human rights cases. This enormous workload (conveniently?) bogged down the Supreme Council. Finally, in mid-1986 the Supreme Council handed down its judgment: twelve years for Galtieri, fourteen for Anaya, eight for air force commander Basilio Lami Dozo, and acquittals for the rest, including the fleeting governor-general of the islands, General Mario Menendez, and navy lieutenant Alfredo Astiz, of whom we shall know more later.

The human rights cases were different. Many active-duty officers had opposed the way their commanders had waged the Malvinas War. They were ashamed of the ineptitude of Galtieri and his collaborators. But none openly disputed the way the dirty war was waged. The officer corps clung to the same story, and to each other. The dirty war, in their view, was provoked in full measure by subversives who threatened to destroy the nation. The only way to defeat an urban guerilla operation was with an urban guerilla operation. Conventional tactics, with concentrated troop strengths and clear lines of communication, would play right into the hands of the terrorists. After noting that the armed forces had "to search for the enemy not only behind a tree or a bush but also, and thoroughly, behind desks, in factories, in classrooms and even, unfortunately, in some cases behind a pulpit," a military journal concluded in 1977 that "the aggressors imposed the law and that is the law that governs and establishes the principles of this war."[13]

The terrorists had already infiltrated military barracks and armories as a prelude to successful attacks. To neutralize infiltrators, the state security forces broke up into secret, autonomous cells, whose orders were communicated orally or implicitly. Supposedly the "individual excesses" were an unfortunate but unavoidable byproduct of these necessary antisubversive tactics. Some did not even consider the excesses excessive, most quotably the governor of Buenos Aires province, General Ibérico St. Jean, who said, "First we will kill all the subversives; then we will kill all their collaborators; then their sympathizers; then those who are indifferent; and, finally, we will kill all those who are timid."[14]

The military judges of the Armed Forces Supreme Council stood solidly behind their former colleagues who now stood before them in the dock, accused under Alfonsín's Decree No. 158 of illegal deprivation of liberty, torture, and murder.[15] The military judges were themselves appointees of the Process. One of them, General Tomás Sánchez de Bustamante, was quoted in 1980 as saying that "there are norms and judicial guidelines that do not apply in the case of subversion. For example, the right to habeus corpus. In this type of struggle the secrecy that must envelop the special operations requires that it not be divulged who has been captured and who must be captured; there must exist a cloud of silence that surrounds everything."[16] Strangely, this blatant conflict of interest did not lead the president to request or the council members to offer their resignations.

Alfonsín's failure to replace the Supreme Council members makes a little more sense in the larger context of his approach. He would allow the military to try its own officers in the first instance, in order to let them clean their own house, but he would provide recourse to civilian courts if the Supreme Council acquitted a defendant or did not produce verdicts within six months.[17] The Supreme Council carried a heavy responsibility in this scheme.

The president ordered the first nine junta members and two notorious torturers (General Ramón Camps and Admiral Rubén Chamorro) to stand trial before the Supreme Council. According to script, after the council condignly punished these protagonists of the dirty war, and the Sábato Commission issued its report on the *desaparecidos*, the public thirst for retribution and information would be slaked. Alfonsín could then issue an amnesty for the rest of the armed forces; Argentina could close a tragic chapter and move on to rebuilding itself. Human rights groups were unhappy with this scheme, but most politicians felt that the dirty war issue had to be laid to rest before the country could realize its hopes.

The Supreme Council, however, would not play ball. It announced itself unable to reach judgments regarding the human rights cases in the nine months allotted (including a three-month extension), but proceeded informally to acquit them anyway. The council reported that the orders issued in the struggle against subversion were "unobjectionable," so the military commanders could only be indirectly responsible for inadequately restraining their energetic subordinates.

The council's focus on only written orders and decrees was too formalistic. It ignored crimes of omission, the probability that illegal orders were issued orally, and "the personality of the cadet, who learns blindly to obey the smallest insinuation of command without discussion, rapidly, in order and silence."[18] The Supreme Council added that the possible bias of witnesses who were relatives of the *desaparecidos* or themselves involved in subversion was of "transcendental importance" in preventing a final verdict. This puzzled those who had thought that the alleged murderers, and not the victims, were on trial. Could the Supreme Council seriously be suggesting that the saga of the disappearances was all a big lie? How could it?

The vast gulf separating Argentines was underscored by the nearly simultaneous release of the Sábato Commission report on *desaparecidos*. The commission and the Supreme Council took identical facts and reached opposite conclusions. Both noticed striking similarities among the grim tales told. Sábato took them at face value, and

> inferred that human rights were violated in widespread and official form by the repression of the Armed Forces. And violated in a manner not sporadic but systematic, a manner always the same, with similar kidnapings and identical tortures in every extension of the national territory. How can that not be attributed to a methodology of terror planned by the high commanders? How could they have been committed by perverts who were acting for their own account under a rigorously military regime, with all the powers and channels of communication that such a regime supposes? How can one speak of "individual excesses?" From our information it emerges that this technology of Hell was carried out by sadistic but regimented perpetrators.[19]

The Supreme Council, too, saw conspiracy in the identical accounts of survivors and witnesses, but one of an entirely different nature. Its chairman commented that "the possibility of prior agreement among those testifying, arising spontaneously or by actions of interested third parties, cannot be discarded in view of the fact that certain coincidences in content and style open the field to suspicions. . . ."[20]

The Supreme Council report fell like a bombshell. The government played it down. Others were more outspoken. The head of left-leaning Intransigent party, Oscar Alende, said that "it shows that they did not want to judge their peers." Sábato Commission member, Graciela Fernández Meijide, was not surprised because the Supreme Council's members "are the same who were there during the military dictatorship, are the same who were aware of and endorsed the violations of human rights."[21] Stung by these and more rebukes, the council asked the defense minister to halt the campaign of disparagement. Borrás coolly replied that, in a democracy, a public tribunal "remains exposed" to public opinion, an "invaluable guide" for public servants. General Sánchez de Bustamante abandoned his "cloud of silence" to lead the Supreme Council in resigning en masse.

According to Alfonsín's amendments to the Military Justice Code, the Supreme Council action sent the cases up to the Federal Court of Criminal Appeals. Videla showed the most galling hypocrisy. Throughout his presidency, he had answered charges of human rights violations by piously maintaining that civilian courts remained open and operated to protect the citizens—when they could find them. Now Videla himself refused to submit to civilian courts, arguing that he had a constitutional right to be tried exclusively by his "natural," i.e. military, judges. The "natural judge" clause of the Constitution states that no inhabitant may be "removed from the judges designated by the law" prior to the act in issue. Videla argued that as a soldier his natural judges were those of the Armed Forces Supreme Council.[22]

Videla had a perfect right to press that argument vigorously in court. But the Supreme Court rejected it, on grounds that military courts had no constitutional jurisdiction over crimes allegedly committed against civilians in the absence of a formal state of war. The case having passed from the Supreme Council, the Federal Appeals Court now would take over.[23] Videla then boycotted his own trial, refusing to designate defense counsel, offer evidence, or formulate allegations. So now the courts (purged of Videla appointees) were not such a bastion for the defense of citizens. Further, this citizen deigned to exalt himself over the Supreme Court as interpreter of Argentine law. He wanted to be defendant and judge in his own case, just as he had earlier been prosecutor and judge in the cases of the defendant-enemy-victims of the dirty war.

Meanwhile, Minister of Defense Borrás could not find respected retired officers willing to serve on the now vacant Supreme Council. The ranks had closed in opposition to the Radical government, so Borrás had to invoke his legal power to summon retirees to serve on the Supreme Council. No sooner had the new council convened than it released navy lieutenant Alfredo Astiz, the most notorious dirty warrior of all. In 1977, in an apparent case of mistaken identity, this hero had felled a fleeing Swedish teenager, Dagmar Hagelin, with a bullet to the back of the head. Then he infiltrated a human rights group that was trying to locate *desaparecidos*, posing as a brother of one of the missing. Astiz, also known as "the Blonde Angel," put the finger on two French nuns, Sisters Alice Domon and Leonie Duquet (aged forty and sixty-one), as they emerged from a group meeting. Neither Hagelin nor the nuns ever reappeared.[24]

The Astiz case did not become notorious for its outrageousness, but because the Swedish and French governments pressed vigorous protests. Perhaps to give Astiz a chance to vindicate himself, the navy gave him command of the unit that occupied South Georgia in the Malvinas conflict. Alas, soldiers in uniform present more of a challenge than nuns or the back of a seventeen-year-old girl. Apparently the garrison commanded by Astiz surrendered to a smaller British landing party without resistance.[25] That valor landed him before the Supreme Council in the Malvinas trials (in which he was acquitted, as noted above).

The Hagelin case became a tug-of-war between the military and civilian branches of government, precisely because it *was* typical. If a young, active-duty officer like Astiz could be prosecuted, the whole officer corps would be at risk. Consequently, Astiz was to be saved at all costs. The reconstituted Supreme Council released Astiz on double-jeopardy grounds (he had been acquitted for lack of evidence in 1981). The civilian Federal Appeals Court reversed the double-jeopardy finding and remanded the case to the Supreme Council for adjudication on the facts. The Supreme Council then reacquitted Astiz for lack of evidence, and the case returned yet again to the civilian court of appeals, which absolved Astiz on grounds that the statute of limitations had run out on his alleged crimes.

Meanwhile, the Argentine nation became transfixed by "The Trial," the long-awaited confrontation between the first nine junta members of the Process and their accusers. Commencing in April 1985, with witnesses testifying through August, attorneys arguing in September, and the decision handed down in December, the trial gripped the Argentine public as thoroughly as Watergate gripped the American public a decade earlier. Contending passions ran high. In Argentina, novelty increased the fascination: public trials are extremely rare, and McCarthy/Watergate-type hearings unknown. This made for some confusing moments. When the presiding judge recited the traditional pretestimony admonition to tell the truth on pain of punishment for perjury to former president, General Alejandro Augustín Lanusse, the general took umbrage at the implicit challenge to his honor and veracity. It took a couple of minutes to persuade Lanusse that the warning was customary, not personal, and that he must indeed proceed with his testimony.

To give some sense of the trial itself, it may be useful to set forth some first-hand impressions I jotted down one day at *Tribunales*, the grand old edifice where it was held. Security was reasonably tight at both building and courtroom entrances, where passes were examined. The neoclassical courtroom itself was wainscoted in dark wood. The hardwood benches that ran down the center of the courtroom were filled by invited guests. Corinthian columns separated the lower and upper galleries to the sides, reserved for the press and public, respectively. Beyond the bar, the twenty-six defense attorneys and two prosecutors sat at tables. Behind the dais of the six judges, a gold crucifix hung in an archway dominated by a stained-glass tryptich of the national seal of Argentina.

Stories emerged in layers, as in a movie where the same scene is played over and over from different angles. First was the case of Señorita María Livia Formiga. Her landlord testified that soldiers and plainclothesmen came, announced themselves as police, destroyed his tenant's apartment and took all her possessions, including her collection of Italian records. Two sisters told of frustrated efforts to file a writ of habeus corpus and futile entreaties to UNESCO, the OAS, the U.S. and Italian embassies, military commands and government ministries. The father explained that his daughter worked as a nurse in a medical research center in Buenos Aires but traveled two or three times a week to La Plata, where she taught Red Cross courses and where she was kidnaped. Señor Formiga was told that four nurses were taken at once; that Monsignor Grasselli had a card file but said that his daughter did not appear in it; that on 20 January 1978 Task Group 113 released her and she left the police station (though no one saw her at liberty); that in 1979 or 1980 a naval captain saw her at the Naval Mechanics School in Buenos Aires (the most notorious detention center); and that a colonel told him that "the bodies aren't delivered." A defense attorney tried to ask the witness whether Señorita Formiga was a member of the Montoneros or other subversive organizations, but the court held the question inadmissible.

A forty-year-old soldier from the Seventh Regiment of La Plata took the stand. He immediately denied that he had been involved in any antisubversive activity, though he admitted that he took in furniture and other items brought in by other soldiers, and that various receipts bore his handwriting.

> "What rank did you have?" prosecutor Strassera inquired.
> "I don't remember."
> "Were your orders verbal or written?"
> "Oral."
> "To whom did you deliver the things brought in to you?"
> "To the deposit."
> "In whose charge?"
> "Nobody's."

The widow of President Lanusse's press secretary, Edgardo Sajón, testified. A few days earlier her suspected widowhood had been confirmed by one of her husband's torturers, who revealed that Sajón had been electrocuted while strapped nude to a billiard table.

Former President Lanusse reluctantly provided the biggest story of the day when testifying of the recovery of the corpse of his relative and high-ranking diplomat, Elena Holmberg.[26] She had disappeared on 20 December 1978. Her body was not identified until 11 January 1979, although it had been recovered from the Tigre estuary to the River Plate in Buenos Aires forty-eight hours after her disappearance, still wearing a signet ring with the initials "EH." First Corps Commander Suarez Mason accompanied Lanusse to the Tigre police station to recover the body and reproached the responsible officer for slowness. "What do you want?" the man replied. "You have thrown over 8,000 bodies in the river."

Similar testimony went on day after day. It filled the newspapers. A new weekly, *The Trial Diary*, began publication and quickly became a bestseller. New and more lurid details emerged; even the military's most ardent defenders had trouble explaining how fellatio, compelled of a woman detainee, helped achieve the goal of the Process to promote Christian values. Many people had ignored the Sábato Commission report or discounted it as a leftist ploy. But now, with respected newspapers reporting the same events in equally shocking terms, the facts of the repression could only be denied by a monumental act of self-deceit.

The prosecutor's summation took place over four days and resonated with the eloquence born of struggles against injustice. Throughout, Prosecutor Strassera sought balance by roundly condemning the subversion that spawned the repression, while insisting that cause did not justify effect:

> The guerillas kidnaped, tortured, and killed. And what did the state do to combat them? It kidnaped, tortured, and killed on a scale infinitely greater and, which is graver, outside the juridical order instituted by the government itself, whose framework it sought to show us was exceeded by the seditious. How many victims of the repression were guilty of illegal activities? Never shall we know, and it is not the fault of the victims. . . .
>
> It is clear that, apart from simulated confrontations and assassination of prisoners, there were real confrontations in which members of the Armed Forces and security forces lost their lives at the hands of the armed bands that were terrorizing the popula. Bn. but these criminals should have been judged, not tortured and murdered. If it had been so, those officials today would be heroes. All that effort was squandered by the commanders.[27]

Strassera then detailed the hundreds of counts filed against the ex-commanders: homicide, illegal deprivation of liberty, torture, aggravated robbery, extortion, kidnaping, concealment, and more. Before asking for sentencing, the federal prosecutor addressed the court:

We Argentines tried to obtain peace founded in oblivion, and we failed. . . . We searched for peace by way of violence and extermination, and we failed. . . . From the moment of this trial and the sentences I propose, we have the opportunity to establish a peace based in remembering and not in forgetting, in justice and not in violence. This is our opportunity; it may be the last.[28]

Strassera then pleaded that life terms be given to five of the six members of the first two juntas, and that the other four receive between ten- and fifteen-year terms.

The defense attorneys advanced various arguments: that the trial itself was unconstitutional and supported subversion, that their clients were not directly responsible for the "excesses" of the dirty war, that the dirty war was necessary, that the victims were subversives (and implicitly deserving of their fate). Of the accused, only the heavy-browed, would-be populist hero, Admiral Emilio Massera, rose in his own defense. His words went beyond that of defense counsel in letter, but not in sentiment:

I have not come here to defend myself. No one has to defend himself for having won a just war. And the war against terrorism was a just war. If we had lost we would not be here—neither you nor us—because some time ago the high judges of this court would have been replaced by turbulent people's tribunals. . . .

But here we are. Because we won the war of arms and lost the war of minds. . . . [M]y accusers are those whom we defeated in the war of arms. . . . The victors are accused by the vanquished. . . .

[T]he enemy knows that the Armed Forces of today are as able to defeat it as the Armed Forces of yesterday. . . . I believe myself to be responsible but I do not believe myself to be guilty. . . .

My future is a cell. . . . Of only one thing am I certain. That when the news reports disappear, because history outshines it, my children and grandchildren will utter with pride the name I have left them.[29]

After weeks of deliberation, the court issued its judgment: five convictions and four acquittals. Videla and Massera received life terms; Videla's successor, Roberto Viola, received seventeen years; Massera's successor, Armando Lambruschini, and Orlando Agosti, the third member of the original junta, both received shorter terms. Acquitted were Omar Graffigna, the third member of the second junta, and all the members of the last junta who would, however, later be convicted in the Malvinas War trial.

The trial was neither a witchhunt nor a whitewash. That is not to say that political considerations were absent, any more than they are absent from the

U.S. appellate courts, but rather that the results could be read consistently with both the evidence and the law. The judges conducted the proceedings with scrupulous fairness. The public was enlightened. Justice was done.

The close of the trial of the ex-commanders brought to the fore the hundreds of charges remaining against other military officers for human rights abuses committed during the dirty war. In April 1986 the government set guidelines for the defense of "due obedience" to orders as a defense against criminal sanction, and urged the military prosecutor to proceed more rapidly in these cases because, in the words of the new defense minister, Dr. Germán López, "justice delayed is justice denied."[30] In response to these developments, one of the six jurists who had presided at the ex-commanders' trial resigned, an indication that the balancing act required to manage the dirty war issue would continue on the razor's edge for a long time to come.

THE MILITARY-INDUSTRIAL COMPLEX

Not surprisingly, over the years the Argentine military has become an economic powerhouse, in land, labor, and capital. The army is one of the biggest landowners in Argentina. By 1983, there were 153,000 soldiers in uniform, and military spending comprised 12 percent of the national budget. Each branch of the armed forces owns or controls a domain of large state enterprises. The air force writ runs to aircraft production, the national airlines, air insurance, and travel agencies. The navy presides over a complex including a merchant fleet, shipyards, weapons research and production.

The army has the big kid on the block, drily denominated the General Directorate of Military Factories, known as FM. FM was Argentina's first state-owned heavy industry, born of the vision of General Manuel Savio, who saw Argentina's industrial incapacity as a grave weakness that the army could greatly reduce. The Great Depression cut Argentina off from its traditional source of capital imports, Great Britain. The Second World War confirmed that the British would no longer be in a position to supply Argentine needs for arms or capital investments. This development could lead to disastrous consequences if Argentina were drawn into the war, especially since the Government's pro-Axis sympathies led the United States to embargo arms shipments to Argentina while generously supplying archrival Brazil.

Although free-market conservatives controlled the Congress, by 1941 Argentina's disquieting isolation earned their consent to the creation of FM. The law creating FM called for research and development of Argentine industrial and mineral capabilities to ensure the ability to mobilize industry onto a wartime footing.[31] Once established, Argentina's newly developed strategic industries would be divested to the private sector.

Somehow expansion, not divestiture, became the norm. For all their talk of free enterprise, the military governments after Perón had little desire to reduce their own economic influence by giving away FM installations. Philosophically, officers felt more at home with the statist solution; vital tasks should be left to the government on national security grounds. This began in the military sphere, with arms factories, but in time it spread throughout the economy, sometimes on the flimsiest grounds. "Telephones. Yes. Lines of communication. Better let the army have a hand in the National Telephone Company." And so on. The boards of directors of state enterprises provided an excellent source of retirement income for ex-officers.

Vested military interests in continued state ownership became an enormous obstacle to privatization plans. Even Martínez de Hoz, the great free marketeer, could not cajole (let alone force) the military to surrender to the free market. "We couldn't privatize," complained one former economics ministry official from the Process. "As they say, the army has everything on the ground, the navy everything in the water, the air force everything in the air." Civilian governments generally lacked the free market instinct, as well as the political clout, to attack this bastion of military privilege.

So military enterprises grew and grew. By the 1980s, they employed over 40,000 and billed some $1.5 billion in sales annually. In its strong years, FM comprised 5 percent of gross domestic product.[32] It operated fourteen military factories directly, producing weaponry, explosives, chemicals, steel, electrical conductors. It maintained a hammerlock on the mining sector. But FM's direct activities tell only a part of the story; it also holds large shareholdings in other companies and mixed state-private enterprises, especially in the fields of steel and petrochemicals production. That included 99.9 percent of the shares of Somisa, Argentina's largest steel company.

FM progressed far beyond Savio's wildest dreams, perhaps beyond his wildest fears. Its mandate grew apace with its scale. In addition to supplying for war, FM became charged with the task of stimulating industrial development in low profit or long lead-time industries. FM historians cite Robert McNamara to justify this approach; the former secretary of defense had said that "security is development and without development there can be no security." So FM expansion into the private sector helped prepare military factories for quick wartime mobilization, by keeping them fully-occupied producing consumer goods in peacetime. With this strained logic, FM became a producer of armchairs, subway cars, hunting arms, and ammunition. Seventy percent of total sales went to the private sector; 98 percent of the receipts of the giant Zapla steel furnaces in Jujuy Province came from the private sector.[33]

Through their own companies and influence over other state enterprises, the armed forces squatly occupied an important segment of the internal market. This afforded enormous influence over Argentine economics and politics. Through this complex, the military controlled budgets and jobs; it could favor some concerns by investing in them and squeeze out others by competing with them. Its weight in the corridors of political power gave it a leg up in getting a hold of government funds. Since the state contributed half of the national total in fixed capital investment, it became prudent in private companies to appoint a well-connected, retired officer to the board of directors. The military companies themselves also directed substantial revenues to the armed forces.

Inevitably, military production ran up the diseconomies of scale typical of unwieldy state enterprises. Until 1980, FM received substantial government subsidies and tax breaks. This favoritism encouraged inefficiency in FM enterprises, while stacking the deck against private enterprises who could not successfully enter the market due to the monopoly competition. According to National Deputy Alvaro Alsogaray, FM poured "hundreds of millions of dollars" into Hipasam S.A. to mine iron ore in northern Patagonia, an investment "that will never produce any benefit."[34] Duplication of effort is the rule; the army and the navy each produce their own gunpowder, as well as a host of other products.

Getting back to basics, we find Argentine arms production falling short. During the Malvinas War, weapons reportedly jammed and misfired. One obvious way to expand markets is through exports, but FM has never succeeded in this field. Exports have generally accounted for only around 5 percent of total sales. As a semi-industrialized country, Argentina should be well placed to sell lower-cost, lower-technology weapons in the multibillion dollar per year Third World arms market.

Brazil, for instance, now exports $1.4 billion worth of armaments yearly, including a forty-ton battle tank, rockets, and the Tucano trainer aircraft, which was adopted by Britain's Royal Air Force. From modest beginnings a decade ago, Brazil has become the fifth leading arms exporter in the world, behind the United States, Soviet Union, France, and Britain.[35] Argentina's historic failure to succeed in the export market testifies starkly against the quality and efficiency of national arms production.

Cutting FM and other military enterprises down to size could prove critical to the long-term effort to keep the military out of politics. Instead of breaking up FM, however, Alfonsín just put a civilian in at the top. The new director, Raúl Tomás, as secretary of defense for production, acquired authority over the whole military-industrial complex. Tomás was more eager to consolidate than to divest his new portfolio. No selling-off of companies or divisions unrelated to military needs was proposed in the first three years of civilian rule. Perhaps few of these losing ventures would attract significant private investment. On the other hand, some military enterprises are profitable, and others manufacture such basic industrial products that a market is assured and investors would surely appear in a stable economic climate.

FM officials blame the private sector for the failure of privatization plans, arguing that investors are so risk-averse that they will not bid for military companies unless at a heavily discounted price and, even then, insist on tariff protection and subsidies. "We are willing to sell off operations at a fair price," one senior FM official told me. "But we are not going to give them away." Businessmen reply that the "fair price" is whatever they will bid, not a sum preordained by FM bureaucrats. Both arguments have merits, but the upshot is that privatization remains elusive.

Eventually, a reform plan emerged, but privatization had no role in it. To the contrary, the Alfonsín government decided to place FM and all other military enterprises under a new, still larger, state holding company. Supposedly, this consolidation would reduce the notorious duplication of effort typical of multiservice production, and permit non-FM, government auditors to reduce inefficiency. If this theory succeeded in practice, it would be the first time.

The statist approach of creating a still more concentrated military-industrial leviathon is typically Argentine. It will not help keep the military out of politics for good. All the next military government would have to do to restore the good old days would be to replace the civilian head of FM with its own general.

Meanwhile, apart from severe budget reductions that all state enterprises now endure and the unwanted, unwonted experience of following orders from a civilian boss, life in FM continues much as before from the military perspective. The top management and board of directors are now dominated by civilians, but active duty officers from generals on down continue to abound in important positions. The two major division chiefs (production and development) are military officers, as are the managers of all the military factories.[36]

More importantly, the second-tier, civilian managers who have always run FM on a day-to-day basis continue to do so today. These careerists have always outlasted their military superiors, who routinely rotate out of FM in a couple of years. The sinecures for retired officers are fewer, but the dismantling necessary to destroy FM as a military power base is nowhere in sight.

SECURITY RISKS

Argentine soldiers never battled foreign foes between the bloody Paraguayan War over 100 years ago, which wiped out two-thirds of the Paraguayan adult male population, and the Malvinas War of 1982. Meanwhile, the turn-of-the-century conversion of Argentine defense forces from provincial militia into a large standing army created a large standing threat to civilian rule. There have been border disputes with Chile and Brazil, but far too limited to justify Argentina's military investment.

To justify their size and budget, the armed forces oversell the threats they face. The late General Juan Guglialmelli, editor of the leading Argentine strategic journal, *Estrategia*, used to describe Brazil's imperialist designs in the Southern Cone so ominously that one would have expected an invasion into Argentina's remote Northeastern provinces years ago.[37]

Ideological threats have been taken more seriously. Conservatives are obsessed with communism; the outbreak of subversion in the 1970s (which their own repressive policies encouraged) vindicated their fears. They allege that Cuba and the Soviet Union armed and funded the guerillas in Argentina.

Even assuming that the Argentine military had its hands full with threats both external and internal, that does not explain why it had to destroy constitutional government. After all, bullets should prove equally fatal to the enemy whether or not a general occupies the Casa Rosada. The Allies won World War II without trashing their own constitutions or allowing soldiers to take over the reins of government. In combating the subversion of the 1970s, why were the Argentine armed forces unable to wage battle without breaking the law?

There was a pretext and a reason. The pretext was that communism in Argentina could only be thwarted by a no-holds-barred counter offensive. Subversives could not be permitted to succeed because they enjoyed the protections of a constitution they were bent on destroying. That argument will not hold. The government of Isabel Perón was as anticommunist as they come, to the point of signing paramilitary, anticommunist death squads a blank check. Moreover, the Peronist government by decree had given the armed forces virtual carte blanche in the "annihilation" of subversion. The former junta commanders defended themselves during their trial by saying they had only acted in fulfillment of civilian orders. Then why did they need to kick out the civilian government?

The true reason for military coups is that the armed forces are thoroughly politicized. The military both takes the initiative and serves the wishes of civilian politicians. Either way, political considerations, not national security risks, provoke military coups. The five coups prior to 1976 prove the point.

What security threats did President Alfonsín face? Crime was one. Felonies have increased markedly in recent years. During Alfonsín's first year in office, crime reports became increasingly alarming. Several gun stores were stripped of rifles, pistols, and ammunition. A team of five armed robbers calmly went from room to room of the four-star Salles Hotel in downtown Buenos Aires, taking two-and-a-half hours to relieve guests of their money, jewelry and, more disturbingly, passports. Small-scale political bombings were common, reaching a crescendo just before the 1985 midterm elections.

Military officers were fond of warning of a possible revival of subversion in Argentina. The growing threat of international terrorism reinforced the speculation. The Shining Path guerillas were rumored to have set up a temporary camp in Tucumán, the province that the ERP had tried to "liberate" ten years before.

Retired military officers said that subversives were already in action, trying to regain power legally through the infiltration of leftist political parties.[38] The chairman of the General Staff, General Julio Fernández Torres, warned that indirect subversive aggression "is in clear development in the fields of psychological operations, the gathering of information and resources" and other actions.[39] The Alfonsín government roundly denied that there was any evidence of a subversive comeback and stressed that it would aggressively thwart any subversion the moment it appeared.

Subversion being secretive by nature, it is impossible to say whether or not it was afoot, in the absence of overt acts. A few things, though, can be said. First, the subversives of the 1970s were crushed, so any revival would be an impressive feat. Second, the socioeconomic conditions of Argentina in the 1980s could conceivably support new revolutionary movements. The increasing economic and political frustration of Argentina today could nourish the roots of such a movement. Third, "psychological" subversion is an infinitely elastic concept; if two Argentines saw a communist meeting, one might call it subversion and the other democracy in action. So one should be careful with definitions. The more broadly one defines subversion, the sooner the need for a military response becomes accepted.

Fourth, motives exist for sounding the alarm that subversion is back. Retired military officers psychologically need to defend their sacred institution against the calumnies permitted by democracy. Encouraging rumors of subversion could justify past actions and insulate them from present attacks. Extremists from the political right gain by fostering the image of subversion by the political left. This fact begins a game of mirrors. In the words of one observer, a "bomb could have been planted by an officer, who wanted to embarass his superiors, who wanted to put pressure on their commander, who wanted to discredit the government that blamed the guerillas, who claimed credit for one of their cells, which tried to contact the officer to pay him for more bombs. . . ."[40] The possibilities are endless.

In short, any enemy of the Alfonsín government or of democracy gains by the increase of domestic violence. Subversion would discredit the government and raise the prospects for yet another coup. Radicals saw the whole subversion issue as a chimera.

The debate over whether subversion was or was not on the move should not obscure a critical fact: subversion can be defeated by a civilian government. The Italian and German governments brought the Red Brigade and Baader-Meinhof gangs to heel in the 1970s without a military government. ("Yes, but the Italians lost fifty judges," replied a former justice minister of the Process.) It can even be argued that the Peronist government had brought the ERP to heel by 1976 without a military government.

The prerequisite is a government willing and security forces able to act effectively. Since Alfonsín would be the biggest loser of a subversive outbreak, he would probably be willing to act decisively. Defense and Interior officials have said so, and there is little reason to doubt them. So if the armed forces ousted Alfonsín on these grounds, subversion would be the excuse, and politics (as usual) the reason. The armed forces stand to be the biggest winner from subversion; it would vindicate them and bring them back into government, where they can give themselves bigger budgets and better jobs. That in turn would raise serious questions as to who, in fact, is planting "subversive" bombs today.[41]

Indeed, suspicions of the military and its friends seemed well-founded when, in May 1986, an unarmed bomb was discovered at a military base during a visit by Alfonsín. The bomb was hidden under a sewer within two yards of the route of the president's car. When it was successfully detonated—with the press in attendance—the question became whether the bomb was meant as a warning and show of force or whether it was a botched assassination attempt. Neither interpretation was heartening.

The Argentine military is too big and too important. It burdens the economy and threatens the Constitution. Arrogating to itself the role of Protector of the Fatherland, it has replaced the electorate as the ultimate arbiter as to who shall govern Argentina.

Yet the armed forces are a symptom as well as cause of Argentine political instability. They acted when civilian political institutions were weak or irresponsible. Their adventures were always encouraged by civilians. As Samuel Huntington has written, military coups have civilian causes.

Recriminations aside, how can the armed forces be kept away from civilian politics? Both military and civilian reform are necessary. The Argentine armed forces must be trimmed to a size large enough to meet their obligations, small enough to be controlled. The officers must be taught to value obedience to the Constitution above the malleable fatherland concept. They must learn to respect that document though they cannot soon be expected to cherish it. As General González said, "The day in which we military men stop deluding ourselves with the fugitive scintillations of adventures from other parts, we shall discover that our mission is to be at the service of democracy and our duty to accept the decisions of the citizenry, maintaining freely elected authorities without interference of any sort in the life and decisions of the parties."[42]

Civilians must learn to leave the armed forces alone. Yrigoyen and Perón converted the officer corps from devoted professionals to a thoroughly politicized and often divided interest group. Last year's election losers must be dissuaded from becoming this year's coup-mongers. Argentine political leaders have a long way to go before learning this lesson. Peronist party leader Herminio Iglesias said: "If this is democracy, give me anything but democracy." The Argentine people also have a long way to go before they can be expected to defend democracy in Argentina. Unfortunately, until now they have had little inclination to do so, for reasons which become clear in the next chapter.

CHAPTER 6

Significant Others

Liberty and authority are not written, they are not decreed; they are created, they are constructed through education. They are not made in the Congress, but rather in hearth and home. They do not live on paper, they live in man.

—JUAN BAUTISTA ALBERDI

At the age of ten, a student is forced to memorize Eva Perón's ghosted autobiography, *My Mission in Life,* while the Argentine Constitution gathers dust in the corner. At twenty, she wants to join the Peronist party, but it is banned. So she joins the Socialist party, even though it does not represent her views, but soon this party, too, is banned. At thirty, she lives in fear of falling in the crossfire of warring factions. At forty, she opens her daily newspaper to find that a group of congressmen have arrested an attorney whose testimony offended them, then personally raided his office and carted away his files before he was released. She has not learned democracy, has not lived it, has not even seen it practiced responsibly. A sad little tale, duplicated millions of times in Argentina.

The citizen is the building block of democracy. No democratic system can survive if the citizens do not believe in it deeply, understand their own rights, and respect those of others. Democracy requires more than mere voting. We have seen how Peronism and the military experience have constricted Argentine democracy. Now we will see that even the democratic institutions themselves imbue the citizen with cynicism instead of democratic sentiment, while a principal defender of social reform in Latin America—the Catholic Church—is a principal defender of authoritarianism in Argentina.

THE CHURCH

Argentina is predominantly Catholic, and the Church bears an imposing presence. Religious columns and clerical statements appear regularly in the newspapers. The depth of religious belief is another question. It is striking that many Argentines cross themselves when they pass by churches, even while hanging on for dear life to the overhead railings of the city buses that careen recklessly through the bustling streets of Buenos Aires. "Yes, but they never go in," scoffed one close advisor to Alfonsín.

What has the level of ecclesiasticism and lay adherence got to do with politics? Lots. The Church has played a powerful political role in Argentina. The less lay support has existed for that political exercise, the more Church actions risk running athwart the popular will, the supposed sovereign in a democratic society.

Since Argentina was a Spanish colony, the Catholic Church naturally enjoyed substantial prestige and influence even before the declaration of independence.[1] Political crisis struck in 1880, when the anticlerical, liberal (some even say Masonic) government of President Julio A. Roca banned Catholic instruction from state schools and stripped Catholic marriage services of legal effect.

As liberals came to appear anticlerical, clerics became profoundly antiliberal. The hierarchy avoided direct political action, however, until it supported the Uriburu coup in 1930. At that time, the antiliberalism of the Church meshed nicely with European currents then in vogue: corporativism, fascism, and nazism. The Catholic nationalism still present in Argentine politics was born in this era, wedding cultural conservatism with political authoritarianism. Elements of the Church supported the Axis in World War II.

During the war, the Church also formed an alliance with organized labor. Perón added the armed forces to create the triple alliance of Justicialism: Church, military and unions. But in his second presidency, Perón's attack on the Church led to a novel situation: the liberals and the Church dropped their traditional enmity and joined forces against Perón. This tactical alliance with the economic liberals to unseat Perón did not mean that the Church suddenly became "liberal" in the North American sense. To the contrary, the hierarchy remained corporativist in outlook. So, when the anticorporativist Illia came along, conservative elements of the Church went along with the coup by Onganía, who imposed the most illiberal, culturally reactionary policies seen to that day in Argentina. A scant twenty-eight hours after Illia had been physically removed from the Casa Rosada, Onganía was sworn in, with the archbishop of Buenos Aires at his side. This was an apt token of the regard in which the Church held democracy.

But times were changing. The three-year Vatican II ecumenical council deeply divided the Argentine Church. One conciliar constitution of Vatican II, "The Church in the Modern World," emphasized the importance of human liberation in *this* life, as well as the next. It condemned atheistic socialism and liberal capitalism as causes of contemporary social turmoil, and alluded to underdeveloped countries as victims of crass capitalism.[2] Young priests took this message to call for a fundamental reordering of priestly functions, for the curing of social ills that afflicted vast segments of the Latin American population.

Thus was born the Third World Priest movement and the Theology of Liberation. The doctrine promotes liberation in three stages. Analysis, usually Marxist, must reveal the forms and authors of oppression. Then, "consciousness raising" makes the exploited aware of their condition. Finally, the exploited classes struggle against oppression, peacefully if possible but, according to some, violently if necessary. During the late 1960s, the old guard in the Church continued to support the Argentine military government, while the Third World Priests openly supported its violent overthrow.

The breach opened in the early 1970s. The Montoneros, spawned from within the lay group, Catholic Action, made their move. Catholic schools and seminaries became breeding grounds for urban terrorists. In response, the wayward priests were ruthlessly crushed. Two bishops died in suspicious automobile "accidents." A leading Third World priest was gunned down while leaving a Church where he had just performed a marriage ceremony. Several other priests were murdered, and dozens of other clerical and lay religious figures disappeared.[3] The Church remained quiet in the matter, prompting Nobel Peace Prize winner, Adolfo Pérez Esquivel, to say, "A Church that refuses to recognize its own martyrs is a Church that has lost its soul."[4]

To be sure, the Argentine Episcopal Conference condemned torture as immoral and expressed "serious concerns" over the numerous reports it had received of disappearances, kidnapings, and torture, and called the methods employed a "sin." That looked good for the record. In practice, unfortunately, some priests strayed from these teachings, working hand in bloody hand with the security forces devoted to the extirpation of subversion. The Sábato Commission concluded that "there were members of the clergy who committed or supported with their presence, with their silence, and even with justifying words these same acts which had been condemned by the episcopate."[5]

Several Sábato Commission witnesses testified as to the presence of priests and even bishops in the clandestine detention and torture centers, or to their roles as middlemen. According to one witness who solicited information from the military vicar, Monsignor Grasselli, the monsignor "consulted a metal file box and told me that it was better that we should remain quiet and not make much noise. . . ." Another testified that Monsignor Grasselli showed her a list of *desaparecidos*, with the names of the dead marked with a cross.[6]

Although the 1970s were hard on the Church, it continued to play an important secular role. Traditionally, the Church is politically strongest when democracy is weakest. When democratic institutions are banned, priests serve as mediators between the government and unrecognized but real powers. In the early 1980s, they intervened in strikes and built a conduit between the military government and the reemerging political parties.

Various Church sectors still sympathize with two politically illiberal currents of Argentine politics: the conservative wing of Peronism and the economic liberalism of the military and business communities. The effort to reconstruct the Church-labor alliance during the 1983 campaign led to public meetings between the unsavory Peronist candidate, Herminio Iglesias, and Monsignor Antonio Plaza.

In modern times, the Radical party has had an anticlerical image. "The Radicals' main problem," said a Peronist strategist, "is that they are antimilitary and anti-Church." That is an oversimplification, for to be anticlerical in the sense of upholding the separation of church and state need not imply enmity to the Church. Indeed, many priests are anticlerical in this sense, favoring their own withdrawal from politics, and devotion to their pastoral duties.

In practice, though, the Argentine hierarchy by no means was prepared to give up on its central political concerns. The archbishop of San Juan lamented a trip of young Argentines to Nicaragua to help reap the coffee harvest.[7] Conservative priests also wage continuing battle against divorce, pornography, and reform of the *patria potestad* laws, which until 1985 gave the father all rights concerning the offspring of a marriage, even if he abandoned the family. In other words, a single mother might raise a son alone from birth, decide to take him to Brazil for his eighteenth birthday, and be prevented by the father, who shows up out of nowhere to deny permission for his son to leave the country.

The Church has taken some encouraging steps. In the 1981 pastoral letter, "Church and National Community," the Argentine hierarchy for the first time formally endorsed a democratic, republican, and representative form of government. Though this call in itself may appear as political interference, historically it was a welcome step forward.[8]

Meanwhile, vestiges of the Third World Priest Movement remain. After the generals departed, a few bishops continued publicly to execrate the dirty war. "The Church committed the sin of omission," said Quilmes Bishop Jorge Novak, by not speaking out against the "blatant disregard for human rights" during the military government.[9]

Where these competing views will lead remains uncertain. From a democratic perspective, recent disclaimers notwithstanding, the Argentine Church remains deeply political. One may sympathize with Church conservatives or liberals, but all continue to stray far beyond the tending of their flocks. So church shows little sign of allowing its separation from state.

Equally disturbing is the content of ecclesiastical contributions to politics. Liberation Theology was developed at episcopal congresses in Medellín, Colombia (1968), and Puebla, Mexico (1979). The Medellín Congress was the Latin American response to Vatican II and set the Church on a course of social justice. Puebla reaffirmed the Church commitment to the poor and human rights; attempts there by the Argentine delegates to bar the word "liberation" from conference documents were rejected.[10] The documents did not mention the word "democracy," either, though, and many fear the tendency toward Marxism. Pope John Paul II is battling against the interpretation of the scriptures as an allegory of class struggle. But Latin American priests resist Vatican efforts to silence their political voices. In the words of Brazilian liberationist, the Reverend Leonardo Boff, "To deny the existence of class struggle is like denying in the sixteenth century that the earth goes around the sun."[11] Four Nicaraguan priests defied a Vatican edict by continuing to serve in the Sandinista government.

As for Argentina's episcopal mainstream, a 1984 episcopal document, "Together We Build the Nation," gave thanks to God for having returned Argentina to democracy "and for having done so in peace," [sic] which they now hoped to serve, preserve, and strengthen.[12] Yet the letter also condemned the "public accusations" and "calumnies" lodged against certain priests, a clear reference to those alleged to have cooperated with the military repression. At length it attacked the "alarming" growth of pornography. The episcopal letter affirmed that changes afoot in the education system—"including under the shadow of the name of democracy"—were making it too ideological and materialistic. In other words, conservative priests feared Marxist infiltration in the classroom.

There's the rub, for education is seen by churchmen as their domain. One reason why the Church in its day has supported both Peronist and military regimes is that these governments have tacitly consented to respect ecclesiastical dominance in education. It is precisely in this field that the Church has most impeded the growth of democratic attitudes in Argentina. Private (mostly Catholic) schools comprise only 30 percent of the total, but the

Church has often extended its imprint to state education, as well, through its influence in the Ministry of Education and Justice. Its curricular emphasis on order and discipline have left democracy in the back seat.

EDUCATION

Even apart from the Church, the Argentine educational system has done little to nourish democracy. According to human rights activist and educator, Emilio Mignone, "It cannot be doubted that the Argentine school system is darkened by authoritarianism."[13] School texts have drily reported, but not condemned, the repeated military interruptions of constitutional governments. Perón transformed civics courses into indoctrination sessions, to instill unquestioning worship of Eva and himself. The study of democracy returned after 1955, but consisted of "a stuffing of abstract notions, broad definitions, dogmatic condemnations and affirmations, reminiscent of classical history and rhetorical formulations impossible to digest and assimilate."[14] Meanwhile, military coups and civil upheaval outside the classroom underlined the irrelevance of the subject.

The structure of the educational system has reinforced these negative traits. Statism has taken root here as in many other sectors of Argentine life: the Ministry of Education reigns firmly over school districts and curricular requirements, superintendents and principals hedge in their teachers, the teachers give little leeway to the students. Human nature suggests that, if anything, strictness increases the further one descends the ladder; fiat from above fuels resentment that can only be vented below.

Democratic influences in education reached a nadir during the last military government. In recent decades, the "minimum contents" in civics courses (dictated, of course, by the federal government) had all proposed the formation of democratic sentiments and practices in the students. By 1977, however, the word "democracy" did not even appear in the government's requirements.[15]

A review of five textbooks (by three authors) recommended by the Ministry of Education during the last military government revealed that only one contained the term "democracy" in the table of contents. In the relevant one and a half page subsection (in the chapter "Man and his Cultural Achievements") the author wrote that democracy has two aspects. As a "government orientation," democracy is described as "the system in which the people participate in power directly through means of the vote; in this last case they elect their parliamentary representatives (deputies, senators) and the magistrates." That is it for explanation of how democratic government functions—not very instructive or inspiring. More attention was devoted to the second aspect, democracy "as an ideal of life." The subsection concludes with quotations from various popes and St. Thomas Aquinas, noting that Christianity stands neutral before the various forms of government.[16]

The values taught at school during the Process were sometimes far from democratic. Consider these textbook excerpts:

Discipline is the respect of the order established by the school authorities. Without order it is not possible to do any task profitably.

Docility is the internal attitude through which we do not put ourselves in resistance to the tasks of the superiors.

The happy and spontaneous fulfillment of our scholastic duties, always being quick to do what is indicated to us, quick and sincere collaboration with the superiors, are all manifestations of the docility that enormously facilitates the achievement of the aims of education, permitting all energies to be channeled toward them.

Obedience is the virtue by which the established hierarchical order is accepted and the orders it provides are fulfilled.[17]

These passages promote authoritarianism, not democracy. And values cannot change over night. Uniformity remains a virtue even today; every morning the streets are filled with children wending their way, dressed in identical little smocks of white, gray, or blue, as dictated by their schools. Learning is by rote. Accurate regurgitation is rewarded. Unconventional ideas are discouraged or scorned. Naturally, individuality and creativity are stifled.

Teachers also suffered during the military regime. Those who held or encouraged beliefs at variance from those dictated by the government risked loss of job or life. The Sábato Commissions reported the disappearance of 511 teachers, 5.7 percent of the total disappearances documented.[18] Many more fled the country.

The problem extends to the university level. In Latin America, student organizations play an unusually important role in national politics. In Argentina, too, students have long been politicized, though seldom successfully. Free exercise of student political rights may not foster democracy; indeed, when students held the most sway, in the mid–1970s, they sought to impose their own forms of radical orthodoxy. Nevertheless, it seems that brutal suppression of student politics and doctrinal purges of faculties, policies adopted by Peronist and military governments alike, further weaken the hold of democratic values.

These policies aggravate the brain drain, the diaspora of young scholars and intellectuals from the country. It is estimated that 2.5 million people—8 percent of the population—emigrated during the last quarter century.[19] Some people say good riddance to subversive elements. But the pride felt when an Argentine professor of chemistry, Dr. César Milstein, shared the 1984 Nobel Prize for Medicine, was mixed with shame that the scientist had been living in England for twenty-two years. Milstein had emigrated during the 1962 academic purges. The brain drain has many other causes—higher salaries, better working conditions, and the leading lights in most fields are found abroad—but academic repression hastens the exodus, robbing Argentina of a dynamic social force.

The Alfonsín administration recognized the need for educational reform to promote democracy. New civics texts, emphasizing democracy, were introduced. Teachers were encouraged to open up classroom discussions and were invited—for the first time—to attend seminars with education officials from the education ministry. The government also launched a literacy campaign in face of data that, despite Argentina's proud history as the continent's most literate nation, functional illiteracy in fact extended to 30 percent of the population.[20] These changes could not bring quick results and, if not sustained, would bring none at all. For the millions of Argentines already past school age, the damage had been done. They would continue to see democracy as an option, a strategy, a final resort after other governments failed—not as a necessity of dignified civic life.

PARTY POLITICS

In practice, political participation has become a privilege, not a right. In the era of Patriotic Fraud, one could speak, but not vote freely. Under Perón, one could vote, but not speak freely. During the last military government, one could neither speak nor vote freely.

Since politics has been practiced sporadically, it should be no surprise to find in the parties a certain lack of seriousness. Having been detached from reality by force, they have become detached from reality by nature. Parties tend not to be the route to power, so they have not borne the burden of responsibility or coalition-building that are the hallmarks of successful, democratic opposition. Nowhere is this clearer than in the Radical party which, after nearly a century in existence, has never remedied its notorious economic ignorance (the architects of the Austral Plan were not longtime Radicals) and has prided itself for its "intransigent" heritage, the refusal to enter coalitions or compromise on principles, no matter the cost. It is as if the Radical party has in some ways remained frozen in its pre-1912, revolutionary form.

This is not to say that *politicians* have been unimportant. Quite the contrary. Civilian politicians have been active and agile in the rough-and-tumble of Argentine politics. No military coup has ever been carried off without a coterie of civilian urgers. Many of these civilian power brokers have been party leaders. Despite its democratic rhetoric, the Radical party has often been right in there pitching. Conspiracy, though, is no breeding ground for responsible party politics.

Continuous exclusion has fragmented the parties. Only the traditionally successful have an interest in consolidation and papering over internal divisions in hopes of gaining an electoral majority. As for the others, the absence of free competition can have the same effect in the political as well as the economic marketplace: the unsuccessful do not receive the signals (few votes or sales) that tell them when to close shop. Moreover, even those parties whose leaders know they lack support may still stay in the game, for they do not need a large congressional delegation to affect national politics. It is sufficient to use their parties as soapboxes for airing their views in the press.

The result is a hybrid party system. The Radicals and Peronists try to bargain and compromise their ways into majorities. Within the Radical party the historically dominant National Line now accepts the leadership of its former splinter group and rival, Alfonsín's Renovation and Change. Alfonsín, in turn, forged an alliance with the powerful Córdoba Line of the party, and stayed left to keep the young student branch of the party on board. The Peronists, despite their gaping divisions, frantically (though unsuccessfully) sought to patch things up in time to go into the 1985 midterm elections united.

Two other parties aspire to become important swing blocks in the Congress, by presenting clearer political doctrines than exist in the two leading parties. The Union of the Democratic Center (UCD), despite its name, occupies the right side of the political spectrum. It is led by Alvaro Alsogaray, a cogent debater and Argentina's leading champion of free market capitalism. The UCD is the economic liberal's party. ("Liberalism" in Argentina is not political liberalism in the sense familiar to North Americans. As shall be further explained in Chapter 8, it can best be translated as economic liberalism, or even, ironically, conservatism. Argentine "liberals" love Ronald Reagan.) The UCD's support is concentrated in Buenos Aires proper, and it appeals mainly to businessmen and military officers.

Alsogaray plays a one-note trumpet: free market, free market, free market. The fundamental proposal of the UCD is "to replace the present state-controlled (*dirigista*) and inflationary socioeconomic system . . . by a system based on liberty in all fields, on monetary stability, and the free play of market forces."[21] In other words, privatize everything and liquidate the mountainous accumulation of state enterprises. The UCD also calls for opposition to the Soviet bloc and "abandonment" of the Non-Aligned Movement.

Regarding the struggle against subversion, the UCD urged that this "painful chapter" be closed, without judgment of the "legitimate repression during the war." It would confine punishment to crimes committed against lives and (even more precious to the UCD) property "that had nothing to do with the struggle"—an obscure standard if ever there was one. Lest anyone doubt where the UCD stood on the issue, Alsogaray stated that he considered that all *desaparecidos* were killed in combat, including those detained in their homes. He called the Sábato Commission report "a lie from beginning to end," and chillingly told a hostile radio interviewer that the newsman was already "on file."[22]

Alsogaray's outbursts suggested that the UCD's attachment to democracy is suspect. Alsogaray himself has had no problem selling civilian government down the river before. Even if one discounts his youthful involvement in the Uriburu coup and forgives his participation in the government that ousted Perón, it is not easy to explain in democratic terms why he defended the 1966 coup in a tour of Europe and the United States shortly afterwards. In 1984 Alsogaray relentlessly heaped abuse on Alfonsín, just as he had upon Frondizi a quarter century earlier.[23] He complained that Alfonsín would not sign an IMF agreement. When Alfonsín did sign an IMF agreement he complained that it would bring on recession.

Alsogaray had had a chance to put his theories into practice in his two brief stints as economy minister. His results were mixed. He did reduce inflation, but at the cost of paying employees with bonds instead of cash, a cruel and one-sided austerity measure. Moreover, this free market hero privatized no state enterprise, lowered no tariffs, and maintained a single, fixed exchange rate for a year and a half. There is room to doubt his fine theories would fare well in practice today. The Argentina economy has been so insulated from competition for so long that rapid exposure to free competition could lead to wreckage, not reform, of the economy. After all, when Martínez de Hoz tried to convert Argentina into a free enterprise economy, he triggered the biggest string of bankruptcies in Argentine history.

There is also reason to doubt that Alsogaray's free market theories would promote true democracy in Argentina. Their social sink-or-swim component promises to intensify the distributive struggle that has so much contributed to political instability. Alsogaray enjoyed the political support of much of the armed forces, which he showed no disposition to cage. Within his own party Alsogaray has sought to rule like a monarch. The one additional seat won by the UCD in the 1985 congressional elections went to Alsogaray's daughter.

At the other end of the political spectrum is the Intransigent Party, created in the 1960s when the Intransigent Radicals split into Frondizi's developmentalist and Oscar Alende's more socialist approach. The Intransigents draw on the two "great historical movements" of this century: the democratic revolution of Yrigoyenism, which introduced widespread popular participation in Argentine politics; and the social revolution of Peronism, which brought organized labor theretofore unknown power and prosperity.

Alende, like Alsogaray, is an old-time politician (governor of Buenos Aires Province from 1958 to 1962) and a powerful speaker. At a time when the workers' traditionally Peronist loyalties came under pressure from the 1983 electoral defeat and subsequent fissures in the movement, his party offered a clear alternative. It openly adopted Peronist rhetoric in an effort to woo the working class, hailing the three "banners of popular revolutionary nationalism": popular because it sought to destroy the oligarchy, revolutionary because it battled against dependence, national because it deplored imperialism and embraced Latin American integration.

The Intransigents, though, lean far left of the Peronists. Peronism calls for liberation, but this is lip service; in practice it is ready to deal with all powerful interests—imperialist, oligarchic, or otherwise. Intransigence takes the theme of liberation and turns it into a talisman, reiterating its revolutionary aims over and over. The Intransigents also oppose the old guard Peronist hammerlock on the unions, criticizing them for being "more interested in settling partisan feuds and attending to their personal benefit than in upholding the legitimate claims" of their members.[24]

How do the Intransigents propose to liberate Argentina? It is hard to tell, since they never get past platitudes. Here is the two-step schematic. First, the economic liberalism of Alsogaray must be abandoned as a recipe for dependence, facilitating the exploitive collusion between local oligarchs and foreign imperialists. Then, emancipation can begin, by "awakening the political participation" of the people, converting land from private ownership to a social good of production, and relying on the state "to guarantee to every human being the security of being the master of his own destiny."[25]

In a country where a grotesquely oversized state has become the greatest obstacle to the reduction of inflation and increase of productivity, the statism of the Intransigent Party seems strangely misplaced. Yet it is not, for Alende's vision of reality is of an Argentina whose sovereignty is "trapped in hege-monic U.S. projects and in the interests of the multinational corporations." So monstrously tenacious are these imperialists that only people and state, united, can wrest national autonomy from their jaws.

The Intransigents are best known for their suggestion to repudiate Argen-tina's foreign debt. This is Alende's siren song: a break with the IMF "would not bring any grave consequence for our country, because it is an entity that represents banks. They possess neither ships nor guns. . . ."[26] Alende should know better, as a longtime national politician. Either he is a fool, which is un-likely, or a demagogue, irresponsibly inflaming public opinion in a bootless cause. For however unjust the imposition of repaying the debt on those who did not personally contract it, rob it, or enjoy it, default just is no alternative for a country, like Argentina, whose livelihood depends on foreign com-merce.

Should Argentina default, Aerolineas Argentinas jets might fly away and never return. Beef and wheat shipments could be confiscated on arrival at foreign docksides. Argentina's foreign creditors could judicially attach every-thing not nailed to the floor in Argentina in order to satisfy their claims. Alende knows that, or should.[27]

Despite their defects, the UCD and Intransigents at least provide clear choices: conservatism v. socialism, right v. left. They are counterpoints to the hybridized Radical and Peronist parties. The UCD could conceivably attract traditional Radicals and conservative, Peronist union leaders. The Intransi-gents share many views with young Radicals and even Alfonsín's Revolution and Change line, and could appeal to rank-and-file workers sick and tired of the Peronist "thieves" who lead them. By presenting this stark option, these two idea parties could force the two major parties to act more decisively, to avoid erosion of their voting bases. The best the UCD and Intransigents could hope for is the realignment of the Argentine party system around the right-left poles familiar in Europe and North America. Such a realignment is not likely, since both Alsogaray and Alende are septagenarians without a broad political base or clear successors, but its prospect should be salutary.

A host of other parties are active in national politics. Most are vehicles for a prominent politician or vocal minority to get their viewpoint into the press. As Huntington wrote, in the praetorian state all actors do what they know best, so politicians orate. To make noise is to attract notice and possibly to in-crease influence.

The most prominent minor party is the Movement for Integration and De-velopment (MID), led by former president Arturo Frondizi and his former economy minister and Sancho Panza, Rogelio Frigerio. The MID and the Intransigents were the two fission fragments of the split within the Intransigent Radicals after Frondizi's fall in 1962. Lo this past quarter century, the MID has stood firmly behind "developmentalism," a pragmatic strategy that welcomes foreign investment to promote basic industries in Argentina. This industrial emphasis makes developmentalism palatable for Peronists and militarists alike, and MID leaders have always sought to ingratiate themselves sufficiently with the prevailing kingmaker to secure an important governmental role. Scruples do not phase them. They were perfectly happy to participate in the unseating of Illia (whose cohorts had, as we recall, helped unseat Frondizi) and in 1984 made a spectacle of themselves by allying with the reactionary, Herminio Iglesias branch of Peronism.

One would think that, as the last surviving elected president in Argentina, Frondizi would prefer the dignified role of elder statesman, urging his fellow citizens to remain calm and constitutional during the nation's current tribulations. Wrong. He and his party are among the shrillest Cassandras foretelling the disastrous end the Radicals are hastening. Since the MID offers no democratic alternatives to this impending doom, it does not take a genius to see the implication of Frondizi's posturing.[28]

Historically, Christian, Socialist, and Communist parties have all had their moments. Now they are feeble. Christian parties have ranged from the most conservative to the most liberal in Argentine politics, but their aspirations have never been fulfilled. The Socialist party has a proud heritage but was eclipsed by the rise of Peronism and never recovered. The Socialists have now split into three parties, as have the Communists, who are well-funded, well-organized, and unpopular. All these leftist parties combined obtained less than 4 percent of the vote in the 1983 elections.

In the provinces, *caudillismo* lives. There are Radical and Peronist parties, but often the real power rests in the hands of independent provincial parties. In the 1983 gubernatorial elections, independent parties won three provinces —Corrientes, Jujuy, and Neuquen. These parties provide the balance of power in the National Senate. Strong family control exists in some provinces, especially those least developed, least changed since the nineteenth century heyday of *caudillismo*. Thus pairs of brothers serve as governors and national senators in Neuquen and La Rioja. A father-son team plays the same role in Catamarca. Both leading candidates for governor of Corrientes were from (estranged branches of) the same family.

The independent provincial parties have tended to lean more toward Peronism on national issues. The urban-based Radicals never made as much room for rural interests as did Perón. Perón himself was a *caudillo*; the majority of his working class support came from new arrivals from the provinces, and the creole nationalism that Perón preached proved far more appealing to outlying provincial leaders. The crucial role provincial parties now play in the national Congress, however, encourages them to refuse the role of automatic Peronist allies. A senior Radical official in the Senate said that "the independents are getting maximum advantage" from the Radical-Peronist battle for the swing votes they hold.

Despite the reflorescence of political parties since 1983, many citizens remain indifferent. In Argentina, one must formally "affiliate" oneself to become a member of a party, so joining a party represents a greater commitment than Americans attach to "being" a Democrat or a Republican. Most Argentines are members of no party. After the 1983 elections, the level of voter identification declined, reflecting voter skepticism that political parties can solve Argentina's problems. By mid-1985, 47 percent of voters polled expressed no party preference, with Radicals and Peronists only attracting 22 and 10 percent of the balance.

CONGRESSIONAL FOLLIES

The Capitol is a slender-domed, ornate structure built in 1906, during the days of political stability. Now, after an eight-year lull, the surrounding neighborhood of sagging roofs and boarded-up façades again bustles with activity. Political talk fills the cafes. Inside the baroque edifice, lengthy neglect bears its scars. Paint peels from yellowing walls with greasy smudges. Congressional comportment is in similar disrepair. Though they have scarcely had time to tire of their new duties, many deputies cannot be bothered to show up for debates.

The Congress has long behaved irresponsibly. As early as 1929, the Chamber of Deputies was reported to be "full of rabble and unspeakable hoodlums. The parliamentary language used up to then had been replaced by the coarse language of the outskirts of the city and the Radicals' committees. . . ." The next year, the Chamber spent four months of its five-month session debating elections of new members, and failed to pass a single bill.[29] In the 1930s the Congress was sullied by its collusion in the fraud rampant in national politics. During Perón's heyday, serious debates descended into mud-slinging matches. Once Perón silenced the opposition, the rubber-stamp Congress became a den of obsequy. In 1966 the Radical minority in Congress could not cope with the efforts of their opponents to undo Illia's government simply by refusing to pass a budget and starving it of funds. The 1973 Congress opened inauspiciously with the blanket amnesty, which loosed hundreds of terrorists from the Villa Devoto and Caseros jails in Buenos Aires.

And now? Congressional behavior has not improved much. How could it? There has been no opportunity to practice. In Brazil, apart from three brief closures, the Congress continued to operate even during twenty-one years of military government. Argentine military governments tolerated no such jabbering, however controlled. Even when Congress has existed, the concentration of power in the hands of the president has always overshadowed the legislature.

Over the years, impotence has bred incompetence. Able people have gone into more productive fields or left the country. So when the gavel opened the congressional session following the 1983 elections, only a handful of those present had ever before served in the National Congress. Most of the experienced politicians were concentrated in the Senate, which operated in the fairly effective, collegial manner expected of upper chambers.

The Chamber of Deputies, however, was another story. Sessions often would not begin until 11:00 P.M. Quorums could not be mustered. Aimless debate dragged on for months, while waiters circulated endlessly with trays full of *cafecitos*, demitasses filled with strong black coffee. Faced by a mountain of undecided legislation, the lower chamber burst into frenetic action in the final three days of its first session, passing over 200 bills. Some were considered for only minutes or even seconds.

Congressional investigations have been equally unimpressive. The case of the Italo electric company is illustrative. In 1978 the military government agreed to purchase Italo, whose board of directors had earlier included Martínez de Hoz. The company was bought for $350 million after its worth had been appraised at $35 million just three years earlier. Deputies smelled a scandal.

The congressional committee called upon former economic ministry official and attorney, Guillermo Walter Klein, to testify. Klein apparently enraged the deputies by boasting that he was the "number two" of Martínez de Hoz and by refusing to divulge a list of his clients, on the grounds of attorney-client privilege. The deputies cited Klein for contempt and hauled him before a judge. Before he could be released, the deputies rushed over to his office (without a judicial warrant) to carry out a personal raid on his files, which they carted away in boxes. The next day, a Senate committee, a federal prosecutor, and a federal judge also raided Klein's offices.

Kleingate became one of the leading stories of the year. Italo Committee members alleged that the presence of files of so many foreign clients showed that Klein's office was a center of intelligence and espionage.[30] One Peronist deputy, Héctor Basualdo, claimed he was shot at in a basement parking garage by a would-be assassin who escaped, although the deputy returned his fire. (The only shells or bullet marks found from this alleged assault were from Basualdo's gun.) When federal judge Néstor Blondi ordered the committee to return Klein's files, on the ground that it had taken them without a judicial warrant, Peronist members filed a motion to impeach Blondi. Martínez de Hoz was briefly jailed after he testified before the Italo Committee. When Judge Blondi released him, the committee chairman accused the judge of "ideological complicity" with the former minister.[31] Whatever the merits of the case, the carnival atmosphere created by the deputies' cavalier approach to constitutional rights, to the judiciary, and to their own responsibilities discredited them and the chamber they represented.

Growing pains are inevitable, but congressional behavior should improve. Time will bring experience, a keel sorely lacking today in the Lower House. Time will also bring elections, and the defeat due to poor performances. (The chairman of the Italo Committee, a Radical, lost party support and thus his seat in the 1985 midterm elections.) Perhaps most important, Congress must become an important center of decision; responsibility promotes maturity. One important aspect of maturity is the realization that, although Congress has the power to destroy an elected government, in doing so it also destroys itself. De facto governments just have no time for Congress. That is a simple lesson, really, but one that has yet to be fully understood.

PART III

THE STAKES

CHAPTER 7

The Laws

... government is the potent, the omnipresent teacher. For good or for ill, it teaches the whole people by its example. Crime is contagious. If the government becomes a lawbreaker, it breeds contempt for law; it invites every man to become a law unto himself; it invites anarchy.

—JUSTICE LOUIS BRANDEIS

In Argentina, Justice Brandeis's warning has come home to roost. At least once a decade, generals have seized power illegally. Even elected governments have at times flouted the Constitution and laws. In popular perceptions, policemen are corrupt, judges biased, and attorneys unscrupulous. Little wonder that callous disregard of the law and its purported enforcers now pervades society at all levels, top to bottom, right to left.

A democracy must be ruled by laws, not men. Argentina has been ruled by men, not laws. Every usurper touts the democratic 1853 Constitution, while breaking the most basic rule of the game: governments must be chosen by voters, not cabals. Other rules have received and other citizens have offered no greater respect. To the extent he could get away with it, each man became a law unto himself.

It should be no surprise that there can be no such thing as a lawless democracy; the surprise is that Argentina is a lawless state. After all, it has a distinguished legal tradition. The 130-year-old Constitution enshrines a host of individual rights and a U.S.-modeled, democratic system to protect them. Argentine jurists have made important contributions to international law, such as the well-known Calvo Doctrine.[1] Attorneys today play a pivotal role in society and government.

Yet law has failed democracy. Confronted by official lawlessness, the courts have repeatedly abdicated their responsibility to protect the Constitution. Legal proceedings often have merely provided a figleaf to cover the depradations of state-sanctioned lawbreakers. People fear the police so much that many choose not to report crimes. Forms are observed, while norms are abused.

Illegality is not rampant. Many laws are enforced. Most streets are safe to walk by day or night. Downtown Buenos Aires feels far safer than Manhattan. The large legal community can ably assist client to form a company or defend against criminal charges. No, the problem is *selective* illegality—specifically, constitutional illegality. The legal community has stood by mutely as generals ejected elected governments by force, blindly as thousands of people disappeared. The Argentine legal system is like a low horsepower engine; it runs fine on the straightaways, but stalls out on the hills.

Now, after many years of neglect and abuse, the Constitution is weak. It has been so stifled so long that it cannot at the snap of one's fingers be restored to ruddy vitality. Alfonsín campaigned to make the Constitution the cornerstone of law and democracy. But he alone could not repair the damage without a national change in attitudes. How did Argentina get into this mess, and how can it get out?

THE CONSTITUTION

During the summer of 1852–53, José Gorostiaga began to sketch the outlines of Argentina's constitution in his lodgings above Merengo's Pastry Shop. For intellectual guidance he consulted the writings of Juan Bautista Alberdi, an Argentine lawyer for English traders, exiled in Chile. Alberdi's famous opus, *Bases and Points of Departure for the Political Organization of the Argentine Republic*, promoted a U.S.-style constitution. A draft text was debated for ten consecutive evenings and then adopted by the constitutional congress. Critics of the Constitution disparage its hasty framing; on average, each article was discussed for less than twelve minutes.

Despite its North American focus, the Constitution retained one characteristically Spanish feature: strong centralization. The president was made the "supreme chief of the Nation" for a six-year term (though he could not succeed himself) and granted the authority to declare a "state of siege" whereby constitutional guarantees are suspended when internal unrest, in the president's view, endangers the Constitution or constitutional authorities. To encourage growth and civilization, clauses promoting European immigration were included.

The Constitution also grants the federal government the right to "intervene" in a province "to guarantee the republican form of government" or to repel invasion. A similar authority formally exists in the U.S. Constitution, too (art. 4, sec. 4), but has never been used. Argentine presidents have often resorted to intervention, appointing a delegate to supervise the "normalization" of province. President Yrigoyen intervened in the provinces to replace political enemies with allies. In a last-ditch effort to save his presidency from an anti-Peronist coup, Arturo Frondizi intervened in provinces won by Peronist gubernatorial candidates. Military governments routinely intervene in all the provinces. Together, the state of siege and the power to intervene have crippled Argentina's supposed federation.

The long presidential term is not strictly an asset; it increases executive pressures as well as powers. As aggravation mounts, the prospect of waiting three or four years more for a change becomes unbearable.

Had the presidential term been four years, even allowing reelection, Argentine postwar history may have turned out differently. Perón was able to avoid ouster for over nine years. Had he retired in glory after eight, the Peronist v. anti-Peronist struggle that beset Argentina for a generation thereafter and produced three coups just might have been avoided.[2] Perón even lasted more than three years into his second term. Frondizi served nearly four years and so did Onganía (unelected but initially popular). Illia and the last Peronist government lasted three years each. A shorter presidential term might have served as a safety valve, depriving coup-plotters of the broad support critical to their success.

A shorter presidential term is not the only possible safety valve. A parliamentary system provides another: flexible government. In a parliamentary system, the president acts as head of state while the prime minister runs the daily affairs of government. When the prime minister finds he no longer commands a majority in parliament, he resigns. The government falls, but the regime survives.

Since Italians comprise the largest ethnic block in Argentina, their homeland provides an interesting comparison. At first glance, the Italian parliamentary system appears an odd example of stability: more than forty governments in the last forty years. But a second look reveals that many ministers reappear in many governments. That includes prime ministers; the release of Palestine Liberation Organization commander, Abu el-Abbas, in the wake of the *Achille Lauro* hijacking brought down the government of Bettino Craxi, which was replaced by the government of . . . Bettino Craxi. And even though until 1982 it was a one-party (Christian Democrat) show, that does not obscure the fact that there were no successful coups and that electoral losers—notably the powerful Communist party—have respected the winners.

Throughout, the regime was never mortally threatened, never abandoned democracy and the rule of law—even when facing grave terrorist violence from the Red Brigade on the left and neo-fascists on the right. Italy has found a way to vent frequent political swings and crises without punting its constitution. It may profitably instruct its South American cousin.

A strong executive has a corollary: a weak legislature. Partly by design and partly by custom, the Argentine National Congress is less active than reactive. Lack of practice has worsened the problem. During the first two Peronist presidencies, the Radical block in Congress faced the dilemma of making little difference or making no difference when faced by large Peronist majorities and a president who jailed Radical leaders. Military governments resolve this cruel choice by dissolving the Congress. Recently revived under the return to democracy, the Argentine Congress has, unfortunately, lacked an independent power base to defend the Constitution. It has been a sideshow—sometimes all too literally—to Argentine politics.

STATE OF SIEGE

The Argentine Constitution contains a rich array of individual rights and protections. Many mirror the U.S. Constitution, such as the equal protection and the privileges and immunities clauses. Argentine citizens enjoy the right to work, to petition the authorities, to travel freely in and out of Argentina, to publish ideas through an uncensored press, to use and dispose of property, and to profess religion freely. Prerogatives of birth, personal privileges, and titles of nobility are forbidden. The rights to trial, to defense, and to refuse to testify against oneself are guaranteed. Arrests are only permitted on written warrants.

Article 23, however, has made a mockery of these noble protections. It allows the suspension of constitutional rights during a "state of siege." These are the fateful words:

> In the event of internal disorder or foreign attack endangering the operator of this Constitution and of the authorities created hereby, the Province or territory in which the disturbance of order exists shall be declared in a state of siege and the constitutional guarantees shall be suspended therein. But during such suspension the President of the Republic shall not convict or apply punishments on his own authority. His power shall be limited, in such case, with respect to persons, to arresting them or transferring them from one point of the Nation to another, if they do not prefer to leave Argentine territory.

States of siege have been imposed or extended over thirty times, in all or part of the country. Causes have ranged from riots to Pearl Harbor. Some have been short. In 1958 Arturo Frondizi declared one to break a strike against the national oil companies, and lifted it three months later. In October 1985 President Alfonsín declared a sixty-day state of siege in response to a wave of bombings, and lifted it two weeks early.

Other states of siege have been long. Following the *cordobazo*, Onganía imposed a state of siege that remained in force nearly four years, until it was lifted for the 1973 elections. A year and a half later, Isabel Perón declared a state of siege that was not lifted until the day of the 1983 elections.

A state of siege has two immediate effects: it frees the government from restraint and strips the citizen of protection. This may not significantly alter daily life—especially when continued for many years. But in extreme circumstances—precisely those that most test the nation's constitutional fabric—the state of siege can transform history. It can convert a nation's legal system into a tool of tyranny. If the circumstances are dangerous enough to provoke the suspension of constitutional guarantees, can the vestigial guarantees provided in Article 23 itself be assured? Theoretically, Article 23 confines the president's power to arresting and transferring persons within Argentina, if they do not choose to leave the country. He cannot convict or punish people on his own authority.

During the Process, the government was not even satisfied with the plenary powers conferred by Article 23, as it trampled those few rights supposedly assured under a state of siege. The military government immediately suspended the right to leave the country so, once in custody, the citizen had no legal escape. The ban on conviction and punishment was respected in letter but not in spirit. Conviction and punishment per se were not authorized, but limitless detention and interrogation were, provided that "half-conclusive proofs" of guilt were found.[3] Some detainees languished for years without even being charged. Many others were tortured and disappeared. These poor souls would have fared better if they had been merely convicted and punished.

Two structural defects in Article 23 encourage its abuse. First, no time limit is set, so the citizen can be and has been denied constitutional guarantees for years on end. Since a state of siege arrest is only terminated by the exercise of the option to leave the country or the cessation of the state of siege, the suspension of the right to exile permits eternal detentions.[4] Second, "conviction" and "punishments" are broad terms that can be evaded by resorting to unconventional sanctions, such as lengthy detention, torture, and disappearance. Transfer is allowed under a state of siege; in the jargon of the clandestine detention centers, "transfer" became synonymous with "execution".

Other safeguards were supposed to be available under the judicial power, which theoretically remains unimpaired during a state-of-seige. Habeus corpus writs may be petitioned to compel the release of a detainee held in violation of Article 23 (i.e. one who has been convicted or punished by presidential authority). Also, the Supreme Court held that the president could not delegate his power to arrest and transfer citizens. This nondelegation rule should limit the number of people held under a state-of-siege to countable, nameable proportions. It should also prevent presidents from hiding abuses behind a mantle of ignorance, as they did during the Process. "There may be a few excesses, of course," they piously intoned. "But this is a war. We cannot monitor every operation in detail."

These built-in safeguards were no help. Habeus corpus—which literally means "produce the body"—only works if you can find the (some)body in question. During the Process, people disappeared, and often the police, armed forces, and government all denied knowledge of their whereabouts. The detainees and their relatives were tragically out of luck. Finally, the president not only delegated responsibility, but also allowed the struggle against subversion to be waged without his knowledge by autonomous "cells," which were thought necessary to prevent infiltration in the security forces and to fight the guerillas on equal terms.

True, the courts remained open throughout the struggle against subversion, while the Congress, political parties, and unions remained shuttered. The few decisions that granted a habeus corpus writ provided a figleaf, a "discourse of rationality," that the military government could point to in defending its record.[5] Freedom granted one victim obscured perdition for thousands. Victims less notorious or influential than Jacobo Timerman could not escape.

STARTING OVER?

This sad story raises a basic question: did the Argentines choose the right constitution? Some nationalists condemn the document as a North American import untailored to Argentine reality. In a monograph, entitled *The Fetish of the Constitution,* José María Rosa argues that Alberdi's anglophilia ruined the Constitution from the outset. Alberdi, says Rosa, believed that the Argentine people could not accustom themselves to Anglo-Saxon, liberal laws. Alberdi, however, also believed that the only worthwhile constitution was the Anglo-Saxon, liberal model found in France and the United States. Those two beliefs, Rosa concludes, led Alberdi to eliminate native Argentines from the new constitutional scheme and replace them with Anglo-Saxon liberals.[6]

Rosa has a point, albeit overstated. Alberdi did argue that it was utopian to think that in 1852 the Spanish-American race, newly formed from a "gloomy colonial past," could immediately achieve representative democracy. "We need to change our people, unfit for liberty," wrote Alberdi, "for other people fit for it, without abdicating the type of our original race. . . . it is necessary to foster in our soil the Anglo-Saxon population."[7] This statement shows that Alberdi did not wish to sell out his own race, but to improve it through the values that spawned the modern world. The European revolutions of 1848 and the long-delayed demise of the Rosas dictatorship infused Alberdi and his Constitutioin with republican exhilaration. Perhaps this republicanism was premature, but it was not treasonous.

Nationalists argue that Alberdi's national self-deprecation converted the Constitution into a "statute of dependence." Its pro-Anglo-Saxon bias played right into the hands of the Argentine ruling classes, who justified their monopoly on political power by suggesting that the common people were not yet ready for true democracy. The Constitution, while formally establishing a democracy, in fact sanctified the oligarchy. Rosa argues that the 1826 Constitution, by contrast, was truly Argentine; it permitted the rule of popular and effective *caudillos* over a robust federation of autonomous provinces.[8] The system may have been immature, but at least it did not create a constitutional house of cards that in practice worked only to facilitate the exploitation of the many by the few. At least it did not convert Argentines into second-class citizens in their own land.

Less mystical objections weigh against the Constitution of 1853. The Constitution may have failed in practice because it almost ignores the most powerful forces in Argentine politics: the military, organized labor, and the Church. Some provisions favor them—mandatory military service, the right to bargain collectively and strike, the official support for Roman Catholicism. But none restrain them. If the Constitution had taken hold, this omission would not have mattered; generals, unionists, and bishops would simply lobby, as helpful contributors to the constitutional scheme. But coups have gutted the constitutional center, and these institutions have filled the vacuum. Now, if the Constitution cannot beat them, perhaps it should join them, or at least set some ground rules.

However valid these constitutional critiques, viable alternatives do not readily appear. Rosa's romantic suggestion to return to the good old days of the Confederacy of 1826, when *gauchos* rode the plains and *caudillos* ruled the provinces, ignores the suffering these petty despots inflicted upon individuals unable to protect their own rights. Besides, Argentina cannot now revert to a simple, agrarian society of less than a million souls. The return to a loose confederation of *caudillos* would only fracture further an already divided society, and could only succeed with the natural emergence of dozens of able leaders. Now it is hard enough to find one. The problem is not that the Constitution of 1853 is inappropriate, but rather that it is ignored.

BITTER EXPERIENCE

The Argentine bench and bar have been no more successful than the Congress and executive branch in supporting constitutional rule. The judiciary has never been able to protect itself, let alone anyone else. The problem is not lack of authority; the judicial power article of the Argentine Constitution closely follows its North American model.[9] The Supreme Court has jurisdiction to decide constitutional questions arising under congressional laws. Judges are granted tenure during good behavior and their compensation is not to be diminished "in any manner" while they remain in office. The one variation from the U.S. scheme is ironically prescient: the president is expressly barred from exercising or arrogating the judicial power.

The long descent began 10 September 1930. Four days earlier, General José Uriburu had ousted Hipólito Yrigoyen and proclaimed himself president. The Supreme Court faced a dilemma. If it held the usurpation unconstitutional, its decision (unsupported by physical force) could be ignored and the judges (unprotected by physical force) could well be dismissed, thereby depriving them of the opportunity to try to keep a modicum of constitutional control over the new, de facto government. On the other hand, if it adopted the so-called "de facto doctrine," which held that governments unconstitutional in origin could be constitutional in practice, it would set a dangerous precedent (that coups are constitutional) and compromise its image as an independent branch of government (especially since the Court's members were already seen as anti-Yrigoyen conservatives). In a one-page opinion, the Court upheld the de facto doctrine, thereby ratifying the illegal government.[10]

This tactical retreat sealed the Court's fate. The year 1947, when President Perón instigated the impeachment of the three anti-Peronist Supreme Court justices, marked a watershed. Before that year, all Supreme Court justices left the bench through death, retirement, or resignation. Since then, the Supreme Court and the rest of the Argentine bench have been sacked en masse five times.

The loss of judicial tenure (regardless of "good behavior") has brought the worst enemy to an effective judicial system: instability. Instability ruins essential ingredients to a healthy jurisprudence: doctrinal gradualism, predictability, and independence. When judges are replaced slowly, constitutional doctrines usually change gradually. When changes are gradual, the constitution can appear to be a lasting but evolving document, one that recognizes important long-term developments but not fads. This continuity is essential to the stately image of a constitution.

More practically, sudden changes of judges can create sudden changes in doctrine, destroying the predictability that law must have for its just application. Finally, the politicization that comes with wholesale changes of judges reduces the possibility of an independent judgment of constitutional questions. The new judge may either fear for his job or simply agree with the president who appointed him. (During the Process, judges had to swear by the Act of the Process as well as the Constitution.) Either way, independence and justice are compromised.

The Argentine judicial system suffers from other defects. One is its relative seclusion. Public hearings could enhance the image of fairness, but Argentine courts continue to use an anachronistic written system. Cross-examination is rare. Lawyers deliver writs to court employees and wait for a response. In practice, judges often do not read these submissions, and the secretary of the court (a sort of assistant judge) wields decisive power. It is a black box system; you insert your card, wait, and out pops the answer.

Soon after my arrival in Buenos Aires a young lawyer invited me to visit the central courts in Buenos Aires. I eagerly accepted, in anticipation if not of Perry Masonesque drama then at least of a good look at how Argentine lawyers practice and judges preside. Instead, we walked from one office to another. Court employees stood behind counters; behind them, long metal shelves were stuffed with bulging files. This was a daily ritual. My acquaintance handed in a few pleadings at some of these "courtrooms" and asked to see the files on the other cases he was following at others. Where the judge, his secretary, or opposing counsel had added another document since the day before, the young lawyer furiously scribbled down notes to show his senior colleagues. No bench, witness stand, or jury box. Just bureaucracy.

It is not a system to inspire trust, but then it was not designed to be. In the colonial era Argentine judges were barred from giving reasons for their decisions, because to do so would affront the absolutist notion of the King's Justice. The courts, guided by God and monarch, owed explanations to no one, be they parties or public. Indeed, to provide any would suggest room for doubt, even error. That would not do.

In Argentina, moreover, judges serve investigative and prosecutorial functions, remnants of Europe's inquisitorial past. These adversarial roles vis-à-vis defendants may interfere with the blindfolded neutrality of justice. Judges leave the courtroom to visit the scenes of the crime. Shortly after Alfonsín's inauguration, judges appeared hovering over newly-opened mass graves filled with bullet-riddled skeletons. The scene presented a good photo opportunity, but was inflammatory and unnecessary: inflammatory because it suggested a judicial bias against the Process, unnecessary because the prosecution could be relied on to present evidence of the location and condition of the remains in court.

As prosecutors, Argentine judges have the right in criminal cases to commence proceedings on their own initiative. This has led to unseemly rushes to claim jurisdiction over important cases. Haste may suggest that the judges have a particular interest to see a case resolved a certain way, or that they do not trust their fellow judges. Neither prospect promotes the image of justice. In Kleingate, two federal judges seized jurisdiction over different aspects of the case; one judge ordered the congressional deputies to ignore the other's order to surrender the seized documents to the Court. In 1983, when Argentine Central Bank president González del Solar signed a debt renegotiation agreement submitting Argentina to the jurisdiction of New York courts, an unhappy citizen flew to the polar province of Santa Cruz to file a complaint before Judge Pinto Kramer. The plaintiff had correctly sized up his judge, who obligingly had González del Solar arrested and jailed on his return to Buenos Aires. The grounds: the Central Bank president had violated Argentine sovereignty by submitting debt renegotiation agreements to the jurisdiction of foreign courts. This fatuous ruling was quickly reversed, but shows how deeply politics infect the judicial process.

Beyond politics, another reason for poor judges is poor conditions. First consider the physical danger. Two days after 370 terrorists were set free under the 1973 amnesty, the Congress cravenly dissolved the special federal court that had been established to try terrorist crimes. Two of the nine ex-judges from this tribunal narrowly escaped assassination attempts. A third, Manuel Quiroga, was less fortunate; he was fatally machine-gunned in downtown Buenos Aires.

Even after Alfonsín's election judges who sought to try right- and left-wing terrorists were physically threatened and intimidated. Just before Christmas 1983, Federal Judge Nicasio Dibur and his family were warned that they would all be killed if he persisted in investigating the right-wing terrorist group, the Triple A. The car of the judge's assistant was wrecked. In downtown Rosario, the apartment building of another judge involved in the Triple

A cases was sprayed with bullets. Some regular forces were implicated in these intimidation efforts. A trial judge in Tucumán Province, a former guerrilla stronghold, requested personal protection, and complained that the chiefs of the Army Fifth Infantry Brigade and Nineteenth Regiment were "seriously interfering" with his work.

What is the recompense for running these risks? Miserable. Even Supreme Court justices barely make over $10,000 per year. The failure to index judicial salaries in a country with triple-digit inflation was finally held to be a salary reduction while in office and, therefore, unconstitutional. Nor is bravery rewarded. In 1983, with the military government still in office, federal judge Oscar Salvi jailed retired Admiral Emilio Massera (member of the 1976 junta that overthrew Isabel Perón) on charges related to the disappearance of businessman Fernando Branca. Branca shared an interest with Massera in a woman and a ranch, and disappeared on 28 April 1977, the day he was to go sailing on Massera's yacht. Never before during the Process had a judge dared to act against any military officer, let alone one of the most powerful men in the country. To be sure, it would have been much harder for Salvi if the murder had been part of the subversive struggle instead of a traditional lust-and-money case, if the victim had been a communist instead of a businessman, and if Massera had not been trying to position himself to win the upcoming presidential election as a populist in the mold of Perón. (Perón had promoted Massera to commander of the navy over several senior officers.) Nevertheless it was a bold step; caution required Salvi to sleep away from home and to prepare a safe house should he need to abscond.

The young judge immediately was hailed a national hero. Weekly news magazine covers featured his photograph, captioned "The Face of Justice" and "The Judge without Fear." But within weeks of Massera's detention, Salvi was unceremoniously taken off the case, supposedly on grounds of bias. So much for the judge who dared to challenge the Process.

Like the bench, the Argentine bar is filled with able and honest attorneys. Legal education, though, shares the defects of primary and secondary education, producing students who can state and apply rules, but who cannot easily question or justify them. "They are never taught to ask 'why?'," complained one law professor. A blue-ribbon panel designated by the University of Buenos Aires agreed, finding that recent law graduates "lack sufficient capacity . . . to imagine original solutions and critically to evaluate the rules, which they tend to apply mechanically, or to put them in a social context."[11] The causes are several. First, legal curricula are encyclopedic, pursuing the objective "as impossible as it is useless of knowing all the Law, instead of providing conceptual tools . . . to find, interpret, and apply juridical norms." Most students take the same twenty-eight courses, from Roman law to Aeronautic law. The panel also found curricula to be too rigid and anachronistic, and criticized "the dogmatism with which teaching tends to be imparted, in presupposing that a given quantity of information must be transmitted" and the lack of time to give courses intended "to generate critical reflection."

Many attorneys emerge from this process perfectly able to draft a contract in accordance with the Civil Code or to advise a client whether a proposed transaction must be approved by a ministry, but reluctant to challenge the logic—or constitutionality—of a statute or decree. This reluctance at times has been reinforced by danger; during the Process, around 100 lawyers disappeared. To challenge the Process at all in those feverish days could be suicidal. The few lawyers who dared to present petitions on behalf of suspected terrorists immediately became suspected subversives themselves.

FOLLOW THE LEADER

Its institutional shortcomings inevitably affect the popular perception of the legal system. Whether they reflect or induce endemic corruption is now moot. Either way, today illegality is integral to everyday life. The underground economy may comprise one-fifth of the Argentine output; its principal virtue after efficiency is its use for tax evasion, estimated at 50 to 60 percent. The only effective taxes are those imposed on companies too big to evade without notice, and those taxes that are automatic—value added taxes, stamp taxes (e.g., for liquor and cigarettes), gasoline taxes, withholding taxes on exports and workers' salaries. Personal income taxes just do not get paid. "I would not pay a cent to those butchers," one wealthy but left-leaning landowner told me in a downtown café during the military government. When I saw him four years later, Alfonsín was president. Was the landowner paying taxes now that democracy had returned? "Well, no." Once one gets out of the habit of paying, it is hard to go back. Since everyone has been alienated by one government or another, everyone has had a pretext to stop paying.

Why should people pay the government? It just wastes their money, or worse. From the economic standpoint, it makes sense to evade taxes, for the worst thing that can happen is that you will get caught and have to pay what you owe and perhaps a fine. Tax evaders are seldom jailed. The fines are not onerous enough to deter them. And occasionally there are tax amnesties.

Anyway, if the tax inspector is after you, bribe him. Bribery—*coima*—is the daily lubricant for those who want to get things done. If you want to sit in a good movie seat, to buy a car without waiting, to import foreign goods without paying duty, the standard practice is to slip someone a bribe. Twenty years ago John Gunther quoted an Argentine as saying, "There are two kinds of officials. Those who take a bribe and perform and those who take a bribe and do not."[12]

"If I need to bribe someone to make a deal go through, I do it," one businessman readily told me. "It's automatic here, a part of our lifestyle. A policeman stopped me for jaywalking and was about to give me a ticket. Before I knew it I had slipped him a few hundred pesos and he was gone." Another told me that "the tax inspectors came one day, and started going through our company files. We had a big, undeclared tax liability just sitting there. They stayed for weeks, but did not find it. It was really getting on our nerves. So finally we showed them a tiny thing we hadn't paid, we added on a small bribe, and they left. We figure that the whole payoff cost us only about one percent of what we really owed." I asked whether all tax inspectors took bribes. "They are all bribetakers," he replied. "And why not? They get paid next to nothing." Other people echoed these sentiments. Whether or not these charges of widespread bribery are true, they illustrate the cynicism felt toward government officials and the apparent willingness to buy them off.

LAW AS CLARION: REVIVAL OF MORALITY

During the 1983 campaign, the Radical party sought strength from Argentina's tattered Constitution. This was less witless than the preceding pages might suggest. For one thing, the Radicals had little choice. Without the military or union tools to compel obedience, they needed a popular theme to earn it. The invocation of morality and legality allowed the Radicals to convert physical weakness into political strength. Their forced isolation from power left them less experienced but also less corrupted than either the armed forces or the Peronists.

Still, the Radicals could not take over by default. The Peronists remained strong, while memories of their pathetic government had softened in comparison with the subsequent tragedy. Moreover, since the Peronist party's inception, it had never lost a free election. The Radicals would need a positive program if they hoped to prevail.

Invoking the rule of law was essential to that program. Here was a value that could be lauded as both antidote and preventive to the depravity rooted in Argentine politics. It was a value that evoked a grateful welcome from citizens tired and frightened of anarchy and repression. The Radical party platform of September 1983 outlined the legal steps it proposed to prevent future coups d'état.[13] It repudiated the Supreme Court's "de facto doctrine" that had ratified *coups* for over fifty years. Torture would be outlawed and its practitioners severely punished. Censorship would be lifted and habeus corpus restored.

Once in office, Alfonsín acted quickly on his promises. Three days after his inauguration, he opened an address to the nation with these words: "The democratic government has announced its firmest determination to restore a state of law in Argentina." He then ran through a litany of bills to be submitted to Congress. One revoked the amnesty the military government had granted itself just before the elections. Another reformed the Military Code of Justice. Others reformed prison sentencing, repealed the former government's antiterrorist legislation, increased the penalties for crimes of rebellion against the constitutional order (i.e. coups d'état), and ratified several United Nations and Latin American human rights pacts. These reforms were promoted as a radical departure, one that would not merely excise the abusive laws promulgated since 1976, but would also prevent the military from returning to power, and make them accountable to civilian authorities for crimes committed upon their fellow Argentines.

What did Alfonsín hope to gain from this invocation of the rule of law? He wanted to set a new tone for Argentine politics, to replace perfidy and intrigue with morality and decency. It would help avert the unpleasant surprises that had become an Argentine way of life. The return to legality soothed raw political nerves. It provided a rallying point. The greater sense of security helped sustain Alfonsín's popularity, the president's greatest political asset. In 1952, Perón had been able to impose a crushing austerity program without losing the support of the workers, who remembered that he had given them benefits and dignity. Perhaps Alfonsín hoped that he too would be able to survive political difficulties, through the support of the people who remembered his gift.

In the long term, Alfonsín's continuing campaign for legality could help instill the political system with the legitimacy it had lost through prolonged governmental lawbreaking. Legitimation of the rule of law could, in turn, reinforce reliance on constitutional methods to achieve political office and exert political power. The revival of a presumption against overthrowing elected governments might one day save civilian government, when general impatience (in *both* senses) returned to Argentina.

LAW AS PRETEXT: THE DIRTY WAR

The question of what to do about the dirty war stirred deep emotions. Harsh punishments might deter future plotters but, if excessive, might sooner or later provoke military retaliation. They would weaken and demoralize the armed forces, depriving them of a vested interest in the new civilian order. Worse, the more severe the punishment, the less willing the next military government would be to relinquish power, for fear of similar treatment. Many people attributed the tenacious hold of Pinochet and company in Chile to fears of an Argentine-like accounting should the army there ever step down. Punishment that did not go far enough, however, would fail to satisfy the public outcry for justice, and could make the new government appear as an accomplice after the fact.

One way for a politician to protect himself is to pass the buck onto the law. A convincing legal argument can partially excuse an unpopular policy. The unpopularity remains, but at least the president may avoid some of the blame by declaring himself bound by legal necessity.

For Alfonsín, the issue at hand was how to deal with the officers accused of human rights abuses during the dirty war. He had repeatedly promised justice during the presidential campaign. But how far would he go? Would only the top commanders be tried? Or would their electrode-wielding subordinates also face prosecution? Would the Nuremberg doctrine—that following orders is no defense against crimes against humanity—be applied? And who would sit in judgment—military or civilian courts?

These choices were deeply political and provocative. But Alfonsín wanted to calm citizens, not inflame them. To the extent that the chosen procedure seemed fair on its face, he could claim that it was legally rather than politically motivated. That could defuse criticism of his decision.

President Alfonsín ordered military officers charged with crimes related to the antisubversive campaign to be tried by military officers in military courts under military law.[14] That would please the Armed Forces, but anger human rights activists. To even the balance, Alfonsín provided for civilian review of military sentences. He also stipulated that if the military tribunal failed to reach a verdict within six months, then a civilian court of appeals could take over the case. In future, common crimes committed by military personnel during peacetime would be tried in civilian court. Alfonsín also proposed to the Congress that severe sanctions against torture and rebellion be imposed. Since these proposals were prospective, they could not be applied against crimes committed during the Process.

Human rights activists knew that they were being thrown a sop. They strongly opposed allowing the military to try these cases, fearing not only lenient treatment for the perpetrators, but also an irresistible opportunity to do away with damning evidence. Civilian review could accomplish little if vital evidence were conveniently lost during trial. Moreover, the limitation of prosecution to the former junta members and their most sadistic subordinates seemed likely to result in the de facto amnesty of virtually all of the hit men. Peronist Senate leader Vicente Saadi called the arrangement "a concealed amnesty for 98 percent of the criminals."[15]

In response to these charges, Alfonsín declared that, under Supreme Court jurisprudence, "military courts are entitled to pass judgment on crimes committed by military men in military zones or in connection with the discharging of their duties."[16] The president asserted that his hands were tied by Article 18 of the Argentine Constitution, which guarantees that all citizens have the right to be tried by their "natural judges." Alfonsín interpreted that article to guarantee military jurisdiction for civilian crimes committed by military personnel.

The president's argument was plausible, but forced. It could more persuasively be argued that Article 18 requires that *civilian* courts try the dirty war cases. A war was never declared, the crime was homicide, the victims were civilians—surely civilian judges were the "natural judges" required by Article 18 of the Constitution. The mere fact that the criminals wore uniforms should not transform the crime and jurisdiction from civilian to military. If the Military Code of Justice provided otherwise (which it did), then *it* was unconstitutional, in granting excessive jurisdiction to military tribunals. Indeed, the Argentine Supreme Court admitted that the Military Code did unconstitutionally extend the jurisdiction of military tribunals over civilian crimes, but upheld Alfonsín's scheme on the grounds that, nevertheless, the justices did not wish to apply formalistic legal reasoning to frustrate the method chosen by Congress to deal with the dirty war issue.[17] That analysis sounded more in politics than in jurisprudence.

The point is that plausible legal arguments cut both ways, either for or against civilian jurisdiction over military personnel accused of common crimes. The deciding factor in Alfonsín's legal analysis must have been political. He did not want to admit that the armed forces frightened him enough to curb his zeal in prosecuting human rights violations. By clothing his position in an argument of constitutional necessity, he could explain to the armed forces that he had no choice but to prosecute them and to the Mothers of the Plaza de Mayo that he had no choice but to allow the trials to be conducted under military jurisdiction.

9. President Vìdela meets with Cardinal
Antonio Samoré, an emissary sent by Pope John
Paul II in 1978 to persuade the Argentine and
Chilean governments not to go to war over the
Beagle Channel boundary dispute.

10. A typical Buenos Aires scene: thousands in the Plaza de Mayo cheering the hero of the day. Here the occasion is President Alfonsín's hundredth day in office.

11.　Jose Alfredo Martínez de Hoz—minister of economy and perhaps the
most powerful civilian in Argentina from 1976 to 1981.

12 & 13   Videla's handpicked successor as president, General Roberto Viola was ousted in a 1981 palace coup by General Leopoldo Galtieri (on the following page), whose Malvinas misadventure hastened the return to civilian government.

13.   General Leopoldo Galtieri.

14. The Atucha-1 nuclear power station, located on the Paraná River about 100 kilometers northwest of Buenos Aires.

15. President Raúl Alfonsín.

LAW AS OBSTACLE: ISABEL AND THE BEAGLE

Naturally, the law sometimes stood in Alfonsín's way. When it did, political needs sometimes prevailed over legal punctilio. Take the case of Isabel Perón. Following her release after five years of house arrest in southern Argentina, the former president moved to Madrid. There she remained out of reach of claims against her for the diversion of more than $3 million in public funds. Meanwhile, the Peronists in Argentina remained strong enough to obstruct Alfonsín's initiatives, but too divided to agree on common policies. The president wanted to reach a *modus vivendi* with the Peronists, to avoid a political stalemate. With whom could he speak? Alfonsín needed an interlocutor. The only Peronist leader who could even pretend to speak for the whole party was Isabel Perón.

The former president could not easily be convinced to return to Argentina to negotiate. She had had enough of politics and had no desire to come home to be sued. But Alfonsín deemed her participation so important that he proposed, and Congress passed, a law relieving the former president from any possible civil liability.

Even if the statute was unquestionably legal, it did little to foster the image of legality and morality so dear to Alfonsín. To grant immunity always risks undercutting the laws whose sanction is avoided, especially when legality itself is only weakly established. Setting *one* person apart is particularly damaging; legislation affecting a nameless class at least preserves an element of neutrality. For the president who had authorized the "annihilation" of subversion to be excused, while those who faithfully carried out her orders were not, seemed to many to be capricious and unjust.

Alfonsín also stretched legality for political aims when negotiating the Beagle Channel Treaty with Chile. Dispute over the three islands of Picton, Lennox, and Nueva dated back over 100 years. Though these desolate and rocky outcroppings never aroused such intense national sentiment as did the Malvinas Islands (many Argentine maps showed the Beagle trio to be Chilean), the dispute had festered for years. The two nations nearly went to war over them at Christmastime 1978, but were stopped through eleventh-hour papal intervention.

Alfonsín wanted to terminate this latent conflict, both to promote peace and to remove the one potential conflict that could justify continued arms expenditures. He did not, however, wish to sign a treaty that could expose him to nationalistic attacks by the Peronists and the military that he had sold out Argentina's national heritage and sovereignty. Gaining sovereignty over the islands through diplomacy would be next to impossible, though, since two international mediation efforts had already awarded them to Chile: one by the Vatican and another by an arbitration panel of the Queen of England. (The adverse British decision further fanned political passions.) Working through papal mediation, Argentine and Chilean negotiators quickly reached an agreement that granted the islands to Chile and certain compensatory rights to Argentina.

Alfonsín was convinced that most Argentines wanted to avoid war with Chile and cared little about the three small islands. So he decided to conduct a public "consultation," a national referendum wherein the people would vote for or against the draft treaty. That way, the passive protreaty majority could outvote the vociferous antitreaty minority, and protect Alfonsín from nationalist attacks. The trouble is that the Constitution does not authorize consultations. Indeed, Article 22 provides that "the people neither deliberate nor govern, except through their representatives and authorities created by this Constitution."

In defense of the referendum, Radical lawyers argued that Article 22 limits the people, not the government. Since the Constitution does not prohibit the government from consulting the people, the referendum was valid. That is a weak argument, hairsplitting between popular "deliberation" and government "consultation." Had a popular majority voted against the proposed treaty, the government would not have signed it. That looks awfully like an unconstitutional form of deliberation by the people through the means of a referendum.

In the event, the Beagle treaty referendum proved a great success for Alfonsín. The Peronists fought openly over how to approach it. The official party line urged "militant and active abstention," while many leading Peronists, including 1983 presidential candidate Italo Luder, supported a "yes" vote. The Peronist boycott lost momentum when a thirty-five-year-old quotation was published, wherein the First Worker himself had suggested that the islands were not worth fighting over and might just as well be dynamited.

On 25 November 1985 the treaty gained an 81 percent affirmative vote in the referendum, on a 71 percent turnout. Compared to the traditional 85 percent turnout for presidential elections, this high turnout for a nonbinding "consultation" appeared directly to repudiate the Peronist leadership. It also appeared to be a ringing vote of confidence in Alfonsín, who had campaigned actively for the treaty.

Alfonsín's dilemma between legal nicety and political necessity intensified in the final months of 1985. By October, he seemed at last to have consolidated his political control. The Austral Plan had slain—or at least stunned—the dragon of inflation. The people responded with their favor (80 percent supported him) and the IMF with $235 million in hard cash (from a standby loan that had been blocked for six months). The trial of the former juntas had withdrawn the shroud of disingenuous ignorance surrounding the military repression of the 1970s, and had earned the backing of 90 percent of the Argentine people. Few tears would fall when the convictions were issued. Meanwhile, the Radicals seemed destined to handy victory in the upcoming November elections, the first midterm balloting to be held in twenty years.

The right wing observed these developments with profound unease. They had been unhappy to leave government in the first place, and had in no wise tempered their ambition or affinity for privilege. Now their tactical, *reculer pour mieux sauter* retreat threatened to develop into a permanent, forced retirement. What could they do about it? The elections would not help. Their favorite candidate, Alberto Alvaro, had been outflanked in his preachy economic liberalism by the president's stunning initiative. Their next preference would have been a Peronist victory. The military could deal with the Peronist leadership pragmatically, as one power broker to another. The Peronistswere so busy fighting each other, though, that they posed little threat to the Radicals. No, the electoral route held no charm for the group Minister of Interior Antonio Troccoli euphemistically called "the recently unemployed."

Unrepentant miscreants therefore returned to a tried and true method: violence. Violence seeks results, not by physically preventing an enemy's advance (e.g., by interdicting supplies), but by frightening him into cooperation (e.g., through fear of terrorism). What better target, then, than Argentina's children? Elementary schools became the most popular targets in a spate of over forty bombings and 1,800 bomb threats. The explosions were timed to avoid loss of life, but one killed a passerby in Córdoba. (Though evidence was scarce, the government and most Argentines believed that the right wing was responsible for the bombing campaign.)

The objective, at least at this early stage, was intimidation, not mutilation. The message: normal life cannot continue under democracy, without the consent of its would-be wreckers. If you want your child to grow up whole, do not shun and degrade the military forces, which alone can deal effectively with social violence (especially if they and their allies refrain from it).

Alfonsín wanted to act decisively to quell this nascent insurgence. Acting on a tip, he arrested six civilians and six military officers for presumed responsibility for the bombings. But the president had no hard evidence. Now his legalism returned to haunt him. Citing the new habeus corpus law passed by Congress and signed by Alfonsín, a federal judge ordered the release of several of the detainees.

On October 25 Alfonsín responded by declaring a state of siege—a grim reminder of the bad old days—which permitted the president to arrest persons on his own authority, without meeting the usual evidentiary prerequisites.

A few days later, the president addressed the nation. He spoke in words that all Argentines understood.

> [L]ike a terrifying ghost emerging from the past, an absurd and sinister terror has sought to prevail over our conscience and over our people's [peaceful] coexistence. . . .

> I will not condemn these insane ghosts. Whoever has placed bombs at a school has already condemned himself. This violent action has neither political nor social meaning. It does not even represent a wrong or absurd path in support of reasonable demands. It is plain madness. It is the madness of the professionals of violence, who have nothing to do in a society that detests violence and that rejects the humiliation and tyranny of the past. The recently staged attacks, the threats, and the psychological campaigns were not caused by violent social conflict. They were caused by professionals. The time for clarifying some things in Argentina has come. What do these disrupters want?

> Although this may seem incredible and absurd, they want to seize power . . . . by creating insecurity, a feeling of impunity, giving rise to the idea that democracy is incapable of defending the citizens. . . .

> These disturbances are not taking place in a virgin society. This community unfortunately is well-experienced in political instability, it knows full well the siren calls of the minority groups that begin by casting doubts on the honorability or the efficiency of democracy and end by vesting themselves with the will of the entire community and restricting the people's freedom without even blushing a bit. . . .

> Undoubtedly they do not know but they will soon learn that democracy is not weak. . . . Democracy and the government will fight.[18]

The courts now upheld the arrest of the twelve. Most Argentines reacted calmly. They believed the president when he said that the state of siege was declared only against the "professionals of authoritarianism," and that the citizens would continue to be free to exercise their rights fully, whether they commended or criticized the government. Besides, Argentines had lived with a state of siege for the better part of twenty years, and in far worse circumstances. True to his word, beyond the initial arrests the president in fact did not suspend any constitutional rights or interfere with the electoral campaign, now in its final two weeks.

The declaration of the state of siege seemed not to affect the midterm election results. The Radicals won 43 percent of the popular vote, easily defeating the divided Peronists, who slipped to 34 percent. The Radicals thereby expanded their majority in the 254-member Chamber of Deputies by nearly a dozen seats. The leftist Intransigents picked up four seats; Alsogaray's party gained one.

Still, Alfonsín must have made his declaration with extreme reluctance. He knew that while a state of siege would undermine the government's campaign for legality, the appearance of weakness could undermine the government itself. Unless the Alfonsín government served its full term, its commitment to the creation of a government of laws would come to nought.

The Argentine people, as well as the terrorists, needed to know that Alfonsín would not yield to such affronts to social peace. The last Radical president, Arturo Illia, had been ousted twenty years earlier as an honest fellow but ineffectual leader. Alfonsín determined not to follow suit. "We have all learned how much it costs to ignore signs of danger," he declared. "[T]o understand why such a firm answer is needed, we simply have to look at what is at stake, at the risk that our country might be diverted from the road it has begun to tread."

Alfonsín's strong image had its price. Many presidents had been forceful, but none had infused Argentine national life with respect for the rule of law. Alfonsín had promised to change that, to show that legality was practical as well as admirable. The state of siege stood as an implicit admission that he, too, doubted that democracy could work in Argentina, that the nation could be governed within its own legal framework even if a few malefactors tossed a few bombs at it. While the state of siege offered short-term political advantages, it hurt the long-term effort to bring Argentina under the rule of its own magna carta.

The Isabel Perón immunity, Beagle consultation, and 1985 state of siege were not blatantly illegal. They show, however, how political expedience sometimes outweighs juridical purity. Alfonsín's own strategy reflects the stunted legality of Argentina. While urging renewed respect for the law, the president himself uses legal forms to shore up his political position. It is a devilish problem. Alfonsín needs every tool at hand to maintain his authority. The law is one of his most powerful. Yet every gain won by politically wielding the rule of law undermines the effort to restore a lasting presumption of constitutionality. That presumption is essential to deterring coups. If carefully nurtured, it could one day save democracy in Argentina.

CHAPTER **8**

The Economy

The country will emerge strengthened in its democratic institutions at the end of the period of economic reconstruction if it is able to mobilize itself with consensus and political will. This is the challenge, this is the responsibility of the social sectors and the Government. The world is watching the restoration of democracy in Argentina with satisfaction; let us also show it a country on the move, headed to occupy a place among the progressive, cooperative, and dynamic nations.

—JUAN V. SOURROUILLE

Argentina *defines* stagflation. From 1950 to 1985 annual inflation climbed unsteadily but inexorably from 25 percent to nearly 1000 percent, only twice dipping below 10 percent. In the same period, per capita income in real terms grew 0.7 percent annually, compared to 3.4 percent in Brazil and 2.2 percent in Mexico. The last fifteen years of the period were the worst, with about 200 percent average annual inflation and a per capita decline in national income.[1] Depreciation outpaces capital formation; the productive base is literally shrinking. The engine is racing, but the clutch is disengaged. The peso printing presses keep rolling, but the population grows no richer.

The recent bout with thousand-percent inflation had to be lived to be understood. Before the introduction of the austral currency in June 1985, a friend held up a one-peso note one day at the Richmond Cafe over lunch.° (Actually it was an old 10,000 peso note, but a 1983 currency reform dropped four zeros from the currency.) "At this price, my father could have bought a 5,000-acre ranch in Entre Ríos Province, in the late 1940s," he said. This sum

---

°The analysis in this chapter refers to historic economic trends. Since it would be inaccurate and unfair to burden the new austral with all the baggage of the unlamented peso, this chapter will refer to Argentine currency in pesos except where australes are specifically at issue.

—one new peso, one million 1946 pesos—had shrunk in value to less than one-fifth of one U.S. penny. More recent comparisons are scarcely less astounding. The pre-1983 one million peso note, now worth ten centavos, will not buy a stick of gum by the time you read this sentence. Ten years ago, it bought a brand new Ford Falcon.

In my first eight months in Argentina, newspapers leapt from 20 pesos to 130 pesos, orange juice from 80 pesos to 490 pesos, a furnished apartment from 60,000 pesos to 264,000 pesos. Although in dollar terms prices varied little or even declined, that was cold comfort to the peso-salaried worker, watching his pay packet shrink before his eyes as the month wore on. All who could do so bought dollars on the black market. Everyone did as much of their monthly buying as possible as soon as they got paid. Few workers have large freezers, so they must buy food—one-third of the basic family budget —throughout the month. In addition, pay increases often lagged behind price increases, eroding the value of the worker's salary even before it arrived.

After so many years, Argentines have learned to cope with high inflation. Workers moonlight; the additional peso cash flow throughout the month can go to groceries, freeing part of the monthly wage for immediate purchases, before it depreciates significantly. Checks and invoices are pre- and post-dated to shave payments and pad billings. Businessmen have necessarily become expert financial managers to protect their assets from erosion. For this reason, the financial sector itself has swollen to hypertrophic proportions. The number of private commercial banks and finance companies more than doubled from 1976 to 1983. Those with adequate funds, information, and access to the financial markets can speculate, often with spectacular success.

The inevitable result is decline; from its pre-1930 position among the top ten nations in living standards, Argentina has now slipped back to around fortieth.[2] Stagnation and inflation combine to stifle the economy. Determining which of these two problems is the chicken and which is the egg is an interesting academic question. Whatever the answer, though, the principal effect is a societal return to the law of the jungle.

Chronic inflation is a plague. While still economy minister, Bernardo Grinspun boasted that he was not concerned by 700 percent annual inflation so long as other leading indicators kept pace with it. Perhaps the desire to reassure the populace led him to make this foolish remark, but foolish it was. With triple-digit inflation, confidence vanishes. This is not surprising. Money is supposed to be a storehouse of value. It is the lubricant that allows society to advance from primitive forms of barter (beads for food, for example) to complex forms of cooperation, in which each citizen exerts real effort in return for artificial tokens of value.

The worth of these bits of metal and paper consists in popular trust and belief. If people believe 1,000 pesos will buy one steak, or two packs of cigarettes, or one hour of manual labor, then the metal and paper have value. Increasing prices erode the value of money everywhere, but within reasonable and foreseeable limits, people easily accommodate and retain their faith in the little pieces of metal and paper.

But when twenty pesos today are worth only two pesos a year from today (as happened in Alfonsín's first year in office) faith in local money disappears, taking with it the basis of trust among business, labor, and government. Prices become a battleground of social struggle. No one is willing to sacrifice short-term gains for long-term hopes because no one knows what the long-term looks like, except worse. An economist might say that the discount factor is so high that the long term becomes essentially worthless. It becomes *irrational* to plan or to invest in major projects. Since there is no stability, there is also no capital investment and no growth.

Now foreign debt adds to Argentina's litany of woes. In 1976, when the Process began, foreign debt stood at less than $10 billion. After seven years of military rule, it had reached $45 billion. Thus Argentina earned the dubious distinction of becoming the world's third largest debtor, after the roughly $100 billion each chalked up by Mexico and Brazil. More dubious still, Argentina obtained relatively few productive assets through this enormous mortgage on the future—some new machinery, a nuclear power station, and the beginnings of an enormous hydroelectric dam at Yaciretá. Vast sums were diverted to two bristling arsenals (one before and another after the Malvinas War), and the construction of a couple of stretches of super-highway around Buenos Aires (chiefly beneficial to owners of weekend country homes). At least the Brazilians completed a large number of major capital projects with their loans. Argentina had embarassingly little to show by comparison.

What happened? In fairness, Argentines do not deserve all the blame. One must also consider the international banking climate in the late 1970s. The major banks were glutted by petrodollars, deposited by OPEC governments unable after the 1973 oil crisis to absorb the $60 billion windfall in their struggling young economies. The banks were desperate to lend out these deposits, in order to earn the interest from borrowers that would enable them to pay the interest due to their OPEC depositors and earn some profit besides. "Recycling," the bankers' savior in the seventies, has boomeranged into the international debt crisis of the eighties. For instance, Manufacturers Hanover lent $1.3 billion to Argentine borrowers and $5.2 billion to the three other largest Latin debtors, a sum representing 10 percent of the bank's total assets. The Argentine government seemed a good credit risk ("governments never default"), and the dollars flowed freely.

At the same time, Martínez de Hoz was attempting the radical transformation of the Argentine economy, from a closed, inefficient, inflationary past to an open, efficient, and stable future.[3] To stop inflation, he sharply limited the printing of pesos. In the past, pesos had been printed freely to cover the huge deficit run up by Argentina's many inefficient state enterprises. Now there were fewer pesos, so government agencies borrowed dollars to cover current expenses. Thus, the government deficit accounted for $20 billion of the total debt.[4]

Borrowing dollars became even more attractive, as the Argentine peso shortage combined with the foreign banks' dollar surplus to make the dollar very cheap in Argentina. The Argentine peso became grossly overvalued in international terms, creating the era of the "sweet money," or *plata dulce.* Dollars became so cheap that anyone of any means could afford to buy them, a move facilitated by the removal of longstanding legal restrictions against the import of foreign capital. Imports became dirt cheap and a national shopping spree began.

That added to the deficit, but not nearly as much as did "the bicycle." In one such venture, a borrower might obtain dollars at 12 percent interest per year, convert them to pesos, and lend them at 8 percent *per month.* That could yield a whopping 55 percent annual return in dollar terms, for the fixed dollar devaluation rate moved steadily along at about 1.8 percent per month. Since, for the sake of "stability," the dollar devaluation table was set and established several months in advance, this enormous profit could be made essentially risk-free. After the bubble of the grossly overvalued peso inevitably burst, in April 1981, the happy profiteers sent their bicycle winnings to banks in the United States, Switzerland and other suitably discreet locations. During the *plata dulce era* over $20 billion left Argentina.[5]

Like all sprees, the sweet money left a crushing hangover. After the Alfonsín government renegotiated the debt, it stood at nearly $50 billion dollars. That sum represented 75 percent of gross domestic product. By 1984, the annual interest obligations alone—$6.5 billion—were equal to two-thirds of total export earnings. The price of profligacy would be austerity (recession is the harsher term); the government's 1985 five-year plan projected a modest 4 percent annual growth, resulting in a 25 percent reduction in the debt by 1989. Predictably, though tragically, the burden of these lean years would fall not on the revelers, but rather on the salaried workers. Yes, they too had benefited from the sweet money, but far less than they would have to pay. Pessimism swept the land.

THE DEMOCRATIC CONNECTION

Inflation, stagnation, and debt together paint a sorry picture, but what does it all have to do with democracy? India is not the only country poorer than Argentina to be democratic. In Latin America, Costa Rica has had a working democracy for two generations, with a per capita income just over half that of Argentina. Conversely, prosperity does not guarantee stability or democracy. Sometimes economic growth can even impair democracy. As people become better off they become better able to press greater claims. If these claims go unsatisfied, a crisis of expectations arises. Impatience provokes unrest. Indeed, most revolutions occur when economic situations are improving.[6]

Nevertheless, Argentina's economic problems have a great deal to do with the failure of democracy. Three words tell why: stability, compromise, and power. The first two are closely related. Stability promotes the patience and compromise necessary to democracy; if one forbears today, she can still benefit tomorrow. A stable economy enhances the appeal of real investment versus fast-buck speculation. Investment opens a virtuous cycle by stimulating growth, which further facilitates compromise and, hence, democracy. At this point, democracy promotes the very stability it requires. The virtuous cycle continues. In twentieth century Argentina, it has yet to begin.

Finally comes the question of sheer power. As in many countries, in Argentina the rich and powerful are often the same people. As in few democracies, however, in Argentina many of the rich and powerful stand resolutely against popular participation. Their affection for things European extends to the theater, museums, and restaurants, but not to the streets. It is striking to the foreign visitor to hear well-educated, seemingly progressive Argentines suddenly assert that the average Argentine is far too brutish and uneducated to manage his or her own affairs.

The political credo of the powerful is libertarianism—the best philosophical defense of the strong against the weak, because it exalts the unobjectionable goal of liberty. Libertarianism holds that efforts to equalize wealth or opportunities between rich and poor are an assault against the liberty to keep what one has earned, be it social rank or income. Once one accepts its premise—that all humans are created equal—the internal logic becomes unassailable. It just seems *unfair*, if all are equal, to take from the diligent to give to the slothful.[7]

It is not unfair. For just as absolute political freedom leads to tyranny of the strong, so absolute economic freedom leads to tyranny of the rich. Moreover, the premise is bogus. All Argentines are not created equal. Over 50 percent of national income goes to the wealthiest fifth of Argentine households, while less than 5 percent goes to the poorest fifth.[8] Those born into the establishment are coddled by an old-boy network as hermetic and effective as exists in any European capital. It has long been so.

The wealthy have survived the vicissitudes of the last fifty years rather well. They may have fewer servants and mansions, but compared to their countrymen they cannot complain. Wander around the wealthy Barrio Norte area of Buenos Aires and you will swear that the so-called Argentine economic crisis is a myth. Lushly-appointed boutiques and well-stocked antique shops line the streets. Sales may be down, but these luxury establishments are still in business. The wealthy neighborhoods stretch out along the muddy estuary of the River Plate: Palermo, Belgrano, San Isidro.

If one remembers that in a city of over 10 million even the wealthiest 2.5 percent comprise over 250,000 people, the possibility of economic deprivation returns to mind. Sure enough, a short drive away from the river reveals modest working class neighborhoods. The outskirts of Buenos Aires are peppered by vast shanty towns. These *villas miserias* give the lie to the candyland image conveyed by the Barrio Norte. The well-to-do shift uneasily when confronted by the *villas*. "They're mostly Chilean or Bolivean refugees. The only Argentines are newcomers from the provinces. They'll be out of there and into a decent job and home within a year." At best, this is wishful thinking.

For play, seasonal sojourns to Paris are rare now, but the Uruguayan beach resort of Punta del Este has mushroomed into an Elysium of posh summer homes, as luxurious as those of any wealthy American suburb. These monuments to the era of sweet money are surrounded by Peugeots and BMWs in the summer; for most of the year they stand vacant. Punta was largely developed with black market money, and it has somewhat replaced Mar del Plata (the Miami Beach of Argentina) as *the* place to go in summer. "I hate it," one *porteña* told me. "The social life there is even more intense than in Buenos Aires."

Emphasizing the conspicuous aspects to the rich-poor distinction in Argentina serves a purpose. Alone, ostentation is offensive. When wedded to lack of economic and political opportunity, though, it can be explosive. It can explain the undying devotion of the workers to Perón, who gave them dignity and higher incomes. Democracy is a side issue, or worse, a sophistry used to justify the subjugation of the less privileged. There is justice to this complaint, for the wealthy have only been able to obtain and maintain political power through fraudulent elections or military coups. They are too few and isolated to succeed democratically.

In sum, economic relations have done much harm to Argentine democracy. Stagflation saps the political system of the resilience necessary to political give and take. Inequality has been exploited by all parties to justify naked power grabs that further aggravate the problem. The upper classes object to participation of the untutored lower classes. The lower classes support governments that protect their interests, by whatever means. As always, the players all descend to the zero-sum game.

A DIAGNOSIS

"Could not all this flesh/keep in a little life?" lamented Prince Hal over the prostrate figure of Falstaff at the Battle of Shrewsbury. So might Sarmiento and his peers look down in sad wonder that all Argentina's natural wealth could not keep in a little prosperity. After all, the fifty years prior to 1930 witnessed impressive growth—approximately 5 percent annually—even though the political system remained closed to many.[9] It is hard to understand how the next fifty years turned out so miserably. The reason lies in the deep division between two fundamental visions of Argentina, which begat a number of other cleavages, each one deepening the economic morass into which the nation sank. This is not a Marxist dialectic with inexorable historical outcomes, but rather a picture of extreme polarization leading to vacillation and stagnation. The result is not the triumph of socialism over capitalism, but the triumph of failure over both.

For generations, the seminal division has pitted agricultural against industrial strategies for the Argentine economy. Traditionalists believed—and believe—in the classic agricultural export model, the backbone of the half-century surge after 1880. Argentina would export beef and grain to Europe and receive foreign capital in return. The formula succeeded until 1914. The British imported Argentine grain and beef (especially after the nineteenth century invention of refrigerated ships), and built Argentina the most extensive railway network in South America. The British also brought Argentina its first bank, insurance company, telegraph, and postal system.

The greatest flaw of the agro-export model is that it leaves the Argentine economy too exposed to the viscissitudes of the international market. World War I decimated Argentine imports. British resources were devoted to defeating the Kaiser, leaving hapless Argentine customers without coal for their trains. Argentine locomotives were forced to burn corn stalks and straw instead, at considerable loss to efficiency.

After war's end, the agro-export model revived briefly, before the Great Depression dealt a still more grievous blow. Again imports dwindled, leaving Argentine industry to its own devices. This time the worldwide collapse of demand decimated Argentine exports, too. An economy that depends on a single sector is brittle, and cannot easily adapt when that sector is depressed. When the key sector is exports, quirks of international markets can be devastating.

Even without crises, the agro-export model has defects. For if world prices of manufactured goods increase faster than prices of agricultural products, every year the same volume of exports brings in fewer imports, fewer foreign earnings. The unfortunate exporter in this case inevitably faces what are called "deteriorating terms of trade," a concept popularized in the 1950s by Argentine economist and international diplomat Raúl Prebisch. Traditional or raw material-based export economies—a group that includes most nations of the Southern Hemisphere, including Argentina—have suffered deteriorating terms of trade for many years.

Argentina's terms of trade have deteriorated 20 percent since 1980. (One might think that Argentina's high inflation would make its prices increase faster than world levels, but this is not true in real terms because, for all but the sweet money years, devaluation outpaced inflation.) In 1985, Argentina exported 51 percent more grain than in 1980, but earned scarcely 5 percent more revenue.[10] Agricultural exports thus must continually increase just to bring in the same amount of money. Otherwise, export earnings and economic growth both recede.

For these and other reasons, most nations opt for industrialization as the key to development. Diversification brings resilience; a recession in one sector can be compensated by growth in another. Industrialization also increases economic independence, insulating the country from foreign embargoes. Finally, industrialization implies the production of more sophisticated products. These, when exported, have a higher value than do the primary products that go into them. The added value, in turn, increases *real* prices of a country's exports, helping to improve the national terms of trade.

Argentine industrialism began in the early twentieth century. It received its first major push, ironically, from the Great Depression; Argentine industry was forced to manufacture unavailable goods, formerly imported from Britain. By 1945, industrial output equaled agricultural production as a share of gross domestic product. After the Second World War, Perón adopted an "import substitution" policy, raising tariffs on imported goods to protect nascent Argentine industry. He wished to substitute formerly imported goods with domestically-produced replacements.

Factories sprung up in a belt around Buenos Aires, manufacturing shoes, refrigerators, and furniture. But Perón's policy was clumsy. By focusing tariffs on consumer goods, he mainly encouraged the development of light industry. This was all well and good, but capital investment in heavy industry would have stimulated economic growth more effectively by facilitating the development of downstream sectors.

Also, tariffs were so high and long-lived that what began as a shot in the arm for new Argentine industry eventually became an addiction, an excuse for gross inefficiency. If a U.S. box of pencils cost $1 but incurred a $1 import duty, an Argentine company could make pencils that cost $1.50 and still undersell the foreign competition at a profit. Argentine industry grew accustomed to being coddled against the chill winds of competition, and remains inefficient and protected to this day. When Martínez de Hoz put the exporters on cold turkey in 1979, reducing maximum tariffs from 210 percent to 100 percent in one fell swoop, hundreds of Argentine companies went bankrupt.[11]

Other industrialization strategies were attempted. Much of the heavy industry gap was filled by the Military Factories directorate, especially through the establishment of steelworks and petrochemical plants. FM combined bureaucratic inefficiency with military unaccountability. President Frondizi's "developmentalist" approach from the 1950s to the present has called for basic industries to propel Argentina into its fully developed potential. Argentina thereby created an infrastructure of transport, energy, and most basic industries, albeit at a high cost.[12]

One Argentine friend blamed attitudes for the lack of private sector impetus to industrialization. "There is no entrepreneurial class in Argentina. You will notice that the upper classes and intelligentsia think that trade and merchants are low class. They want nothing to do with them. Banking, agriculture, and the professions—these are O.K." In Argentina, unlike more advanced countries, the middle classes have not been dynamic agents of growth.

So Argentine industry remains a bitter disappointment. Productivity is low. Tariffs and government subsidies still protect inefficiency. Sudden economic policy reversals are the norm. In the past thirty years, there have been thirty-six economy ministers, many of whose first acts were 180 degree reversals from their predecessors' policies. The fear of giant devaluations destroying one's peso assets at a stroke keeps everyone on their toes.

In this febrile atmosphere, business confidence is minimal. So is investment. Consequently, Argentine industry is filled with aging and obsolete machinery. That suppresses overall efficiency and worker productivity. The workers demand wage hikes, but since productivity is stagnant, any increases must come out of the owner's profits or capital, which then reduces funds available for investment. Investment remains low, industrial plant keeps aging, productivity keeps falling—leaving workers and management to keep battling it out in the zero-sum game.

STATISM V. LIBERALISM

This economic paralysis suggests two possible responses, one statist and the other liberal. In one, the government is the main problem solver. In the other, government is the main problem. Under the statist approach, if the private sector refuses to invest, the government will. If a major company is about to go to the wall, the government will take it over. If people are out of work, the government will hire. To a large extent, since Perón's first presidency, the Argentine government has played this guardian angel role. In 1943 there were a dozen state enterprises; now there are nearly 300. The government contributes 40 to 45 percent of gross fixed investment and employs around 20 percent of the national labor force.[13]

Liberalism, in the Argentine sense, is a subset of libertarianism. The liberals argue that this statism is neither more nor less than the major cause of Argentina's economic stagnation. They are not political liberals, but economic liberals, who share the classic free market views of Adam Smith, David Ricardo and, more recently, Milton Friedman. If only the state would get out of the way and let free market forces govern, all would go right. Through prices, supply and demand would efficiently determine the allocation of resources. The overgrown, inefficient state would stop draining valuable economic resources from potentially profitable enterprises. Efficient companies would prosper, losers would fold, and growth would revive. Investments would also become attractive in this fresh environment, promoting a sound basis for continued growth through new technology and increased worker productivity. The zero-sum game could be consigned to the dustbin of history, in favor of more trivial pursuits.

Economic liberalism is analytically powerful, because it revolves around a great truth: humans by nature are selfish. Its attraction is that it transforms the individual vice of greed into the social virtue of progress. If everyone selfishly seeks to acquire goods, then they will act industriously to produce them, in order to make trades. Individual initiative and diligence are rewarded by increased income.

Meanwhile, the increased production resulting from enterprising efforts benefits the whole society (say supply-siders and trickle-downers). Rich capitalists help poor workers, in order to expand the market for capitalist goods. Thus Henry Ford doubled his employees' wages in order to create a mass market for his Model T's. A rising tide lifts all boats. Those who remain poor despite these opportunities do so because they are lazy or incompetent. Diligence is rewarded and sloth punished. The social Darwinist aspects of the theory justify the unequal distribution of wealth inherent to capitalism. The logic is internally consistent, and comforting to the prosperous.

Two basic problems beset liberal theory. One was noted earlier; the premise is wrong. All men and women in Argentina are not born equally, in either advantages or opportunity. Second, at this stage, liberal theory cannot easily be put into practice in Argentina. The economy has been swaddled for decades in state protection; it has grown soft and indolent. Sudden exposure to the harsh free-for-all entailed in economic liberalism wipes out local businesses, unprepared and unable to compete successfully. They either lose out to foreign competition, or collapse under the weight of their own inefficiency. Hypocritically, many self-styled liberals are first to line up at the trough of state subsidies.

Whether liberals or statists have the better case, one thing is certain: the present mixture of both statist and liberal traits in the Argentine economy has brought about the worst of both worlds. As some say, Argentina has socialism without a plan, and capitalism without a market. The result is drift and decay.[14]

One need not accept liberal doctrine to reject the statist approach. Today virtually everyone admits that the state is grossly inefficient. It got that way in stages. First came the strategic phase, when Perón nationalized the major industries. National security theorists willingly sacrificed efficiency for the sake of establishing "strategic" industries—communications, roads, fuels, steel—under state control, in anticipation of the imminent World War III that Perón expected between the United States and the Soviet Union.

Then came the bailout phase. From 1966 to 1983, the military and Peronist governments increased the number of state enterprises from around fifty to three hundred. Instead of strategic industries, though, the new state industries ranged from sugar refining to textile manufacturing to catering. Most were taken over because they were losing money, and the government wanted to minimize bankruptcies and unemployment increases in those troubled years. Of course, state takeover did not reverse these companies' unprofitability, so the major difference was that these losses now came out of the taxpayers' instead of the owners' pockets.

Meanwhile, the performance of the major state enterprises is a national scandal. YPF (Yacimientos Petroliferos Fiscales) is said to be the only state oil company in the world that loses money. The state-run railways employ 2,150 agents per passenger mile, or more than three times the Western European average of 715. The railways lose $1 million per day. Entel, the state telephone company, is a nightmare. In Argentina, there is one Entel employee for every fifty telephones, compared to an average employee/telephone ratio of 1:200 in Europe. With this abundance of staff, however, the telephones still do not work. Around one-quarter to one-third of one's calls are misdirected through crossed wires to other telephones. If a customer receives his bill late or torn, he must go in person to a different office to pay it.

Still, perhaps unhappy telephone users should not complain; many people cannot get telephones at all. Some people who have been waiting for a dozen years are still waiting. The presence of a telephone can add $5,000 or more to the price of a house in Buenos Aires. The rats' nest of telephone wires above downtown Buenos Aires testifies to a common self-help solution adopted by many businessmen: patching one's own line into an existing Entel connection. Apart from the direct waste of such an overstaffed, underperforming enterprise, the time lost by telephone users in misdirected calls and grossly inconvenient bill-paying must cost the nation an enormous amount of lost work-hours. Forays into the state enterprise bureaucracy result in Kafkaesque nightmares of delays, misinformation, and futility.

The Argentine banking sector employs one person for every $60,000 in the system; in Japan the ratio is one employee per $3 million. In Buenos Aires government buildings one commonly sees three operators tending a single elevator (which of course needs none). Really, this overemployment is disguised underemployment compensation, but in such a haphazard form that waste and injustice are inevitable. The only needs test that counts is the need to know someone to get you a sinecure.

The efforts by Martínez de Hoz to open the Argentine economy to free competition stumbled over state enterprises. His professed intention was to reduce the role of the state in the economy, but in fact he increased it. The military junta would not let the economy minister transfer inefficient state enterprises to the private sector, or trim their corpulent payrolls. No service was the least disposed to deliver any of its vassal state enterprises up to the free market. On the contrary, during the tenure of Martínez de Hoz, the government purchased the only major private airline, Austral; a major electrical company, Italo; and created a host of new state enterprises.[15] Nationalization was a way at least to keep the lid on the number of bankruptcies caused by unaccustomed free market forces.

Had he gotten past the junta, Martínez de Hoz would have faced another problem: finding buyers. Who would want to take on these leviathans, their losses, and their truculent unions? Those state enterprises most likely to be privatized were not the major seven, controlling the oil, gas, hydroelectric, telephone, telegraph, mail, and railway sectors. Far more likely candidates for the auction block were the many other enterprises nationalized later, that is, those that were taken over because they had been losing money. Few entrepreneurs were stout enough to bid for such enterprises given Argentina's economic prospects.

In a way, this seemed puzzling. Traditionally, failing corporations are undervalued in the stock market. Consequently, investors willing to take a higher risk, by buying a dubious business, could also reap higher profits, by acquiring it at a bargain price and exploiting its full value.

This buy-cheap, sell-dear approach has failed in Argentina for two reasons. First, whoever has enough money to buy a company, even an undervalued one, could certainly profit more by speculation. Even a thriving business, much less a loser, can hardly manage a 20 percent profit per year in the best of times. Lending on the black market often yields much more. Second, when investors did buy undervalued companies, during the bankruptcies of the early 1980s, many resorted to get-rich-quick schemes instead of trying to run a successful business. For example, an insolvent company's full stock market value could well be much less than the value of its assets. An investor would buy the undervalued company, sell off the assets for a profit, and then declare bankruptcy. This maneuver was called "emptying" the company.

SPECULATION V. INVESTMENT

The overwhelming emphasis on the short-term leads to the third cleavage: speculation versus investment. In short, speculation pays better. Chronic inflation and high interest rates have allowed Argentines with liquid assets to profit handsomely in short term markets, and then invest their gains in stable assets abroad. When a large peso expense accrues, such as a new tax or year-end bonus, businessmen need pesos in a hurry. Thus, holders of pesos and dollars, of liquid and illiquid assets, are constantly gambling against one another. One person's hedge against inflation can become another's bonanza.

Speculation becomes more profitable when the government imposes exchange rate and interest controls. The difference between the official and free (i.e. black) market rates creates opportunities for easy profits. The bicycle was the best known, but there have been others. In a program to promote seed planting, the government once offered credit at concessionary terms to farmers to buy seed. A farmer could borrow money at 10 percent per month and, instead of buying seeds with it, lend it on the parallel market at, say, 15 percent, thereby netting more than a 60 percent annual profit. Beats raising corn and toiling under the noonday sun.

Why is speculation a bad thing? After all, speculators are enterprising individuals who profit under adverse circumstances. Do they deserve that reward? Should they serve as models for others? No. They are social parasites, thriving at the expense of their host. In Argentina, they might even be considered carrion feeders. The worse the inflation, the higher the interest rate, the greater the distortion, the better they do. Funds that could go to productive investment instead end up in their pockets, foreign bank accounts, and vacation homes. They are the masters at staying on the positive side of the zero-sum game, helped by their three principal assets: liquid and unreported capital, good information, and access to the markets. If they win, who loses? Some other speculators, who took the risk and lost. But more often, the government and, through it, the taxpayers (from whose ranks the speculators tend, naturally, to absent themselves).

Why is speculation irrepressible? One reason is that it is so appealing. Although they should not be, the speculators are role models to many who covet their wealth. Even the investor with a social conscience may be drawn to speculate by the absence of a predictable long-term. Why invest in a building if high inflation and interest rates will force you to abandon it before completion? When the government relentlessly spews out more and more pesos, covering its bloated budget with an inflationary tax, why should the person with his or her own resources not seek to protect or even nourish them in the financial market? Once again, the tradition of instability practically compels short-term gluttony. An Argentine must either be a super-patriot or a fool to invest in the long term. It just does not pay.

Under these circumstances, it is surprising that there is *any* private sector productive investment at all. The crisis has worsened in recent years. Since 1970, investment as a share of gross domestic product has fallen from 20 to under 12 percent. Many investors suffered badly since the 1981 collapse. Contractors stopped construction when their financing ran out. Today, half-built hulks of concrete and rusting beams, scattered throughout Buenos Aires and the provinces, bear mute witness to a boom gone bust.

When they reach extraordinary levels, high inflation and interest rates destroy financial instruments designed to provide security and facilitate business. Life insurance virtually does not exist. Banks do not offer mortgages. Major purchases are usually made in cash on the barrel; the difficulty and risks in paying huge sums up front further discourage major productive investments. Shortage of investments in turn suppresses national income and worker productivity.

A natural side-effect of the shrunken production and commercial sectors is an expanded financial sector. To prevent erosion of their assets, everyone must be a part-time financier, from the high rollers to the salaried wokers who buy a few black market dollars whenever they can. In the sweet money days, "banks" sprouted up everywhere. Anyone with a few thousand dollars, a telephone, and a desk could put himself in operation. Even worse, the state helped rip itself off, by guaranteeing all bank deposits. Thus, a two-bit financial operation could attract capital by offering high interest rates, do the bicycle, pay-off depositors while the going was good, and go belly-up when the good times stopped. The "bankrupt" banker's profits by this time could be "invested" in Lichtenstein front companies, while their not-so-hapless depositors (remember they enjoyed the high interest rates) were reimbursed by the government.

These high-flying days halted abruptly in March 1980, with the forced liquidation of the largest privately-owned bank in Argentina, the Banco de Intercambio Regional (BIR). That triggered a panic that left many more banks and finance companies in liquidation. An estimated $2 billion injection averted a general collapse of the private banking system, but investors would no longer invest in the highest yield asset, regardless of its stability. The BIR collapse frightened perhaps $4.5 billion in capital out of Argentina.

In 1982 the foreign debt crisis struck in earnest, and officially available credit disappeared. Companies with lots of cash on hand began lending directly to other cash-short enterprises, bypassing the banking system. Thus began the "interfirm" market for loans, which continues today. Bank credit, under government control, bore a nominal interest rate as high as 17 percent per month. Since inflation surged ahead of interest rates, though, the *real* interest rates were negative. In other words, the banks lost money on every loan. As a result, funds were simply unavailable at that rate. Meanwhile, on the interfirm market, credit could be obtained, but at what a price! In 1984 real annual interest rates of 60 percent or more were common.

The interfirm market made headlines in December 1984 when annualized interest rates nominally exceeded 500 percent. One reason for the December surge was the *aguinaldo*, the traditional bonus of a thirteenth monthly paycheck begun by Perón. The federal government itself was caught in this squeeze. Under pressure from the provincial governors, it withheld payment of year-end bonuses to its employees in order to pay its promised contribution to the provinces. These competing claims highlight the fourth major cleavage: Buenos Aires versus the provinces.

BUENOS AIRES V. THE PROVINCES

This cleavage is one of the least visible to foreigners, who often know no more of Argentina than its capital. Nevertheless, the division is real and has stunted Argentina's political development. As the metropolises of nineteenth century imperial Europe exploited their far-flung empires, often preventing the colonies from developing their own political systems, so Buenos Aires has thwarted the growth of the outlying Argentine provinces. The wars between the capital and the provinces ended in 1880, but the inequality continues to this day.

For example, several presidents used their constitutional power to intervene in the provinces and expel their governments. The tax system is so centralized that national taxes exceed those collected by all twenty-two provinces together by about four times. Consequently, the provinces depend heavily on contributions from the National Treasury to keep afloat. In the poorest provinces of the Northwest, the federal contribution has at times reached 90 percent of the provincial budget.

The frequent overvaluation of the peso has also hurt provincial exports. The fertile lands of Buenos Aires Province support cattle herds and grain production at such a low cost that, even when the peso is overvalued, Argentine prices may still be competitive on the world market. The poorer lands of the provinces raise production costs, however, so that the added penalty of an overvalued peso may price their produce right out of international markets. That is one reason why Río Negro apples and excellent Mendoza wines have not fared better overseas.[16] The provincials also lose out on speculation; those who have the money lack the quick access to market information so important to success. This is even true in the biggest cities of the interior—Rosario, Córdoba, and Tucumán.

What does the plight of the provinces have to do with democracy? Participation. The centralization of economic and political power has destroyed the basis of a pluralist society in Argentina. In a pluralist society, opportunities to participate are widespread. In Argentina, opportunities are concentrated in Buenos Aires. For decades, people eager to get ahead flocked to Buenos Aires. The arrogance of power has settled in the capital, which saps the provinces of many of their best and brightest. Consequently, many provinces remain underpopulated and underdeveloped, prone more to the domination of a few leading citizens or families than to the dynamic political competition of a democracy. President Alfonsín acknowledged this fact when he proposed that the capital be shifted from Buenos Aires to Viedma in Northern Patagonia, much as the Brazilian government had moved its capital from Rio de Janeiro to a jungle clearing dubbed "Brasilia" a generation before.

BLACK V. WHITE MARKET

In such a fractured political economy, it should come as no surprise that much economic activity has gone "underground." The combination of burdensome government controls and cynicism toward the system ensures it.

Despite its sinister name, the underground economy or "black market" simply represents unreported income. The traditional image of black market goods and services—drugs, prostitution, and contraband—make up but a small part of the whole. Bribery comprises another. Many people, however, earn black market income from perfectly legal operations. The only illegality consists in not reporting the income. A restaurant owner under-reports receipts. An importer over-reports costs. Some black markets that are nominally illegal—such as the parallel market in dollars—are so widespread and unsanctioned that they lack all the secretive trappings of movie-style black markets. The major newspapers publish the black market dollar rates daily, complete with opening and closing quotations.

No one knows the exact size of the underground economy, but estimates range up to 20 or 25 percent of the national product. That is why many people are better off than depressing official statistics suggest. If a state employee's official salary has stagnated, and he earns unreported income from a second job, then he may not be better off per hour, but at least his total income has increased. People in the street seem to dress and live better than one would expect in a ruined economy. This is true partly because high inflation encourages maximum consumption and minimum saving, but partly because many earn black market income.

It can be a tough sport. One auto dealer reportedly sold a fleet of new Renault 11's to a well-dressed, chauffeured group of con artists. The parties agreed that the transaction would take place in dollars, for the sake of mutual convenience, while the sales slip would be written out in pesos, to comply with the law. After trading the receipt for a satchel of cash, off drove the proud new Renault owners. Closer inspection revealed that the "dollars" were crude counterfeits, but the dealer was stuck. The swindlers had both the cars and a legal peso receipt, which they could show to any judge.[17] What could the auto dealer say? "That receipt I signed was fraudulent. And the illegal payment I received was counterfeited."

Still, the black market is no laughing matter. Symbolically, it is a slap in the face of the government, showing that the people neither respect nor fear it. (Machiavelli told his Prince that it is better to be feared than respected. You need one or the other, though.) The black market is partly responsible for the large government deficit. Foreign exchange reserves, critical for the payment of Argentina's debt, are also eroded by black market transactions. An importer pays $120 for a $100 Japanese radio, tells the Argentine Central Bank that the radio cost $120, and has his supplier stash the extra $20 in a foreign bank account. An exporter sells a leather jacket abroad for $120, tells the government he received $100, and has his buyer deposit the extra $20 in a foreign bank account.

To respond to abysmal tax collection, the government resorts to more and more draconian revenue measures. The easiest remedy is also the least fair; since those with hideable income do not pay taxes, the government relies more and more on automatic taxes, including value-added taxes, agricultural export taxes, cigarette and alcohol taxes, gasoline price hikes (actually a tax, since YPF is a state enterprise). In this reverse-Robin Hood scheme, the poor pay the taxes for the rich. In 1984, of total government revenues, only 1.2 percent comprised wealth taxes; 2.3 percent, income tax; and 41.5 percent, production and consumption taxes.[18] Haphazard and patently unfair government tax policy frustrates taxpayers' planning and encourages cheating. The 50 to 60 percent level of evasion provokes ever more drastic government countermeasures, and the vicious cycle continues.

Corruption can be less gross, though, as in the case of government pensions. Public officials who served in any position at assistant secretary rank or higher used to receive a pension of full pay for life, provided they held that position for at least forty-five days. Thus it is not uncommon for a retired civil servant to be collecting three or four full pensions. In 1981, a retired major who served during the Process as mayor of a small city and intervenor of the provincial affiliate of a state company was collecting three pensions for an $84,000 annual income. Presumably a retired general could do even better. By contrast, the minimum pension, on which many retired workers depended to live, at that time had yet to reach $3,000 per year.[19]

Is it any wonder that Argentine cynicism is so strong?

PASSING THE BUCK

How are the burdens from these cleavages shared? The traditional government solution has *not* been to reduce state payrolls and programs, but rather to print more pesos. For illustration, state employees now number around 1.8 million. If the average salary were 50,000 pesos per month, the government would have to pay out 90 billion pesos. If government revenues only amounted to 80 billion pesos, the Mint would just print up the balance. Who *truly* pays? Anyone holding pesos at that moment. Since the new pesos are not backed by real goods or services, the addition of 10 billion pesos simply inflates overall price levels, diluting the value of each peso outstanding. If 300 billion pesos are in circulation on payday, the issuance of 10 billion pesos will increase inflation by 3 percent. Yesterday's peso will now be worth 97 centavos.

In essence, printing pesos constitutes an inflationary tax to cover the deficit. This tax is paid principally by workers, merchants, and service suppliers since most salaries, sales, and services are paid for in pesos.[20] Naturally, these people want at least to stay even with and if possible to get ahead of the inflation rate. Thus begins the familiar wage-price spiral.

A second way for the government to cover its deficit is to increase its revenues. Since the income tax collection system is so toothless, the government resorts to the inescapable taxes noted above. Since these taxes are levied on consumption, they too weigh more heavily on those with less income. The reason is that people with less money spend a greater percentage of what they have on consumption. A two pack-a-day smoker pays the same tax whether he earns $5,000 or $50,000 per year. That tax represents a higher percentage of $5,000 than of $50,000. If the richer man used his greater income to buy twenty packs a day, he would equalize his relative tax burden. But who smokes twenty packs a day?

The third method to cover the government deficit is by borrowing. This method may also unfairly burden those least able to pay. For instance, under President Isabel Perón, the government financed its deficit by domestic borrowing. It issued adjustable-rate bonds, whose interest rate increased as a function of inflation. The burden of these bonds fell on small savers. Consider Figure 8–1:

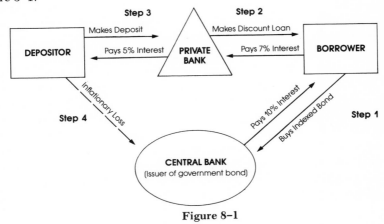

Figure 8–1

People with sufficient resources and information used borrowed funds to buy adjustable bonds. (Step 1.) They then pledged these bonds as collateral in order to take out more loans from commercial banks, which they used to buy more bonds, and so forth. (Step 2.) The interaction between Steps 1 and 2 was another form of the bicycle. In a single transaction, a borrower with no capital could borrow the money to buy the bond by simultaneously pledging the bond as collateral to the commercial bank. As an added advantage, using government bonds as collateral enabled the borrowers to obtain their commercial loans at discounted interest rates. The commercial banks would acquire the funds needed to make these discounted loans from their depositors, who received the passbook rate of interest. (Step 3.)

On balance, this transaction had several results. The government obtained the immediate funds it needed to cover its expenses. The bank received the traditional spread between the interest paid on deposits and the interest earned on loans, 2 percent in the example above. The borrower in the example secured bank loans at a discount to earn a net 3 percent return on its indexed bond (10 percent bond interest received minus 7 percent loan interest paid). Bond indexation guaranteed that the borrower's return on investment would keep pace with inflation. The depositors, out of habit and lack of financial sophistication, earned interest rates lower than those available from indexed bonds and perhaps even lower than the rate of inflation. They lost their potential profit to the financially astute borrowers, while the Central Bank issuance of indexed bonds fueled inflation and further debased the value of their deposits. (Step 4.)

Eventually, as inflation rates grew ever higher than interest rates, people just stopped making savings deposits in pesos. Savings deposits fell as a portion of total commercial bank deposits from over 50 percent in 1970 to around 10 percent in the early 1980s. In 1982 the Central Bank finally eliminated the adjustable bond system of financing the deficit.

The adjustable bond was not the only bad bargain struck by depositors. Interest rate controls were even more destructive to small savings.[21] When the nominal interest rate is lower than the inflation rate, the real interest rate is negative. As mortgagors and student borrowers know, negative real interest rates make borrowing profitable. Negative interest rates can serve a useful fiscal objective of stimulating production and growth, if the borrowed funds are devoted to the purchase of machinery and construction of factories. In Argentina, however, negative interest rates merely dried up both new deposits (who makes a bank deposit to lose money?) and funds available to make bank loans at the official interest rate (who makes a loan to lose money?). Thus arose the interfirm loan market.

Of course, deficits can be covered by foreign as well as local borrowing. In Argentina this method was employed foolishly and irresponsibly. Foolishly, because the government took foreign funds to pay current expenses, rather than to make productive investments in projects that could generate sufficient cash flow to repay the loan. Irresponsibly, because the government increased the debt, and thereby burdened tomorrow's Argentina with today's profligacy. The funds needed to pay interest on the debt are usually obtained from fresh loans provided by Argentina's creditor banks. A stern government austerity program monitored by the International Monetary Fund is the precondition for disbursement of new money. The burden of austerity falls on the peso economy.

It is becoming apparent that the peso economy bears the brunt of Argentina's woeful legacy. It makes sense that the black market continues to grow, since it is a haven from this onerous burden. The wealthiest classes escape most completely, keeping only enough pesos at one time to cover current expenses, much as one keeps a minimum balance in a no-interest checking account.

Austerity is the final solution for a chronic deficit. Call the policy adjustment or deflation, the features are the same: economic contraction through some combination of reduced wages, government spending cuts, and increased taxes. This castor oil approach eliminates the deficit by cutting into living standards and growth. The Austral Plan embraced austerity; in 1985, the Argentine gross domestic product fell 4.4 percent.

SCHOOL OF PLUNDER

The wealthy have betrayed Argentina. They evade taxes religiously. During the Process, they benefited from the greatest transfer of wealth in Argentine history. Before recent reforms, banking secrecy laws made an accurate accounting impossible. There are only a few indicators. Hundreds of new yachts appeared in Buenos Aires docks. Hundreds of new homes appeared in Punta del Este. The wealthy live beyond the nation's means, but never pay in full for their extravagance. They always leave others holding the bag. The mountain of private debt ended up in Argentine bank accounts abroad and conspicuous consumption.

Average, peso-earning Argentines benefited from cheap imports and foreign travel, but did not obtain the lion's share of the benefits. Yet they will bear the lion's share of the repayment burden, because nearly all of the private sector debt has been assumed by the government. The bailout began in

1982. With $5 billion of short-term loans falling due, the Central Bank found that it did not have enough foreign currency reserves to sell to the private debtors to repay the foreign creditors. The Central Bank could not simply tell the local debtors to go out and buy the dollars they needed, because it had banned unofficial foreign exchange purchases in order to keep the value of the peso artificially high.

In order to persuade local debtors to renegotiate their debt repayments rather than to default, the Central Bank offered to *assume* the local debtor's obligation to repay. The system was called exchange insurance. The local debtor would pay in the pesos due on the debt at the official exchange rate, and the Central Bank would issue five-year bonds or promissory notes to the foreign creditor. In this way, debtors would pay off their debts at forty-five to sixty-five cents on the dollar, and the government would eventually pay the rest. In other words, the taxpayers would pay the rest. The debtor profited handsomely.

In Argentina, the wealthy never advanced from exploitation and consumption to productive investment, remaining smugly immune to reform. They came to power through exclusion and they remained exclusive, never willing to share political power freely with other economic groups. It is striking how the wealthy complain even when government policies are most favorable to them. As Perón aptly noted,

> By tragic paradox, the conservative classes lost their instinct of conservation. Their vehement desire to retain all, their eagerness not to give up a single one of their accumulated advantages, did not allow them to see what was manifestly evident: that the desire to preserve all would lead them to lose all.[22]

When other groups elbowed their way into power—the middle class through Radicalism and the working class through Peronism—they applied the lessons they had learned and grabbed for all the could. Politics-cum-exploitation, unsoftened by the *noblesse oblige* of Thomas Jefferson or the Marquis de Lafayette, turned Argentine government into a free-for-all.

CHAPTER 9

The Nuclear Tightrope

Each one of us must with his knowledge, his studies, his self-effacement, his material assets, bend his work and effort toward making this effort successful. The country will owe us in the future a greatness which today we cannot begin to imagine. So be it.

—JUAN D. PERÓN, *on Argentina's nuclear program, 1951*

Try to see it their way. The Argentines believe they have a perfect right to develop nuclear technology. They have devoted thirty-five years and billions of dollars to the cause. From the outset, the government has always insisted that its aims are strictly peaceful, and has never taken any unequivocal steps toward building nuclear arms. Diligence and skill have brought Argentina a mastery of nuclear technology matched in the developing world only by India. It is the scientific field in which Argentina has most distinguished itself internationally.

Argentines claim that their credentials as opponents of nuclear weapons are impeccable. Apart from officially abjuring nuclear weapons on numerous occasions, the Argentine government was a founding member of the International Atomic Energy Agency (IAEA) in 1957 and has accepted that organization's safeguards over all imported nuclear facilities.[1] The government has pledged to require IAEA safeguards on all Argentine nuclear exports, too.

The *real* threat of nuclear holocaust, in Argentine eyes, flows not from the South but from the North, from the bristling and burgeoning nuclear arsenals of the United States and the Soviet Union. "It is *immoral* that some countries have the bomb!" exclaimed one senior atomic scientist. Producing the bomb, he added, is not a technical issue: "The bomb is in the heart." But not in Argentine hearts, he insisted.

Then why do so many people worry and speculate about Argentina and the bomb? Prejudice and sheer selfishness clearly play a part, but valid

171

grounds for concern exist, too. Argentina has engaged in plutonium reprocessing and uranium enrichment, processes which can be used to produce nuclear explosives. These technologies have peaceful uses, but their military possibilities cannot be gainsaid. Significant amounts of plutonium or highly enriched uranium have probably not been produced, but plants involving each technology are under construction.

Argentina's nuclear diplomacy creates more concern. Argentina rejects international inspection for homebuilt items—notably its plutonium reprocessing and uranium enrichment plants, as well as heavy water, uranium dioxide, and zirconium production facilities. Moreover, the government has steadfastly refused to sign the 125-member Non-Proliferation Treaty (NPT), which bars acquisition of nuclear arms by states that did not possess them before 1968. The Argentines assert that the accord is invidiously discriminatory, "disarming the unarmed" while allowing five nations (the United States, Soviet Union, Great Britain, France, and China) to monopolize nuclear weapon possession. The government has signed but not ratified the 1967 Treaty of Tlatelolco, a Mexican initiative to convert Latin America into a nuclear weapon-free zone. All Latin nations except Argentina and Cuba have ratified the treaty, which will not become fully effective until these final two ratifications are deposited.

Argentina traditionally has objected to Tlatelolco on the grounds that the IAEA (backed by the United States) refuses to accept the notion that any nuclear explosion can be "peaceful," though Article 18 of the accord permits "peaceful" nuclear explosions. This scholasticist argument now has been overshadowed by a genuine complaint: the British military occupation of the Malvinas Islands. To the Argentines this unwelcome presence implies an unverifiable possibility that nuclear weapons are deployed in the region, in flagrant violation of the treaty. After all, the cruiser *Belgrano* was sunk by the nuclear-propelled submarine, HMS Conqueror, and the British flotilla reportedly had nuclear weapons on hand during the war. Her Majesty's government, in accordance with longstanding policy, refuses to confirm or deny the rumored presence of nuclear weapons in any military theater. The British policy is understandable, but offends the letter and spirit of the Treaty of Tlatecolco.[2]

Argentina's diplomatic posture is serious. It is logical and fervently supported. Yet nagging uncertainties persist. Argentine allegations of discrimination, accompanied by vague allusions to the possible use of nuclear explosives for peaceful purposes, appear to many as a smokescreen for belligerence. The NPT is discriminatory, but Argentine diplomats concede that Tlatelolco is not. Even Brazil, the other leading Latin nuclear power, has ratified Tlatelolco. Most other Latin nations have submitted to the treaty's controls voluntarily, even though they will not legally be obliged to do so until Argentina and Cuba join, too. In short, doubts persist because Argentina has adopted no categorical international commitment against acquiring nuclear weapons. An Argentine bomb could be built and exploded without breaking a single treaty or agreement.[3]

Other concerns relate to Argentina's political instability. Even if every Argentine leader to date has sincerely opposed nuclear weapons, who knows what the future may bring? The country has for years possessed the technological wherewithal to develop nuclear weapons, but has declined to exploit it. Given this technological capacity, future leaders may reach out for nuclear weapons to divert popular criticism at desperate moments. President Galtieri's surprise attack on the Malvinas Islands reinforced concerns over the possibility of Argentine nuclear recklessness.

A final group of concerns has nothing to do with Argentina itself. States that already possess nuclear weapons naturally worry about those that do not. It is in the self-interest of the nuclear powers to keep the nuclear club small, to pull the ladder up after them. The more members there are in the nuclear club, the more diluted is the influence of each. Sheer probability also enters the calculations; the more parties that possess nuclear weapons, the more likely that one will be used somewhere sometime. This is not to say that the present nuclear powers are inherently wiser or more responsible than the Argentines, or that Argentines are less trustworthy than they. The point is that nuclear weapon technology, once acquired, cannot be unlearned. Those who are already nuclear weapon-states will remain so, for better or worse. The fewer that learn the ugly secret, however, the better. That, at least, is the argument.[4]

Argentines are worried, too, for quite another reason. Economic crisis now threatens to destroy a rare national success story. The Argentine nuclear program has long been a cynosure of national pride. It has chalked up an impressive array of firsts in Latin America: first research reactor, first commercial reactor, first plutonium reprocessing and fuel element production, first reactor export (to Peru). In 1983, Argentine nuclear chief Carlos Castro Madero announced that Argentina had developed its own technique for enriching uranium, a process mastered by only seven other nations in the world. The Balseiro Atomic Centre at San Carlos de Bariloche is the best nuclear training institute on the continent. In addition to five operating research reactors, the 367 MWe Atucha-1 commercial reactor has completed more than a dozen years of high-level performance and a 600 MWe, Canadian-designed station is in its fourth year of operation. Argentine delegates have presided over the General Conference of the International Atomic Energy Agency, adding luster to the national image.

Now more than ever this legacy of success stands at risk. The 1979 Three Mile Island accident did not phase Argentine nuclear planners; indeed, later that year the military government authorized an ambitious program to build four 600 MWe nuclear reactors and a complete nuclear fuel cycle by the year 1997.[5] The nuclear budget quadrupled, approaching $1 billion annually by conservative estimates. (It may have been much more.) Some plants were completed, others begun. Then came the 1982 economic crash, and half-completed projects began to falter for want of funds. The nuclear program was still popular, but hypertrophic. The Treasury simply could not sustain its elephantine proportions.

Alfonsín's inauguration deepened concern among nuclear backers over the program's future. Especially to Peronists, his avowed nuclear pacifism smacked of pusillanimity toward the nuclear powers and concealed the new president's disdain toward technology in general and nuclear energy in particular. The new energy secretary, Conrado Storani, favored hydro over nuclear development. He and other Radicals were not persuaded that the nationalistic value of nuclear independence outweighted the high costs entailed. In Alfonsín's first year in office the nuclear budget was halved. Real salaries plummeted by 40 percent or more. Capital projects froze, while carrying charges mounted for equipment stuck in foreign ports awaiting shipment to Buenos Aires.

What were Alfonsín's true intentions? And what were those of his predecessors? Are Argentine scientists, wittingly or not, headed toward nuclear weapons? And if not, what political attraction has been so powerful as to allow the National Atomic Energy Commission (CNEA) to become the most successful and celebrated Argentine government agency? The answer to these questions requires a historical glance at a nuclear program unlike any other in the world.

A POCKETFUL OF MIRACLES

An extraordinary tale begins the Argentine nuclear legacy. Shortly after World War II, an exiled Austrian physicist named Ronald Richter wandered around Europe in search of sponsors for nuclear experimentation.[6] Brought to Argentina by an ex-Nazi aircraft designer, this beguiling European soon convinced President Perón that he could bring Argentina to the forefront of nuclear technology, and for only a fraction of the investment made by the

Americans and Soviets. Convinced of this get-rich-quick opportunity, Perón lavished Richter with funds and personnel. The president even granted him executive authority over tiny Huemul Island, nestled in a lake district of northern Patagonia called Bariloche, which is known as the Switzerland of Argentina. Surrounded by the majestic Andes and lush greenery, Richter set to work in 1949.

Two years later, Perón and Richter stunned the world by announcing a major scientific breakthrough. Argentina (they said) had successfully demonstrated the process of nuclear fusion, the forcing together of two minute isotopes of hydrogen. Up to that time, the world had only witnessed the inverse process, fission (the splitting of heavy isotopes), so devastatingly introduced at Hiroshima and Nagasaki. Fusion had never before been controlled. For that matter, in 1951, no one had yet demonstrated even an *un*controlled fusion reaction: the fusion or so-called hydrogen bomb. That feat was first announced by President Truman in 1952. Scientists today are still struggling to harness fusion for the production of energy.

"I control the reaction," Richter boasted at the 23 March 1951 press conference. "I make it expand or diminish at my desire." The world's leading nuclear physicists—among them Otto Hahn and Enrico Fermi—immediately discounted the Argentine announcement, which the U.S. State Department labeled as "95 percent propaganda." Perón bristled with indignation. "They have not told the first truth, while I have not told the first lie," he parried. But eventually even Perón began to doubt Richter, whose budget demands grew ever more extravagant and paranoia ever more acute. Argentina's nuclear *Wunderkind* blamed one bungled experiment after another on spies and saboteurs. Finally, in November 1952, after several trips by Argentine scientists to Huemul Island, Richter was exposed as a fraud and sent packing. His staff and facilities were dismantled. After Perón's ouster, a congressional panel determined that Richter had squandered $70 million in his endeavors.

The Richter episode cannot simply be dismissed as a farcical interlude. Peronists—unable to concede that the First Worker was simply conned by a jumped-up fake—even today insist that despite the weaknesses of Richter's specific "theories," nevertheless his experiments launched Argentina's nuclear success story. That is true in one sense; the high priority according the nuclear program under Richter continued after his undoing. Only now, the motive became vindication, not mere recognition.

Fortunately, Richter's successors were more earthbound. Professionalism became the watchword at the National Atomic Energy Commission. Partly this was a simple reaction against the harebrained experiments of Huemul Island. After Richter, Perón entrusted nuclear development to Navy Captain Pedro Iraolagoitia. When the new nuclear chief told Perón that, by and large, competent physicists were anti-Peronists, Perón reluctantly consented to hire them anyway. That shows the seriousness of Perón's commitment, for in all other academic fields, the mere hint of disaffection with Peronism resulted in immediate dismissal or worse. Thus began the CNEA commitment to professionalism over politics, an article of pride to this day. To be sure, politics have always been important, but they do not dominate decisionmaking in the nuclear realm as much as in other programs.

The ouster of Perón initiated a new phase in Argentina's atomic program —the Quihillalt era. Except for a brief hiatus in the late 1950s, Navy Captain (later Admiral) Oscar Quihillalt headed the commission for the next eighteen years, until Peron's return in 1973. Quihillalt (pronounced key-*zhalt*) had had technical training (mainly in ballistics and mathematics) and reinforced Iraolagoitia's commitment to professionalism. He also shared Perón's fierce pride in Argentina's *independent* quest for nuclear technology, in defiance of superpower concerns. Quihillalt, however, also added a new and essential ingredient to Argentine nuclear progress: stability. Quihillalt outlasted five presidents. For a dozen years, he kept his top-level management team virtually intact. Even today, many senior CNEA officials are thirty-year veterans, and many in the second tier have logged twenty years or more. In a country where many ministries average a minister per year, and political purges often flush away hard-earned institutional memories, the CNEA's achievement is still more remarkable.

Stability has paid off handsomely. It has allowed the CNEA to pursue its unwavering goal of independence. It has helped to create a capable work force, imbued by an unusually strong *esprit de corps*. It has allowed the CNEA to participate increasingly in successive nuclear reactors; local content comprised 35 percent of the value of the first atomic power reactor and 50 percent of the second.

The role of the navy cannot be ignored. For thirty years, until 1983, a naval officer headed the CNEA. That did not mean that the program was oriented toward nuclear-armed or -propelled ships or submarines, but rather that the commission enjoyed navy protection in struggles over budgets and bureaucratic turf. That meant a lot during civilian government, and even more during military governments.[7]

The CNEA's autonomy became self-perpetuating. Stability produced results, which in turn helped bring in funding. Success begat success. Presidents were loath to tamper with the one Argentine technical program that worked. By 1974, the commission had built four research reactors, inaugurated its first commercial power reactor (Atucha-1), produced and milled over a thousand tons of uranium ore each year, and reprocessed minute quantities of plutonium on a laboratory scale.

Despite these impressive achievements, the nuclear program at that time remained relatively small—around $250 million per year. The highest single ticket item, the Atucha-1 reactor, had been financed by a 100 percent credit arranged by the German contractor, Siemens. It only cost around $70 million and a 100 percent cost overrun was wordlessly accepted by the giant German electrical firm.

Dreaming Argentine physicists and technicians, though, would soon have a chance to fulfill their fantasies. After three years of Peronist chaos, in 1976 the military returned to power. Now to professionalism and stability would be added a third Argentine atomic legacy: scale.

The new CNEA president was another naval officer, Carlos Castro Madero —the first atomic chief with training in nuclear physics. Top commission officials who had preferred exile to Peronism returned; some of them, including Admiral Quihillalt, had worked for the Shah, helping to get the Iranian nuclear program under way. The young turks who had taken over important positions during the Peronist government were purged. A few disappeared, most notably Antonio Misatich, a physicist who had studied in the United States. His sister, apparently a Montonera, had been killed in a shootout. Misatich himself had become politically active, a surprise to his physicist friends. When Perón returned, Misatich became a leading candidate to head the commission, a gambit headed off by an old-guard maneuver to offer the job to a figure of impeccable Peronist credentials—retired Admiral Pedro Iraolagoitia, Perón's advisor and CNEA chief from 1952 to 1955. In 1976, Misatich joined the long roster of the *desaparecidos*.

The CNEA at once shifted into high gear. The military junta approved plans to complete the fuel cycle—in other words, to build all those facilities necessary to convert raw ore into finely-processed uranium fuel elements, and later to treat and dispose of the irradiated fuel after it was removed from the reactor core. That would make Argentina self-sufficient in the nuclear field. Work continued on a second nuclear power reactor, a Canadian model sited at Embalse, to serve Argentina's third largest city, Córdoba.

A plant was built to supply the uranium rods for the core of Atucha-1, with plans to build production lines for Embalse and Atucha-2—a third power station contracted out to the Germans. Three more reactors were approved for construction by 1997. On the fuel side, a pilot-scale reprocessing plant was begun. After the United States terminated its supply of highly-enriched uranium to Argentine research reactors in 1978, the commission took a daring decision: Argentine scientists would build their own enrichment plant.

A team of scientists and engineers went to work on the enrichment project at Pilcaniyeu, thirty miles from the site of Richter's earlier endeavors. For the next five years they labored in secret, concentrating on the difficult and painstaking gaseous diffusion technology. This was the technology used by American scientists forty years earlier in the Manhattan Project; the gaseous diffusion plant at Oak Ridge, Tennessee, produced the enriched uranium for Little Boy, the bomb dropped over Hiroshima. This was the technology that produced all the enriched uranium for commercial nuclear reactors until 1980.

Gaseous diffusion is a filtration process. Its purpose is to increase the concentration of the easily-split uranium-235 isotope from the scant 0.7 percent level found in natural uranium. The uranium is converted into gaseous form, and the lighter, smaller uranium-235 isotopes pass more easily through a filter barrier than the heavier and slower uranium-238 isotopes, weighed down by their three extra neutrons. The uranium gas that filters through to the other side of the barrier has been "enriched" ever so slightly, perhaps by a factor of around 0.004 percent. The level of enrichment reached depends on how many times you push the uranium gas through the barriers: a few hundred times will give you 3 percent enriched uranium, good enough to run a light water reactor. A few thousand times will give you over 90 percent enrichment, good enough for a nuclear explosive.

Gaseous diffusion presents two formidable technological challenges. First is the barrier; you must find a material with pores so tiny that they discriminate between the chemically-identical uranium-235 and uranium-238 isotopes. Reportedly, the chance discovery of a suitably porous material, perhaps ceramic, precipitated the Argentine decision to try to develop a working enrichment process. The second challenge is to find a way to handle uranium in gaseous form. Uranium hexafluoride (UF_6) is highly toxic, volatile, and corrosive. Special pipes and pumps must be used to contain and compress it. Despite disclaimers that they had received no foreign help, Argentine officials privately said that nickel was secretly imported to plate the plumbing for protection against the destructive properties of UF_6. Notwithstanding this and other precautions, in October 1984 a canister of UF_6 exploded while a technician was carrying it in the Pilcaniyeu plant. The man lost his legs and, soon thereafter, his life.[8]

The crowning moment of the military government's ambitious push in the field of nuclear technology came, ironically, on the eve of its abject retreat from the political arena. Just after the October 1983 elections, Castro Madero learned that the Pilcaniyeu experiment had succeeded. The Argentines had enriched uranium! Castro Madero, bursting with this exciting news, found himself in a political quandary. If he announced the achievement, he would get the credit for it, but would also confirm Radical party suspicions that the military had conducted its own, secret nuclear program.

An announcement might increase Castro Madero's already high national popularity, making it harder for the incoming president to fire him. Conversely, Alfonsín might view an announcement as an effort to preempt his own authority, and repudiate Castro Madero. The admiral could give the president-elect the final say, but what if Alfonsín said no? Castro Madero, never shy to tout his accomplishments, would then have to swallow his greatest of all. Meanwhile, the CIA already suspected an enrichment program was afoot, and a flurry of press attention had followed the publication of a *New York Times* article in September speculating on the prospect. Was Castro Madero stoically to remain silent only to allow the American newspapers to steal his thunder?

In the end, Castro Madero got half a loaf: the glory but not the job. He informed Alfonsín of the breakthrough and, on 18 November 1983—the midpoint of the military-civilian transition—held a press conference where he stated that "Argentina has successfully demonstrated the technology for the enrichment of uranium."[9] Perhaps Castro Madero figured that he might lose his job even if he kept quiet; at least this way he would go out with a bang.

World press notice did not disappoint Argentine nationalists. It is strange how the international press, generally so skeptical, takes nuclear claims at face value. At once Argentina was hailed as the "eighth" nuclear power.[10] A close look at Castro Madero's statement should have restrained such wild speculation. He merely stated that the Argentines had successfully "demonstrated" uranium enrichment and were building a medium-sized plant. He did not say how much if any had been produced, and averred that the enrichment would only be used for peaceful purposes. This was vintage Castro Madero, extracting every ounce of popular acclaim from a statement carefully crafted so as to prevent hysterics in the professional community.

Castro Madero's legacy extends beyond the enrichment breakthrough. He also left behind him an array of ambitious projects in various stages of completion. Castro Madero served at a special moment. The late 1970s were the days of oil crisis, sweet money, and nuclear technology suppliers desperate to make sales in the developing world. Atucha-1 was running well. The country was ruled by military men, as fond of large capital projects as are military men everywhere. The stage was perfectly set for a huge surge in nuclear spending, and the CNEA took full advantage of it. Machinery to produce zirconium sponge was ordered from the Soviet Union; to purify uranium and fabricate fuel, from West Germany. The enrichment and reprocessing facilities also benefited from foreign equipment. Sulzer Brothers of Switzerland provided cooling equipment to Pilcaniyeu. The Ezeiza reprocessing plant is arrayed with microswitches from Honeywell and meters from Foxboro, Massachusetts. The Argentine subsidiary of the Italian company, Techint, reportedly has also been able quietly to direct European technical assistance to the Argentine reprocessing program.

Two grand projects, however, dwarf the rest. The 690 MWe Atucha-2 power station, ordered from West Germany at a cost of nearly $1.6 billion, has already climbed above $4 billion, making it one of the most expensive reactors per kilowatt of installed capacity in the world. A companion, 250-ton heavy water production facility was contracted out to Sulzer Brothers for roughly $250 million. It may end up costing $1 billion. The plant is under construction at Arroyito in the southern province of Neuquen, and CNEA planners nervously hope that it operates soon and well enough to produce the first heavy water load for Atucha-2. If it does not, and Argentina must import heavy water, there will be a lot of explaining to do.[11]

THE GUIDING LIGHT: INDEPENDENCE

For over thirty years, the CNEA has been headquartered in the same building, at the outer limits of Buenos Aires. The white, colonnaded edifice looks stately but worn, and one corner on the ground-floor has been let out to a bank. Across the broad Liberator Avenue lie the verdant and immaculately manicured grounds of the Mechanical School of the Argentine Navy (known as the ESMA), a reminder of the commission's navy links. The tranquil appearance of the ESMA, with its elegant façade kept freshly painted in white with neat dark trim, belies its reputation as the most nefarious torture center in Argentina during the 1970s. It looks more like the manor house in a plush health resort.

It all goes to show how deceptive appearances can be. One would expect the interior of a nuclear agency to be modern and flourescent. At the CNEA, the elevator is the only contemporary appurtenance. The hallways are dark, and a few open doors show old laboratory equipment mixed in with the new. Office paint is stained and cracking. Tarnished silver trophies in a dim second-floor lobby celebrate past CNEA triumphs. In contrast to the nuclear energy division at the U.S. Department of Energy, security at CNEA headquarters is lax. Under democracy, CNEA visitors may find their own way through the building to their appointments, and sometimes are waved through by the guards without even receiving the customary visitor's slip to be signed and turned in before leaving. It is a credit to the commission, really, that it has not diverted more funds from its mission to its lodgings. Only the president's office stands apart, as big as a large conference room, expensively furnished in glass and steel modernity.

A sense of mission pervades these modest digs, and it can be summed up in one word: independence. The quest for independence has driven the nuclear program since its inception. Perón, Quihillalt, and Castro Madero all wanted it. The grail of independence led the Argentine government to buck international trends and choose heavy water reactors over light water reactors. It rejected light water reactors because at the time they depended upon U.S. supplies of enriched uranium fuel, while heavy water reactors used natural uranium, which Argentina possesses in abundance. The quest also led the government to the decision to build its own, complete nuclear fuel cycle, despite the high cost and Argentina's small market. It led the CNEA to resist foreign pressures, even at the cost of tens of millions of dollars or more.[12]

The appeal of independence is easy to see. It has spurred the greatest postwar political movement around the globe, the tottering of colonial empires before waves of nationalist movements in the developing world. Argentines, keenly sensitive to imperial dominance from the North, shared the natural desire for national fulfillment.

Nuclear independence offers special advantages. For good or ill, nuclear fission is the crowning achievement of the modern age. To share its secret is to share its glory, to sit at the head table among nations. Practically speaking, it offers a rare tactical advantage against the major supplier nations in the international nuclear market. "If you don't give it to us, we will build it ourselves—and without your safeguards" is the implicit threat. Thus the Argentines designed their own heavy water plant to pry one loose from the developed nations. "As soon as we published the blueprints based on Argentine designs for international bidding," recalled one CNEA official, "the major suppliers offered to build one using their own, advanced designs." Independence can provide domestic political payoffs, as well, an excellent argument to use in justifying budget increases.

The nuclear commitment was further driven by the creation of the so-called "London Club" of nuclear suppliers. The London Club—comprised initially of the United States, the Soviet Union, France, Great Britain, Canada, West Germany, and Switzerland—agreed to more restrictive export guidelines in the wake of India's detonation of a "peaceful" nuclear device in 1974. This galled the Argentines. After all, nuclear technology was their showcase; they were leaders in the International Atomic Energy Agency. And here, a cabal of select IAEA members was conspiring against the free flow of nuclear technology. Excluded again!

Many CNEA officials still become visibly upset when mentioning the U.S. Nuclear Non-Proliferation Act, signed into law in 1978.[13] The Non-Proliferation Act led President Carter to cut off the supply of highly enriched uranium for Argentine research reactors. This move forced the commission to allow Western Germany to supply the nuclear fuel to be used in Argentina's first major nuclear export—a research reactor in Peru. "Never again," they swore, as Castro Madero launched his own uranium enrichment project.

Independence offers both a goal and an excuse for failure to attain it. It appeals to national pride, while setting the stage to blame failures on the potent imperialist forces committed to the continuation of dependence. But the rhetoric can go too far, and undermine sound judgment. After all, we have not reached the Age of Interdependence by accident. According to the theory of comparative advantage, everyone can be better off if each country produces and exports the goods which it can produce more cheaply relative to other domestic goods, and imports others. The truly independent country cannot reap these benefits of specialization. Simply put, independence is expensive. In a field as technologically complex as nuclear power, it costs far more to design and build nuclear facilities from scratch than to buy them from abroad. During the energy crisis, this extra cost was deemed by many to be justified. The argument ran that energy was not like other goods because it was the lifeblood of an economy, that it was too important to leave to the vagaries of OPEC and other possible cartels. Governments therefore were willing to pay a premium to achieve energy independence, through nuclear power if necessary, because its strategic importance outweighed its economic costs.

In today's market of cheap and plentiful oil and more efficient use of energy, the argument for energy independence is much less compelling. (A new energy crisis could change that, though.) Moreover, it can cost more to buy nuclear facilities from a supplier with fewer safeguards restrictions; in 1979, the Argentines selected an untested German design for Atucha-2 over a Canadian reactor that cost $500 million less and had already compiled decades of operating experience. One principal reason was Canadian insistence that Argentina accept safeguards over its home-built facilities.[14]

Independence can also be provocative, when it entails exploitation of weapon-related technologies. In one sense, provocation is intended; the Argentines want the world to stand up and take note of their nuclear sophistication. But this high profile is costly. After the 1974 Indian explosion, the Canadians—who had supplied the reactor which produced the plutonium for

India's bomb—insisted that the Argentines accept tighter safeguards on the Embalse nuclear power station then under construction. Argentine resistance led to two years of haggling and a $200 million increase in reactor cost, some of which was borne by the Argentines. The most provocative elements of a fully independent nuclear program also turn out to be economically the least beneficial: enrichment, reprocessing, and so-called peaceful nuclear explosions.

Worst of all, from the Argentine perspective, the quest for independence can be self-defeating. The Argentines escaped dependence on foreign supplies of enriched uranium only by subjecting themselves to dependence on foreign supplies of the heavy water needed for natural uranium reactors. They sought, in turn, to escape dependence on foreign supplies of uranium fuel and heavy water by building uranium fuel and heavy water production facilities, but thereby subjected themselves to dependence upon the suppliers of those fuel facilities for at least a dozen years more. And while a nuclear buyer can shop around and play fuel suppliers against one another, once he has contracted to purchase a major facility, he is stuck for years in a weakened bargaining position.

"People think we are technologically advanced because we have many technology transfer agreements," said one nuclear scientist. "That is a way to prolong dependence, because you buy technology that fits others' needs and not your own. Your debt increases, and you become poorer and poorer."

The heavy water plant under construction at Arroyito is the most egregious example. The plant is scheduled to produce 2400 tons of heavy water by the year 2000, while Argentine reactors will probably need no more than one quarter of that amount. Even CNEA officials condemn Arroyito's "pharanoic" scale. As for technology transfer, a much-lauded byproduct of independence, Arroyito is a loser. "Technology transfer?" scoffed one high CNEA official, "the Swiss are supplying everything right down to the faucets."

Out of arrogance, asserted the present CNEA president, Albert Costantini, "we refused to accept further technical assistance from the IAEA in the early 1980s. So the Uruguayans received IAEA assistance in nuclear medicine and now they are far ahead of us in the field, with far better equipment." This is not to say that independence is a bad idea, but only that when it becomes an obsession it distorts decisions. It is and should be a valuable tool in mobilizing Argentine efforts.

THE BOMB

Dangling the possibility of nuclear weapons is the most provocative way to assert independence. Militant Third World politicians make no bones about it. "Can such a nation [i.e. without nuclear weapons] play any role in world affairs?" asked a former member of the Indian parliament, Krishan Kant. "What is required today is for the government and the people of [India] to make up their minds to develop a dedicated nuclear-weapons option so that as and when it becomes necessary it can be exercised."[15] Argentines are less brazen; their European outlook cushions their attacks on the status quo. Argentines can denounce imperialism with the best of the table-thumpers, but underneath many long to be included. After years of condemning the London Suppliers Club, Castro Madero could not conceal his pleasure at being invited to a meeting in Japan in which all other participants were London Club members. "It is a distinction conferred upon Argentina; by inviting us to participate along with advanced countries such as France, England, Russia, the U.S., and Japan. . . . Argentina's advanced position in nuclear development was recognized," he said.[16]

This schizophrenic conflict between Western sympathies and Southern resentment opens a window into Argentine nuclear psychology. For years, Argentines have kept the nuclear weapon option open, without exercising it. They have pursued enrichment and plutonium technologies, but poured much more money into militarily-useless nuclear power generation. They have rejected the NPT and Tlatelolco, but consistently insisted their intentions are peaceful. Even after the Malvinas War in 1982, amidst rumors that the British forces had carried nuclear weapons and that the Thatcher government had considered a possible nuclear attack on the provincial capital of Córdoba, Castro Madero threatened to retaliate only by building a nuclear-propelled submarine, a far less threatening—and more difficult—task than the manufacture of a crude nuclear explosive.[17]

These mixed signals partially reflect ambivalence within Argentina. Most CNEA scientists harbor purely peaceful objectives. A few military men have had other ideas, though they have never carried the day. Mixed signals also have been shrewdly employed by commission officials who know that the prospect of nuclear weapons can help win both military support for nuclear budgets at home and bargaining leverage abroad.

The overall impression created is a policy that "we could if we want to, but we don't want to." In 1978, Castro Madero asserted that Argentina was able to build nuclear weapons.[18] When pressed, officials in both the CNEA and the foreign ministry concede that they exploit this purposeful ambiguity to gain advantages in dealing with the supplier nations. "How are countries rewarded for signing the NPT?" asked one. "They are immediately taken for granted and lose all power to negotiate. We can get far better access to nuclear commerce now than if we joined the NPT. So why should we?"

Why, indeed. This Argentine criticism of the NPT (and there are many more) has merit. NPT parties *are* taken for granted. Meanwhile, those who refuse to join enjoy much more attention and sometimes more support, for they are the nations seen to be nearest the nuclear threshold: Argentina, Brazil, India, Pakistan, Israel, and South Africa. This perverse system of punishing virtue and rewarding vice someday could undermine the whole international nonproliferation regime.

Behind all the diversionary marches and countermarches, little doubt remains that Argentine scientists could produce a working nuclear device, given the political decision and corresponding funds. There are now some 6,000 scientists and technicians at the CNEA, working with the benefit of thirty-odd years of experience in the field. Minute quantities of plutonium were produced in a laboratory-scale reprocessing project in the 1960s, and a larger plant was launched in 1978. Once complete, this plant could produce enough plutonium for one or two bombs per year. Although the plant *could* be fed by irradiated fuel rods from existing reactors, that would require the breach of international safeguards already in place in Argentina. The plutonium could be produced without violating any international commitments, however, if the Argentines expand the capacity of their RA-3 research reactor or build a new, larger research reactor. Raw uranium for the reactor could be mined, processed, and molded into fuel elements within Argentina.

The more direct route to weapon-grade material would be through uranium enrichment. This method would not violate international safeguards. It would not be easy. Although Argentine scientists claim that the Pilcaniyeu facility will be unable to enrich uranium beyond the 20 percent level used in research reactors, foreign analysts remain skeptical, because the same process that enriches uranium to 20 percent can be used to reach 90 percent.

Once enough fissile material is obtained, Argentine metallurgists should be able to fashion an explosive. The charge could be molded by machinery at the Constituyentes nuclear center. To design and build a deliverable weapon would be a greater challenge. If it were done, though, the Argentines already have a suitable delivery system on hand—the Super Entendard jet fighter and the Exocet missile, used with such devastating effect against the British ships in the Malvinas War.

A CHANGE OF HEART

The ascension of President Alfonsín abated concerns over Argentine nuclear ambitions. The new president left no doubt as to his intentions: "Argentina is committed exclusively to the peaceful use of nuclear energy," he often reiterated.[19] Alfonsín joined in a series of meetings with the so-called Group of Six (with Greece, India, Mexico, Sweden, and Tanzania), which periodically issues impassioned pleas for nuclear disarmament. He also threw open the doors of CNEA facilities. In 1980, to enter the reactor construction area at Embalse, I had had to cross a cordon manned by machine gun-toting security guards. Five years later, the only sentry on duty at the plutonium reprocessing plant at Ezeiza was a stray black cat.

In Washington, the new line was welcomed but not embraced. For one thing, the Group of Six invocations were aimed more against the superpowers than against the nth nuclear weapon state. For another, the prospects for adoption of the Non-Proliferation and Tlatelolco treaties seemed no closer. The British presence in the Malvinas, now shored up by a $350 million airport, presented an insuperable political obstacle to Argentine acceptance of the Latin American nuclear weapon-free zone.

Alfonsín surprised many in early 1985 by stating that he would sign the NPT "tomorrow" if the nuclear weapon states observed their own obligations to promote nuclear assistance and arms control. Argentine diplomats, who seemed as startled as anyone by Alfonsín's pledge, hastened to add that this condition could not be expected to be fulfilled in the foreseeable future. Alfonsín, they said, had merely put a fresh face on Argentina's traditional policy. In reality, Alfonsín had at one stroke reversed Argentina's standing objection dating to the NPT's inception in 1968, that the treaty was inherently discriminatory and could *never* be subscribed to by Argentina.

In 1985, Presidents Alfonsín and Sarney signed an Argentine-Brazilian pact for mutual nuclear inspections, to reassure each other that no weapons programs were underway. This time, lower officials loudly insisted that the new system was merely a continuation of longstanding Argentine-Brazilian cooperation. These mutual visits would *not* be safeguards or the equivalent, they added, since safeguards were "too expensive." When confronted with the statement that *rejection* of safeguards had probably cost Argentina much more over the long run than acceptance would have, the officials retreated to the uneconomic-but-always-irrefutable argument of sovereignty. By September 1986, however, the two governments had gone so far as to sign a protocol providing for the prompt notification of any nuclear mishaps, and to discuss electronic monitoring of each other's nuclear facilities.[20]

The minuet between the new pacifists and the old diplomats made little real difference, though. Everyone knew that neither the NPT nor Tlatelolco could be ratified by the Congress. Even many members of the president's own party were expected to vote against the treaties, as Radicals sought to outvie the Peronists in nationalism. As for the Brazilian proposal, Alfonsín had bigger fish to fry than to raise a political ruckus over measures designed chiefly to assuage imperialist concerns.

Besides, budget restraints were making the pacifists' job easier. The CNEA, which had flown higher than most agencies, now fell harder. After the budget reductions, even high-ranking officials and scientists with doctorates were now earning less than $10,000 per year. A few left. More would have, had there been any place to go. The reprocessing plant, originally scheduled for 1985 completion, was pushed back three years. Even the higher priority enrichment program suffered.

Peronists accused the Radical government of intentionally selling out the nuclear program due to their anti-technology bias and weakling pacifism. Radicals replied that they wanted to protect Argentina's nuclear achievements, especially its carefully-nurtured human capital, but the government deficit had to be reduced and the CNEA would have to bear its share. Under the economic austerity plan, no reactors beyond Atucha-2 would be begun before 1989. Meanwhile, investment would shift toward Argentina's newly-discovered, massive reserves of natural gas.

By 1986, however, the government had come around to a more pronuclear stance, evidently persuaded that the technological, economic, and political benefits of a vigorous nuclear effort warranted a greater commitment of resources. President Alfonsín revived plans to complete the nuclear fuel cycle and promised that the needed funds would be made available. A fifteen-year national energy plan called for a doubling of installed nuclear generating capacity by the year 2000.[21]

What role will nuclear technology play in Argentina's future? Probably, it will continue to be an important source of energy. Hopefully, President Alfonsín's successors will share his opposition to nuclear arms development. Most importantly, perhaps, is the lesson the CNEA experience holds for the Argentine people. "The most interesting aspect of Argentina's development of uranium enrichment technology," said Dr. Mario Mariscotti, who directed the research project,

> was that of having successfully faced a technological adventure. There is a terrible culture in Argentina and the Third World; people think technology is out of reach. Refrigerators, cars, even toothpaste, all require technical assistance.

By having this attitude you are lost forever. Now that we have developed enrichment technology, we should show it to the Argentine people and say, "Why not try to make a telephone that works, a railroad suitable to Argentine needs?"[22]

In Argentina, where for too long too much talent has been diverted from production to speculation, where the search for solutions has been replaced by the search for scapegoats, this spirited approach to challenge could offer untold benefit.

PART IV

CLEAVING THE KNOT

CHAPTER 10

Democracy on Trial

The task confronting the lawgiver, and all who seek to set up a constitution of a particular kind, is not only, or even mainly, to set it up, but rather to keep it going. (Any kind of system can be made to work for a day or two.)

—ARISTOTLE, *The Politics*

Can Argentina become democratic and prosperous? The preceding chapters have shown the question to be less one of institutions than of people. American high school civics texts often treat politics as an agglomeration of political parties, federalism, judicial review, and the separation of powers. These issues *presuppose* democratic attitudes. The fundamental rules of the game—that our government should be democratic, republican, and federal—have been universally accepted since their last great test in the Civil War. Questions often arise whether the rules are being broken (Roosevelt's court-packing plan, racial segregation, Watergate) but the rules themselves are not fundamentally attacked. The *interpretation* of the Constitution generates heated debate, but few suggest that we discard the text.

Not so in Argentina. The most powerful institutions—the unions, the military, the Church—have consistently pursued antidemocratic goals. To them, the Constitution has not been an obstacle, but simply irrelevant. The unions were weaned on authoritarianism. Attorneys and judges have been too timid or unsympathetic to defend the constitution that they have sworn to uphold. The military, for want of foreign foes, has become the cottage industry of insurrection warned of by Alberdi. The Church has drilled its flock to obey without question, while supporting military dictatorships. The parties, all of them, including the Radicals, have conspired against democracy.

Raúl Alfonsín stands alone at the helm, the only leader who can steer Argentina through these perilous waters. Alfonsín is an Argentine rarity, combining charisma with democratic impulse. He respects the law. More importantly, he invigorates democracy with pragmatism. Democracy must succeed, not because it is an admirable ideal in the abstract, but because it is a solution, perhaps the only solution, to the chronic problems that have plagued Argentina.

Perhaps a democracy should not depend so much on one man. Are we not confusing democracy with the old model of the *caudillo?* No. At critical moments, when passions run high and patience runs low, even the sturdiest of democracies may fall prey to the demagoguery of a Huey Long (or a Juan Perón) and look for stewardship to a Franklin Roosevelt (or a Raúl Alfonsín). Argentines, even more than Americans, are *personalistas.* It may seem strange that it should require a singular, charismatic leader to establish a routine, pluralistic system. But such are the quirks of history. It makes all the more chilling the menace uttered by the fanatical General Ramón Camps, Jacobo Timerman's nemesis in *Prisoner Without a Name.* Camps, convicted for his role as Buenos Aires police chief and dirty war protagonist, unfortunately retains a strong following among some military officers and other right-wing zealots. He told former *Buenos Aires Herald* editor, Robert Cox, that "when we return to power, my hand will not tremble when I order Raúl Alfonsín's execution."

Alfonsín, however, does not face his great challenge alone. His fate depends on the Argentine people. The whole nation now faces its greatest trial: to abandon government by cabal and to live within the bounds of its own constitution. A profound change in national character must occur before democracy is firmly estabished in Argentina. Now we see glimpses of light. Political debate and artistic expression are reviving. But a generation or more will be required. Without a strong taboo against military coups, that generation needed for change will be repeatedly interrupted, its task left incomplete.

Thus the conviction of the ex-commanders closes one chapter and opens another. It is a fitting way in which to seal a dark and painful past, of disappearances and a pipe-dream Argentine renaissance that sank into an abyss of depravity. Ultimately, democracy will stand condemned, unless four minimal conditions for its survival are met.

TOLERANCE

Democracy is impossible without tolerance among divergent socioeconomic groups. Argentina has never enjoyed that kind of tolerance, for the society has always been deeply divided. With the crumbling of the Spanish

Empire in the Viceroyalty of the River Plate a Hobbesian struggle erupted, pitting Federalists against Unionists in a civil war that ended in the twenty year dictatorship of the *caudillo*, Juan Manuel de Rosas. The fall of Rosas gave rise to a stylized democracy, on paper emulating the U.S. constitutional system, in reality concealing the rule of a narrow group of oligarchs.

The attitude was best exemplified by early Argentine president, Domingo Faustino Sarmiento. On one hand, Sarmiento represented the best traditions of Argentine progressivism. He opposed the tyrant Rosas and founded the Astronomical Observatory of Córdoba. His extensive writings include a sociopolitical travelogue of the United States, reminiscent of if less insightful than de Tocqueville's *Democracy in America*.[1] He visited Horace Mann and is still revered as the father of Argentine public education.

Darker themes, though, also ran through this renaissance man. Sarmiento's most famous book was *Facundo*, the story of Facundo Quiroga, a great provincial *caudillo*, whose fabulous exploits were ended by a bullet in the eye. The book is subtitled *Civilization or Barbarism*, revealing Sarmiento's Europhilia and disdain for native Argentine culture:

> The American races live in idleness, and show themselves unable, even by compulsion, to dedicate themselves to hard and continuous work. . . . It evokes compassion and shame in the Argentine Republic to compare the German or Scottish colony of the south of Buenos Aires [Province] and the [creole] village formed in the interior; in the first, the little houses are painted, the front of each house always tidy, adorned with flowers and graceful shrubbery; the furnishings simple but complete; the crockery of copper or tin, always gleaming; the bed with pretty ruffles, and the inhabitants in continuous movement and action. Milking cows, making butter and cheeses, some families have managed to make colossal fortunes and to retire to the city to enjoy its comforts. The native town is the contemptible other side of the coin; dirty children covered in rags living with a pack of dogs; men lying on the floor and in the most complete inaction; the slovenliness and poverty on all sides; a little table and chest the only furniture; miserable huts for habitation that are notable for their general aspect of barbarity and shiftlessness. . . . .

> Moral progress, the culture of intelligence neglected in the Arab or Tartar tribe, here is not only neglected but impossible. Where to put the school so that children spread out over ten leagues away in all directions can attend lessons? Thus, civilization is totally unachievable, barbarity is normal, and be thankful if domestic customs preserve a small deposit of morality.[2]

Liberalism, yes, for the white man. Education, yes, to bring the benighted savages up to the point where they might earn a say in their own political destiny. Until that time, Sarmiento saw no virtue in popular government. To the contrary, he saw only vice. Where de Tocqueville argued that America's rulers could not govern too badly because they shared the same interests as their constitutents, Sarmiento viewed constituent interests as so base that they dare not be permitted to taint the noble aspirations of the enlightened ruling class.

For the rest of the nineteenth century and into the twentieth, the plutocracy of Sarmiento's successors perpetuated a vast gulf of cultural and economic differences between Argentina's rulers and ruled. At first it did not matter. Government was a pastime; the oligarchs established favorable conditions for economic growth and deferred noisome questions such as the enfranchisement of Argentina's burgeoning immigrant population. For their part, the immigrants coveted the prosperity that had eluded them in their native lands far more than the exercise of political rights.

Argentine society became a two-dimensional façade, fully endowed with civil and economic but not political rights. Once the World Wars halted the Argentine engine of economic growth, the façade began to crumble for want of political legitimacy. The ruling classes had no answer for the excluded masses, ever growing in size and awareness.

Positions hardened. Those in power refused to cede an inch of it. The division into two Argentinas had allowed them to monopolize power, while sowing the seeds for resentment that now would fuel their first powerful opposition. The political system had survived the good times, but bad times threw its lack of popular support into high relief. The extreme position of the elite provoked violent responses: three failed Radical rebellions in one generation; the Peronist movement in another. The Left sees the Right as mass murderers and running dogs of foreign capitalism, while the Right sees the Left as Communists and terrorists. Argentina has never surmounted this polarization. A series of slogans have swept national politics, always posing political conflict as nothing less than a mortal struggle: Sarmiento's Civilization or Barbarism; Braden or Perón in 1945, Liberation or Dependence during the 1970s' Peronist revival, Democracy or Dictatorship today. These antitheses implicitly brand those on the wrong side of the "or" as treacherous sell-outs, *vendepatrias*. They raise the stakes of political argument and thwart consensus. Slogans beget slogans. True dialogue disappears. In response to the now-popular Radical party slogan, "Democracy or Dictatorship," one retired general told me that "the government has a choice. It can either have a republican future, or it can prosecute the former military leaders." The veiled coup threat always lurks—do it my way, or I will destroy you.

These harsh antipathies have frustrated every attempt to establish a viable democracy in Argentina. While bullets have replaced ballots, democracy has appeared to be, at best, a policy alternative, not a way of life. And, as a political alternative, it has not seemed a very attractive one. Despite their much-vaunted European culture, Argentina is steeped in Latin traditions—such as personalism and authoritarianism—that tend to trump the electoral system. One important Latin feature in Argentina is the lack of a sense of rights, of one's own and of each others'. Those who relied on the letter of the law were chumps compared to those who did not scruple to resort to a $100 bribe, an important friend, or a gun. The European-style respect for law has remained but a vague aspiration.

This stunted sense of democracy and of rights has left the Argentine social fabric particularly susceptible to fascism. In the 1930s and 1940s, facism was embraced by the Catholic Church, by important cadres within the military, by the unions. The confluence of these interests created the Peronist coalition. Perón advanced the facism of Mussolini, of mobilized masses from the working and lower-middle classes.

Argentine facism had another strain. The fascist impulse coursed throughout the body politic, running broad as well as deep. It extended to landowning and wealthy classes. These groups eschewed the populist mass-mobilization of Italian fascism for the supercilious, technocratic version of Franco's Spain. This model exalted the highly trained and proficient bureaucrat as an epic hero, wrestling Argentina into socioeconomic modernity.

Even today, many people openly admire Adolph Hitler. In the face of the brutalities inflicted in the 1970s, one tailor complained, *"Esto no es una dictadura, es una dicta*blanda." This play on the word dictatorship—substituting *blanda* (soft) for *dura* (hard)—can loosely be translated, "This isn't a dictatorship, it is a wimpship."

Argentina is now barely reaching the political adolescence of an open society. People air their views, but they do not always listen. Noisy street protests drown out reasoned discourse. It is better than the oppressed silence of yesterday, but it is far from a true interplay among ideas and compromise.

PATIENCE

A half-century accumulation of political rot cannot be removed overnight, least of all by politicians who perforce face their tasks inexperienced and unqualified. "The crisis of confidence is a question of time," Vice President Victor Martínez said in an interview. "The people should give us at least as much time to rebuild the economy as it took the autocracy to destroy it. They stayed for eight years. Inflation cannot be terminated overnight. It takes nine months just to create a human." The vice president makes sense, but try to convince the average Argentine. "He promised everything and has done nothing" is a common complaint about President Alfonsín. People expected prosperity to leap forth from the ashes of a mordant economy, despite their own unwillingness to lift a finger in the endeavor. One taxi driver told me that Alfonsín would not survive his six-year term: "One day the unions will decide they've had enough and they will call a general strike. The country will be paralyzed and Alfonsín will be finished." Happily for Argentina, this prediction has not been borne out.

Impatience appears everywhere. The Peronists staged a half dozen general strikes by Independence Day of 1986. Businessmen clamor for peremptory repeal of all burdensome government controls (though not of all government subsidies). The Mothers of the Plaza de Mayo cannot see far enough past their grief to know that Alfonsín must close that tragic chapter in order to rebuild a working society. The military perches vulture-like, gloating over every civilian misstep and waiting for the day that it will be invited to return to power.

This impatience has two corollaries. The first is short memory. "Democracy is fine, but what has it done for me lately? We have never been worse off economically." The second corollary of impatience is the affinity for quick fixes and miracle cures. "During the last fifty years," said Alfonsín, "The country has cultivated a growing proclivity for direct action, for the antijuridical short cut, for explicit or implicit violence."[3] Alsogaray has the answer today, just as Richter had the answer thirty years ago. But long-term investment? Forget it.

By the midpoint of Alfonsín's six-year term, notable progress had been made on this score. People recognized that prosperity would require redoubled efforts and, above all, time. Shrill demands to renounce the debt and immediately recover lost living standards were little heard and less heeded. Some old-line Peronist leaders still tried this approach, but they were out of tune with both the reformist Peronists and the rank-and-file. This was a hopeful sign.

REALISM

Argentines sometimes display an astounding detachment from reality. It is most obvious in their foreign relations. Cosmopolitan Argentine diplomats, who prided themselves on their sophistication, were convinced that Britain would not fight over a tiny and windswept archipelago, isolated in the cold South Atlantic. *La Nación*, the Argentine newspaper of record, reported that President Alfonsín was welcomed to the U.S. Congress to address a joint session by President of the Senate "Jerry Brush" (aka George Bush).

One day in Buenos Aires I visited a Senate Commerce Committee staff meeting. The staff members included distinguished professors and others who had not been invited to participate in government for many years. Now they could contribute to solving the nuts-and-bolts problems afflicting Argentine commerce in the 1980s. The urgent task they set for themselves: determining what will be the key areas of logic in the first third of the twenty-first century. Incredulously, I listened as the committee director ticked off the items on his agenda: systemic lexicology, the unity of sciences, cybernetics, the future of probabilities. Perhaps the irrelevance of this comical discussion stemmed in part from the greater role the executive branch has in setting commercial policy. But in greater measure it reflected a wild misjudgment about the nature of today's challenges and how to meet them.

Detachment from economic reality is costly. In the field of foreign investment, it has reached the state of schizophrenia. The Argentines blame foreign imperialists for their woes, but protest the closure of an ITT subsidiary in order to protect jobs. Some abominate the giants of the North. One worker told me, "We have fertile soil. We have everything here. We do not have two climates, but four. Throw a seed, and a tree grows. But this country is controlled by the outside, by the great powers of the North." Others beg for foreign investment to put the economy back on its feet.

The "if it's foreign it must be bad" syndrome led to President Illia's disastrous decision to repudiate all foreign oil concessions. For the sake of "preserving the national patrimony," this step cost the Treasury steep penalties for breach of contract and deprived Argentina of its just-earned oil self-sufficiency—a bad bargain, to say the least. Even today, rather than adopting a flexible policy to permit foreign investment to enter the country to serve Argentine interests, many prefer a name-calling approach that hurts themselves more than it does the foreign companies, who move on to more hospitable investment climes.

As one Argentine economist aptly described this quixotic approach, "We have European culture, American-style consumption, and Third World production." This produces a "we deserve better" attitude that undermines the common sense notion that to live better one must work harder. All recognize the need for change, so long as someone else bears the sacrifice.

Take bank employees. They successfully lobbied the Congress to pass a wildly profligate law, which forced employers to pay fired employees for the rest of the workers' lives at full pay if an arbitral tribunal found the dismissal unjustified. This life tenure measure at one stroke would have cost the Treasury an incalculable sum and tantalized bank employees with the prospect of a permanent income for no work if they could provoke their own dismissal in a way unlikely to leave hard evidence for the tribunal's consideration. Fortunately, Alfonsín vetoed the measure, defying the unanimous (including Radical) vote of the Senate.

The government is seen as a pot of gold, endlessly to be tapped. Of course, it is not. In its present size and shape (big and flabby), it saps the economy of vitality and drains resources from otherwise productive endeavors. Argentina has confirmed Max Weber's model of the bureaucratic state.[4] For years, bureaucracy has been Argentina's principal growth industry. The state grows and creates a bureaucracy to serve its increasing demands. But the bureaucracy becomes so powerful that it reverses these roles; ultimately the state serves the bureaucracy.

The Radicals are statists. They have traditionally viewed the state as the solution rather than as the problem. Spain's pragmatic Socialist prime minister, Felipe Gonzalez, was able to learn from Mitterand's mistakes without repeating them. Alfonsín had to learn for himself, following an expansionary economic course until a dogged 1,000 percent inflation rate brought home the lesson.

It makes sense that the Radicals cannot easily eschew a large state. They lack independent sources of power, and so are ill-disposed to part with the one they have: the long-awaited control of the state and the spoils it entails. That made Alfonsín's economic shock treatment of 1985 all the more courageous and, forgive the expression, statesmanlike.

CONFIDENCE

Simon Bolívar may have had the settlers of the River Plate in mind when he lamented that "there is no good faith in South America." Until there is, there will be no democracy in Argentina. Since democracy prospers only in a stable environment, it must be institutionalized. But Argentines remain skeptical. They rally to democracy on call, but do not live it day to day. Rampant tax evasion continues. Unions still strive to win on the streets what they lost at the polls. Generals still strut and make political statements.

Prolonged instability has destroyed public confidence. Quite rationally, Argentines maximize short-term gains. Why should they plan for a long term that has never existed, as the country has lurched from crisis to crisis? Why should they pay taxes to a government that may be gone tomorrow? Why should they defend democracy, when a new military junta may soon throw it away and hunt them down? Herein lies the tragedy, as individually rational behavior produces the collective insanity that has roiled Argentina for generations. A vicious cycle has set in: instability destroys confidence; lack of confidence precludes stability.

This lack of confidence produces the brain-drain, capital flight and the withering of Argentina's productive base. There is no building towards the future. The total value of shares on the Argentine stock market is around $1 billion—less than 2 percent of GDP. This is a gross undervaluation, suggesting enormous untapped profits. Why do investors not buy a company for 10 percent its value, and then run it at an enormous profit? Because they doubt that they will enjoy the stability necessary for successful production. Meanwhile, the present economic instability creates greater opportunity for profit in short-term investments.

But there is hope. There is a sense that this time the effort is different, that it may succeed. With increasing confidence, people are exercising their civil and political rights to assemble peaceably and to exercise free speech. The exercise of liberty reinforces its popularity. Like goodness, liberty is its own reward. It can still be lost, as Solidarity so calamitously learned in Poland, but it will be harder to go back to military dictatorship now.

THE GIANT OF THE NORTH

And what of the United States? Will we ever learn? Must we wait until a situation is utterly irretrievable before it captures our full attention, as with Batista in Cuba, with the Shah in Iran, with Somoza in Nicaragua? By that time, support for democracy is too late. The opportunity has been lost. Democracy has become irrelevant, overtaken by events, and more particularly by the most extreme elements of dissatisfaction within troubled societies.

The United States is doing too little to support democracy, in Argentina and in the rest of Latin America. Sure, the rhetoric is there, but that and fifty cents will buy you a cup of coffee. Where is real help? The Latin Americans, as Henry Kissinger and others have recognized, simply cannot pay the enormous debt that they have contracted on its present terms, without submerging their economies in poverty and deprivation. We know how sorely the democratic system of the United States was taxed during the Great Depression of the 1930s; European democracy succumbed to fascism in the face of that onslaught. The hyperinflation that for a year of Alfonsín's administration seemed ever on the verge of spinning utterly out of control disturbingly paralleled that of Weimar Germany, and evoked images of the Nazi ascendance that it spawned.

But bankers' balance sheets continue to dominate U.S. strategic policy. Former president Frondizi told me that the problem with U.S. policy towards Argentina is that it is always guided first by security interests, second by financial interests, and only third by political interests. The U.S. view is myopic, for by grasping so fervently onto the servile security offered by authoritarian sycophants like Galtieri, or by supporting the elites who have been the traditional clients of U.S. capital, all is lost in the long run. It is time to recognize that democracy *itself* is in the largest national security interests of the United States, that democracy can best assure profitable economic relations among the nations, and that a country can be socialist or socially democratic, without being communist.

Communism has never found fertile soil in Argentina. But Americans encourage communism when they live up to the worst descriptions of "capital in its imperialist phase" expounded in communist doctrine. Thus in Chile, despite hysterical opposition to communism by the U.S. Government (until it learned the Marcos lesson) and by the ruthless dictator, General Augusto Pinochet, the Communist party remains strong.

President José Sarney of Brazil could have been speaking for all Latin American democrats when he wrote:

> I believe there is no greater historical error on the part of the United States in its relationship with South America than the third-class treatment it has given to this continent, as if the whole region were the turf only of the multinational corporations. . . . Latin America, in part as a reaction to U.S. policy itself, is beginning to nurture anti-American feelings where they had not existed before. When problems arise, Washington's concern is security; its solution, military. So the error is compounded. This is how the problem cropped up in the Caribbean, and this is how other problems will arise in our hemisphere.[5]

The U.S. banking community shares a great responsibility for the $350 billion Latin debt. During the 1970s, New York banks were desperate to lend out the petrodollars burning in their hands, to earn the income needed to pay interest to their Arab depositors. They eagerly pushed funds toward Latin American borrowers of any description, with any collateral, for any reason. True, the Argentines bear an equal share of the responsiblity and must now pay for the foolishness and corruption of the Process. But the responsibility should be shared by the U.S. banks more than it has been so far. Instead, U.S. banks have stared down the Latin debtors until the latter, in a weaker bargaining position, have buckled.

One American banker in Argentina told me that although U.S. banking executives are partly responsible for the Latin debt crisis, only the U.S. banks' shareholders have reason to complain on that score. The Latin peoples have no standing against the creditors, and must look only to the ex-leaders of their own corrupt governments for relief. In a narrow sense, he was right. But look past the narrow sense. Those corrupt governments were able to remain in office largely due to the continuing support of the international banking community. When Chase Manhattan's David Rockefeller embraced Martínez de Hoz and his Chicago school of economic philosophy immediately after the 1976 military coup, he was indeed casting a very important vote. It is not outrageous for the Argentine people to look to him and his colleagues for some relief, nor was it surprising that his 1985 visit to Buenos Aires sparked hostile protests.

A golden opportunity now exists in Latin America, despite past U.S. policies. Democracy is gathering momentum. But if democratic governments cannot relieve economic suffering and stagnation, democracy will die yet again. It is that simple. Foreign Minister Dante Caputo has tried repeatedly to bring that message home to U.S. officials and bankers.

Democracy cannot be bought, but where it is so fragile it should be subsidized. That was the idea behind President Kennedy's Alliance for Progress. At that time, democracy across the continent succumbed to the hobnailed march of dictators. Perhaps the tracks they left in the past twenty years have convinced Latin Americans not to give up their freedom so readily. Most people now understand that, once surrendered, liberty cannot easily be regained, and the military juntas and their technocratic friends know no special formula to produce prosperity.

A comprehensive solution to Latin America's $350 billion debt must be found, including further refinancing and probably a write-off of a portion of the outstanding balances, as proposed by U.S. Senator Bill Bradley. The alternatives are grim. The Latin govenments can repudiate their debt, as urged by Fidel Castro, and bring down international banking with them. Or they can pauper themselves to pay, strangling their own economic and political development. Democracy and other moderate forms of government could be an early casualty in either case.

Despite the clear danger, the political will to reach a once-and-for-all accommodation on the Latin debt has not ripened. Foreign aid and international financial policy are increasingly captive to American domestic politics. Protectionism blocks trade concessions. The looming deficit inhibits financial concessions. As *The Economist* editorialized, "Unhappily, creditor countries are still using trade controls to save a few thousand jobs in this or that industry, when what they are really doing is threatening to bust their banks."[6] That is a shame, for a comprehensive compromise provides the only way for the Latin nations to produce and export their way out of the hole instead of borrowing their way deeper in.

The American commitment to good business and anticommunism has led to a preference for military dictatorship over left-leaning civilian governments. This mirrors the Argentine elite's mistake of staking out a maximalist position and thereby provoking the most extreme counterreactions. By seeking everything you end up with nothing. U.S. policy should awaken to that reality before it is too late.

President Alfonsín likes to tell this story: One day in ancient Greece, a man was walking through a city and stopped when he saw a man breaking stones. "Poor man!" he exclaimed, "to be doing such back-breaking labor."

"I am not a poor man and this is not back-breaking labor," the man replied. "I am an Athenian who is building the Acropolis."

To flourish, democracy needs time. Raúl Alfonsín is struggling to buy it, hampered by his dreadful political and economic inheritance. If civil unrest returns, he may lose his race against the clock. The forces of authoritarianism wait eagerly in the wings. The fate of democracy, not only in Argentina but also in the rest of Latin America, hangs in the balance.

Appendix

PRESIDENTS OF THE NATION

President	Year Assumed Office
Bartolomé Mitre	1862
Domingo F. Sarmiento	1868
Nicolás Avellaneda	1874
Julio Argentino Roca	1880
Miguel Juárez Celman	1886
Carlos Pellegrini	1890
Luis Sáenz Peña	1892
José Evaristo Uriburu	1895
Julio Argentino Roca	1898
Manuel Quintana	1904
José Figueroa Alcorta	1906
Roque Sáenz Peña	1910
Victorino de la Plaza	1914
Hipólito Yrigoyen	1916
Marcelo T. de Alvear	1922
Hipólito Yrigoyen	1928
José Félix Uriburu	1930
Agustín Pedro Justo	1932
Roberto Mario Ortiz	1938
Ramón S. Castillo	1942
Arturo Rawson	1943
Pedro Pablo Ramírez	1943
Edelmiro J. Farrell	1944
Juan Domingo Perón	1946
Eduardo A. Lonardi	1955
Pedro E. Aramburu	1955
Arturo Frondizi	1958
José María Guido	1962
Arturo Illia	1963

Juan Carlos Onganía	1966
Roberto Marcelo Levingston	1970
Alejandro Augustín Lanusse	1971
Héctor J. Cámpora	1973
Raúl A. Lastiri (provisional)	1973
Juan Domingo Perón	1973
Maria Estela Martínez de Perón	1974
Jorge Rafael Videla	1976
Roberto Viola	1981
Leopoldo F. Galtieri	1981
Reynaldo Bignone	1982
Raúl Alfonsín	1983

Notes

PREFACE

1. *La tradición republicana* (Buenos Aires: Sudamericana, 1984), and "¿Habitantes o ciudadanos? La Argentina del ochenta y el problema de la identidad política," in *El poder militar en la Argentina 1976–1981*, Peter Waldmann and Ernesto Garzón Valdéz, eds. (Buenos Aires: Galerna, 1983), pp. 7–18.
2. See, for example, Max Hastings and Simon Jenkins, *The Battle for the Falklands* (New York: Norton, 1983), and Martin Middlebrook, *Operation Corporate: The Falklands War* (New York: Viking, 1982).
3. Raúl Alfonsín, *La cuestión argentina*, 2d ed. (Buenos Aires: Torres Agüero, 1984), pp. 201–02.

CHAPTER 1

1. Carlos F. Díaz Alejandro, *Essays on the Economic History of the Argentine Republic* (New Haven: Yale University Press, 1970), p. 201.
2. Robert A. Potash, *The Army and Politics in Argentina, 1928–1945* (Stanford: Stanford University Press, 1969), p. 58.
3. Junta Nacional de Carnes, Secretaría de Agricultura y Ganadería, República Argentina, *Síntesis estadística, año 1981*, p. 10; and Domingo F. Cavallo, *Volver a crecer* (Buenos Aires: Sudamericana/Planeta, 1984), p. 17.
4. See Instituto Nacional de Estadística y Censo, Ministerio de Economía, República Argentina (hereafter INDEC), *La probreza en la Argentina, 1984*. A free food program, called PAN (*Programa de Alimentación Nacional*), was initiated by the Alfonsín government, but its scale was initially unclear.
5. These estimates were made by the Foundation of Development Research (FIDE) on the basis of data from the Central Bank of the Argentine Republic (BCRA).
6. Leopoldo Allub, *Social Origins of Dictatorship and Democracy in Argentina* (Ph.D. dissertation, University of North Carolina, Chapel Hill, 1973), p. 129.
7. See Robert McGeagh, *Catholicism and Sociopolitical Change in Argentina: 1943–1973* (Ph.D. dissertation, University of New Mexico, 1974).
8. "Act Establishing the Purpose and Basic Objectives for the Process of National Reorganization", 24 March 1976, 36B *Anales de legislación argentina* (hereafter *Anales*), p. 1020.

9. For the salutation, see letter from Pío Laghi, the papal nuncio to Argentina, a copy of which appears in Ragnar Hagelin, *Mi hija Dagmar* (Buenos Aires: Planeta, 1984). The mass was one of a series organized by FAMUS (Families and Friends of Victims Killed by Subversion). In the ensuing public outcry, the priest, Father Jorge Triviño, insisted that by "material arms" he did not mean firearms, but the inflammatory rhetoric of his polemical homily had already made its mark.

10. See José Luis de Imaz, *Los que mandan* (Buenos Aires: EUDEBA, 1964) and Alain Rouquié, *Pouvoir militaire et société politique en République Argentine* (Paris, 1978).

11. Domingo Faustino Sarmiento, *Facundo*, 8th ed. (Buenos Aires: Editorial Losada, 1963), pp. 32–33. The quotation in the preceding paragraph appears in Sarmiento's *Obras Completas* (Buenos Aires: Luz del Día, 1949), 36:86–87.

12. Díaz Alejandro, *Essays*, pp. 32, 60–61.

13. *Tiempo Argentino,* 24 November 1984, p. 3. For a more considered analysis of the problem, see Raúl Alfonsín, *Ahora, mi propuesta política* (Buenos Aires: Planeta, 1983), p. 52, where he states: "We accepted as guidelines of life and codes of conduct values that were alien to our culture. We were, we had been the object of indecent manipulation by the consumer societies, which consolidate their welfare on the basis of exploitation of our riches and the deformation of our style of life. . . . Imperialism goes on adopting forms every time more subtle, less gross, but equally perfidious." By his second year in office, Alfonsín softened his approach and did his best to encourage foreign investment. The turning point came in the president's speech to U.S. oil executives in Houston in 1985.

14. V.S. Naipaul, *The Return of Eva Perón* (New York: Random House, 1981), p. 150.

15. *Index Económico* 6:69 (August 1984), p. 2.

16. Allub, *Dictatorship and Democracy*, p. 173.

17. See Arthur Whitaker, *Argentina* (Englewood Cliffs: Prentice-Hall, 1964) for the history of this era.

18. The federal government is authorized by Article 6 of the Argentine Constitution to intervene in a province "to guarantee the republican form of government, or to repel external invasions." Intervention entails the replacement of provincial authorities with a presidentially-appointed administrator, called the "intervenor." New elections are to be held as soon as practicable.

19. Samuel P. Huntington, *Political Order in Changing Societies* (New Haven: Yale University Press, 1969), p. 196. For interesting Argentine approaches to political thought, see Natalio Botana, *La tradición republicana* (Buenos Aires, 1984), and José Luis Romero, *Las ideas políticas en Argentina* (Buenos Aires: Fondo de Cultura Económica, 1975).

20. Before entering government, Foreign Minister Dante Caputo argued that "precisely the absence of a memory of social stability (which permits understanding that objectives are achieved incrementally) promotes the idea among society's members that their demands will be satisfied now or never. No one believes—because all history demonstrates the contrary—that things will improve with time."

In Peter Waldmann and Ernesto Garzón Valdéz, *El poder militar en la Argentina 1976–1981,* 2d ed. (Buenos Aires: Editorial Galerna, 1983), p. 130.

CHAPTER 2

1. FREJULI included Peronists, Frondizi's Movement for Integration and Development, popular conservatives, popular Christians, and other groups. The Radicals, led by Balbín, won 21.3 percent of the popular vote; 29.3 percent went to other parties. Technically, there should have been a run-off election, since the Lanusse electoral law called for a second round should no party reach 50 percent in the first polling. Lanusse decided to declare the Peronists victorious despite their 0.4 percent shortfall, perhaps from fear that the Peronists would win even more votes the next time.

2. For contemporary news accounts and the military version of the events at Ezeiza, see República Argentina, El Poder Ejecutivo Nacional (hereafter PEN), *Terrorism in Argentina* (1980), pp. 77–92. See also Joseph A. Page, *Perón: A Biography* (New York: Random House, 1983), pp. 462–66.

3. The English language classic of Argentine military history of this period is Robert A. Potash, *The Army and Politics in Argentina, 1928–1945* (Stanford: Stanford University Press, 1968). For a broader historic treatment, see David Rock, *Argentina 1516–1982* (Berkeley: University of California Press, 1985). A useful chronology appears in Gerardo López Alonso, *1930–1980: Cincuenta años de historia argentina* (Buenos Aires: Belgrano, 1982). For a general treatment beginning in pre-colonial days, see José Luis Romero, *Breve historia de la Argentina,* 6th ed. (Buenos Aires: April, 1984).

4. See Robert A. Potash, *Peróny y el G.O.U.: los documentos de una loggia secreta* (Buenos Aires: Sudamericana, 1984).

5. Page, *Perón,* chap. 13. For this period, see also Robert A. Potash, *The Army and Politics in Argentina, 1945–1962* (Stanford: Stanford University Press, 1980), *and* Félix Luna, *Argentina, de Perón a Lanusse,* 2d ed. (Buenos Aires: Sudamericana, 1984).

6. Page, *Perón,* chap. 35.

7. Frondizi denied that he made any such pact. When Perón grew disenchanted with Frondizi's failure to reintegrate Peronism into Argentine politics, he released a purported copy of his agreement with Frondizi, which the latter denounced as a forgery.

8. See Rogelio Frigerio, *Crecimiento económico y democracia,* 2d ed. (Buenos Aires: Paidós, 1983), for the fully-articulated expression of developmentalism by its cofounder.

9. Potash, *Army and Politics, 1945–1962,* pp. 271.

10. "Mensaje de la Junta Revolucionaria al Pueblo Argentino," 36B *Anales* 754–55 (28 June 1966).

11. Ibid.

12. "Objetivos políticos (fines de la revolución)," 36B *Anales* 757 (1 July 1966).

13. For a detailed account of economic policy-making, not only during the Onganía period but also for the rest of the postwar period until 1976, see Gary W. Wynia, *Argentina in the Postwar Era: Politics and Economic Policy Making in a Divided Society* (Albuquerque: University of New Mexico Press, 1978).

14. "Ley orgánica de las universidades nacionales," *Ley 17.245*, 27A *Anales* 188 (25 April 1967).

15. Ione S. Wright and Lisa M. Nekhom, *Historical Dictionary of Argentina* (Metuchen, N.J.: Scarecrow Press, 1978), p. 56.

16. PEN, *Terrorism in Argentina*, pp. 21–42.

17. *Ley 20.508*, 27 May 1973, 33C *Anales* 2951. The congressional debate also appears in Norberto O. Beladrich, *El Parlamento suicida* (Buenos Aires: Depalma, 1980), pp. 11–22.

18. Page concludes that "Perón probably tolerated his wife as the least objectionable vice-presidential candidate available to him. . . . He needed a running mate who would not hurt him, who could not claim any credit for his triumph, and who would thereafter be a ceremonial vice-president. . . ." *Perón*, p. 473.

19. *La Prensa*, 2 May 1974, p. 1.

20. Page, *Perón*, p. 425. Page chronicles several other, equally diverting López Rega stories.

21. *La Prensa*, 22 March 1976. The article reported that 445 terrorists had also died in the same period.

22. PEN, *Decreto No. 261*, 5 February 1975.

23. Guido di Tella, "The Economic Policies of Argentina's Labour-based Government (1973–6)," in Rosemary Thap and Laurence Whitehead, eds., *Inflation and Stabilization in Latin America* (London: Macmillan, 1979), p. 184.

24. 36B *Anales* 1020. The other principal documents of the coup were the Act and the Statute for the Process of National Reorganization, 36B *Anales* 1019 and 1021, respectively.

25. Comisión Nacional sobre la Desaparición de Personas (hereafter Sábato Commission), *Nunca más Never Again* (Buenos Aires: EUDEBA, 1984). For one prisoner's experience, grippingly recounted, see Jacobo Timerman, *Prisoner Without a Name, Cell Without a Number,* trans. Toby Talbot (New York: Vintage, 1982).

26. Sabato Commission, *Nunca Más*, p. 223.

27. Ibid., pp. 238–39.

28. The policies of Martínez de Hoz are set forth in detail in his book, *Bases para una Argentina moderna, 1976–80* (Buenos Aires, 1981).

29. For a British account of the Falklands-Malvinas conflict, see Max Hastings and Simon Jenkins, *The Battle for the Falklands* (New York: W.W. Norton, 1983). For analyses concerning the competing legal claims, see Farook Hassan, "The Sovereignty Dispute over the Falkland Islands," *Virginia Journal of International Law* 23:1 (Fall 1982): 53–72; and articles by Mónica Pinto and John M. Lindsey in *Texas International Law Journal* 18:1 (Winter 1983): 1–10, 11–36.

30. Sebastián Soler, quoted in *¿De que república hablamos?* (Buenos Aires: Somos, 1981), p. 109.

31. I am indebted to James Neilson, editor of the *Buenos Aires Herald*, for half of this image.

CHAPTER 3

1. Interviewed in Horacio de Dios, ed., *El tema es la democracia* (Buenos Aires: Editorial Belgrano, 1983), p. 78.
2. Ibid., p. 80.
3. For more biographical data, see República Argentina, Secretaría de Información Pública, *La democracia y su presidente* (Buenos Aires, 1984).
4. For the history of the Radical Civic Union, see David Rock, *Politics in Argentina, 1890–1930: The Rise and Fall of Radicalism* (Cambridge: Cambridge University Press, 1975), and Peter G. Snow, *Argentine Radicalism* (Iowa City: The University of Iowa Press, 1965).
5. *Gente*, 21 February 1985.
6. In *La cuestión Argentina [The Argentine Question]*, 2d ed. (Buenos Aires: Torres Agüero, 1984) Alfonsín asserts that "as bad as it may seem to some, Argentina is a socially democratic country" (p. 111) and that "the increase of wealth within society must be accompanied by a growing participation of all inhabitants in the national income" (p. 202).
7. In Raúl Alfonsín, *Ahora, mi propuesta política* (Buenos Aires: Editorial Planeta, 1983), pp. 21–42.
8. Ibid., pp. 21–25.
9. Alfonsín, *La cuestión argentina*, p. 120.
10. Ibid., ch. 2.
11. República Argentina, Poder Ejecutivo Nacional, *Decreto No. 158*, 15 December 1983. Decree No. 158 was based on Article 514 of the Code of Military Justice, Ley No. 14.029, which states, "When a crime has been committed through the execution of an order of service, the superior who has given it will be the only party responsible, [and] the inferior will only be considered an accomplice when he has been excessive in the fulfillment of said order."
12. República Argentina, Poder Ejecutivo Nacional, *Decreto No. 157*, 15 December 1983.
13. Quoted in *The New York Times*, 19 February 1984, p. E3.
14. Alfonsín, *Ahora, mi propuesta*, pp. 49, 51.
15. Carlos Ares, "El año del presidente," *El Periodista de Buenos Aires* 1:13 (8 December 1984), p. 30.
16. *Somos* 8:423 (26 October 1984), p. 8. The poll cited was taken on 25 October 1984 and combines the opinions of Alfonsín's performance of "very well" and "well." Alfonsín's popularity rose to 80 percent with the introduction of the Austral Plan.
17. Daniel Heymann, "El Plan Austral: una experiencia de estabilización de shock," *Tres ensayos sobre inflación y políticas de estabilización: documento de trabjo 18* (Buenos Aires: Comisión Económica para America Latina y el Caribe, February 1986), p. 160.

18. *La Nación*, 10 February 1986, pp. 1, 3, 5, International Edition.

CHAPTER 4

1. In Argentina, senators are selected by the provincial members of legislatures, as they were in the United States before the Twelfth Amendment. The Peronists did win more provincial elections (11) than did the Radicals (8), giving them a plurality in the Senate. The balance of power in the upper chamber rested in the hands of the independent provincial parties, who won three provinces.
2. Quoted in John Gunther, *Inside South America* (New York: Harper & Row, 1967), p. 180.
3. Juan D. Perón, *El proyecto nacional* (Buenos Aires: El Cid, 1982), pp. 24–25. See also Joseph A. Page, *Perón: A Biography* (New York: Random House, 1983), ch. 25.
4. Juan D. Perón, *Conducción política* (Buenos Aires, 1951), p. 109.
5. Ibid., p. 181.
6. Ibid., pp. 47, 127–28.
7. Juan D. Perón, *La comunidad organizada* (Buenos Aires: Secretaría Política de la Presidencia de la Nación, 1974), pp. 57–73.
8. Perón, *El proyecto nacional*, p. 71.
9. Ibid., p. 71.
10. Sábato Commission, *Nunca más*, p. 296.
11. For an excellent history of the Argentine labor movement, see Samuel L. Baily, *Labor, Politics and Nationalism in Argentina* (New Brunswick: Rutgers University Press, 1967).
12. Ibid., p. 99.
13. Félix Luna, *Argentina, de Perón a Lanusse*, 2d ed. (Buenos Aires: Sudámerica/ Planeta), p. 70.
14. Page, *Perón*, chap. 18, pp. 160–161.
15. Ibid., chap. 20, p. 181.
16. According to Perón, the *caudillo* exploits disorganization to gain power, while a leader, or *conductor*, organizes, teaches and builds the society. *Conducción política*, pp. 146–47.
17. Page, *Perón*, chap. 26, p. 232. See also Eva Perón's ghostwritten autobiography, *La razón de mi vida [My Mission in Life]* (Buenos Aires: Editora Volver, 1984).
18. Other passages from this speech appear in John Barnes, *Evita, First Lady* (New York: Grove Press, 1978), pp. 152–53.
19. Ibid., p. 167.
20. This fate befell early supporters, such as army colleague and Buenos Aires Province governor, Domingo Mercante, and labor leader Cypriano Reyes, as well as later disciples, such as Jorge Daniel Paladino, Perón's delegate in talks with the Lanusse government prior to the 1973 elections.
21. For the party reformists' views on the "Peronist crisis," see Antonio F. Cafiero, "Vigencia del peronismo," *Clarín*, 25 February 1985, p. 15, and José Manuel de la Sota, "Un peronismo para todos," *Clarín*, 11 March 1985, p. 15.

22. Quoted in *La Nación*, 18 October 1984, p. 7.

CHAPTER 5

1. Alain Rouquié, "Hegemonía militar, estado y dominación social," in Alain Rouquié, ed., *Argentina, hoy* (Mexico City: Siglo Veintiuno, 1982), p. 21.
2. *Buenos Aires Herald*, 16 March 1976, p. 8.
3. Quoted in Arthur Whitaker, *Argentina*, p. 25.
4. Alexis de Tocqueville, *Democracy in America*, trans. Henry Reeve, rev. Francis Bowen (New York: Knopf, 1976), 2:270, 267. De Tocqueville's warning is worth quoting at length:

> . . . as among democratic nations . . . the wealthiest, best-educated, and ablest men seldom adopt the military profession, the army, taken collectively, eventually forms a small nation by itself, where the mind is less enlarged and habits are more rude than in the nation at large. Now, this small uncivilized nation has arms in its possession and alone knows how to use them; for, indeed, the pacific temper of the community increases the danger to which a democratic people is exposed from the military and turbulent spirit of the army. Nothing is so dangerous as an army in the midst of an unwarlike nation; the excessive love of the whole community for quiet continually puts the constitution at the mercy of the soldiery.

5. See *Decreto Nacional No. 3397, [Military] Joint Staff Decrete No. 138*, and Ministry of Defense, *Decreto No. 93/84*. See also George Hatch, "Argentina's President Reins in Military," *The Wall Street Journal*, 31 July 1984, p. 34.
6. Interviewed on Argentina Televisora Color, *"30 Millones,"* 18 March 1985.
7. Personal interview, 6 March 1985.
8. *Voz militar* (August 1977), p. 38.
9. Quoted in Richard E. Neustadt, *Presidential Power* (New York: Wiley, 1980), p. 33.
10. Kalman Silvert, *The Conflict Society*, rev. ed. (New York: American Universities, 1966) pp. 209, 219. See interview with the National Defense College director, Rubén Blanco, in *El Cronista Comercial*, 3 April 1985, p. 20.
11. The Rattenbach report was never published, but was leaked and appeared in full. 15 *Siete Días* 858, 859, (23 November 1983, 30 November 1983). See also *Gente* 17:884 (1 July 1982). The whole issue is devoted to the Malvinas conflict and includes interviews with returning soldiers on their diet, clothing, and arms during the conflict.
12. The officers were charged with negligence and premature surrender under Articles 737, 740, and 751 of the Code of Military Justice, *Ley 14.029*, text as amended and published as República Argentina, Ejército Argentino, *Código de justicia militar* (Instituto Geográfico Militar, 1984.) The death sentence is provided for wartime failure to solicit support for military forces by an officer who was able to lend such support, under Article 747.
13. "Las operaciones militares y los derechos humanos," *Voz militar*, p. 38.

14. Quoted in the *International Herald Tribune*, 26 May 1977.

15. The decree bears the signs of its hasty issuance, five days after Alfonsín's inauguration; it charges the junta that took power after the period stated in the decree and is couched in the rhetoric of conviction, not accusation.

16. Sábato Commission, *Nunca más*, p. 402.

17. *Ley 23.049*, art. 10 (13 February 1984), 44A *Anales* 8, amendments to the Code of Military Justice.

18. From the remarks of General González, quoted in Silvert, *Conflict Society*, p. 208.

19. Sábato Commission, *Nunca más*, p. 8.

20. Text of the Armed Forces Supreme Council report to the presiding judge of the Federal Court of Criminal Appeals, reprinted in *La Nación*, 26 September 1984, p. 12.

21. Ibid.

22. *Constitución de la Nación Argentina*, art. 18. Videla's briefs before the Federal Appeals Court and Supreme Court were published by Asociación Jurídica Argentina, *Ante los jueces* (Buenos Aires, 1984).

23. The Supreme Court decision with comment appear in *El Derecho* 109:6037 (Buenos Aires: Universidad Católica Argentina, 27 July 1984,) p. lff. According to constitutional scholar Germán J. Bidart Campos, *both* the Supreme Court decision and Videla's position were incorrect. He argued that the pre-Alfonsín military courts were not protected by the Constitution as natural judge when they presumed to try cases outside the strictly military sphere, and thus converted themselves into unconstitutional "personal fora." But he also maintained that the Alfonsín amendments were unconstitutional, because they effectively placed trial jurisdiction into the Federal Appeals Court, after the acts committed. In his view, the true natural judge was a regular court, which should have been given jurisdiction over the trial. *La Nación*, 26 November 1984, p. 9.

24. The morning of 27 January 1977, Hagelin was approaching a house, in which seven armed persons were awaiting one María Berger, aged 30, whom they intended to detain. Frightened, Hagelin turned, ran, and fell from a single gunshot. O.A.S. "Human Rights in Argentina," pp. 74–77. Sábato Commission, *Nunca más*, pp. 389–90. One reliable source, however, took issue with that account. Also see R. Hagelin, *Mi hija Dagmar* (Buenos Aires: Planeta, 1984.) For the nuns case, see the same sources at p. 111 and pp. 387–88, respectively.

25. See Hastings and Jenkins, *The Battle for the Falklands*, p. 129.

26. Allegedly, Elena Holmberg, who had been posted to the Argentine Embassy in Paris, had seen a junta member, Admiral Massera, together with Montonero leader Mario Firmenich. The Foreign Ministry, then under the control of the navy, recalled Holmberg to Buenos Aires, where she disappeared.

27. The full text of the accusation appeared in *El Diario del Juicio*, 8 October and 15 October 1985.

28. Ibid.

29. *El Diario del Juicio*, 8 October 1985, p. 25.

30. *La Nación* 28 April 1986, p. 1, International Edition.
31. *Ley 12.709* (9 October 1941) 1 *Anales* 53, established Fabricaciones Militares. Savio also successfully lobbied for legislative approval of a national steel plan and the Army School of Engineering. The Savio Law, *Ley 12.987* (13 June 1947) 7 *Anales* 295, initiated Somisa, Argentina's biggest steel company, and the National Steel Plan. For a dated but useful overview of all FM operations, see Fabricaciones Militares, *Visión de una gran empresa*, (1981). More current data on production and revenues for the major FM enterprises appeared in "¿Qué hacer con las empresas militares?" *El Cronista Comercial*, 16 January 1984, p. 2ff.
32. Apart from FM, companies with military involvement include Aerolíneas Argentinas and the related OPTAR travel service, Aeronautics Industries, Naval Shipyards and Factories of the State (AFNE), Argentine Maritime Line Companies (ELMA), General Directorate of Research and Development, North Dock Naval Workshops (TANDANOR), Special Development Company S.A. (EDESA, under the navy), and Domecq García Shipyards S.A. (to build submarines with German cooperation). Alberto J. Ugalde, *Las empresas públicas en la Argentina* (Buenos Aires: El Cronista Comercial, 1984), pp. 145–76. Annual sales reportedly reached $2.2 billion in 1980, a sum which is exaggerated by the over-valued peso of that time. See "Fabricaciones Militares: Los límites de la privatización," *Mercado*, 5 June 1980, p. 21.
33. "Contribution of the Army to National Development Law," Ley 17.633 (12 February 1968). For McNamara quote, see Alberto S.J. De Paula, María Haydée Martín, Ramón Gutierrez, *Los ingenieros militares y sus precursores en el desarrollo argentino, 1930–1980* (Buenos Aires: Dirección General de Fabricaciones Militares, 1980), p. 230.
34. Quoted in *El Cronista Comercial*, 31 January 1984, p. 4. See also Ugalde, *Empresas públicas*, pp. 160–61.
35. See *The New York Times*, 3 November 1985, p. F4.
36. Officers have always been a tiny proportion of FM employees, less than 1 percent, but they have traditionally occupied the highest positions. "Dirección General de Fabricaciones Militares," *Manual de informaciones* 15:1–2 (January–March 1973):63. A mini-rebellion resulting from the argument that by law military officers could only be commanded by other military personnel, under the Military Statute, *Ley 19.101*, art. 5 (30 June 1971) 31B *Anales* 1344, subsided when two senior army officers replaced the new civilian heads of FM's major divisions: Development and Production. See *La Nación*, 14 June 1985 and 26 June 1984.
37. Gen. Juan E. Guglialmelli, *Argentina, Brasil y la bomba atómica* (Buenos Aires: Tierra Nueva, 1976) and *Geopolítica del Cono Sur* (Buenos Aires: El Cid, 1979).
38. A leaked State Intelligence Service (SIDE) report alleged that the Montoneros have been active in Brazil in recent years, and that they have begun to infiltrate the Intransigent and other parties, to build up strength in anticipation of increased future activity. "La conexión de Montoneros en Brasil," *Somos* 8:442 (8 March 1985):16–17.

39. *La Nación*, 12 December 1984, p. 5.
40. Andrew Graham-Yooll, *A Matter of Fear* (Westport: Lawrence Hill & Co., 1982), p. 15.
41. The possibility of military-terrorist collaboration should not be dismissed lightly. Apart from the case of the Argentine diplomat, Elena Holmberg, the 1977 disappearance of the Argentine ambassador to Venezuela, Héctor Hidalgo Solá, has also been attributed to the supposition that the diplomat encountered evidence of such a connection.
42. Quoted in Silvert, *The Conflict Society*, p. 222.

CHAPTER 6

1. See José Luis Romero, *Las ideas políticas en Argentina*, 5th ed. (Buenos Aires: Fondo de Culturo Económico, 1975), part 1.
2. Robert McGeagh, *Catholicism and Sociopolitical Change in Argentina: 1943–1973* (Ph.D. dissertation, University of New Mexico, 1974), pp. 312–13.
3. Sábato Commission, *Nunca más*, pp. 247–59.
4. Personal interview, 25 April 1985.
5. Conferencia Episcopal Argentina, *La Iglesia y los derechos humanos* (Buenos Aires, 1984), pp. 9, 35; and Sábato Commission, *Nunca más*, pp. 259–63.
6. Sábato Commission, *Nunca más*, pp. 259–63.
7. Monsignor Italo Di Stéfano, quoted in *Tiempo Argentino*, 15 January 1985, p. 9.
8. Conferencia Episcopal Argentina, *Iglesia y comunidad nacional* (Buenos Aires: Editorial Claretiana, 1981).
9. Quotations appeared in the *Buenos Aires Herald*, 4 February 1985, p. 7, and 9 February 1985, p. 9. According to Río Negro Bishop Miguel Hesayne, the Argentine people desired that "the human rights violations and the administrative corruption [of the military government] be investigated thoroughly and justice be done." *Buenos Aires Herald*, 5 November 1984, p. 7.
10. Penny Lernoux, *Cry of the People* (Middlesex: Penguin, 1982), p. 429 ff.
11. Barry James, "Church Marxism Worries Pope," *Buenos Aires Herald*, 9 January 1985, p. 6.
12. The text appears in *La Nación*, 11 November 1984, p. 20.
13. Emilio F. Mignone, *Educación cívica I: libro del profesor* (Buenos Aires: Ediciones Colihue, 1985), p. 49.
14. Emilio F. Mignone, *La educación cívica en la escuela media argentina* (Buenos Aires: Comisión Permanente en Defensa de la Educación, 1984), p. 10.
15. Tedesco, Juan Carlos; Cecilia Braslavsky; and Ricardo Carciofi, *El proyecto educativo autoritario argentino* (Buenos Aires: Grupo Editor Latinoamericano, 1985), pp. 57–58.
16. Arnold Spitta, "El proceso de reorganización nacional: 1976–1981," in Waldmann and Garzón Valdés, *El Poder Militar en la Argentina*, p. 92.
17. See Blas Barisani, *Formación moral y cívica III* (Buenos Aires: Editorial Estrada, 1981).

18. Sábato Commission, *Nunca más*, p. 295.
19. For the role of students in Argentine politics, see Snow, *Political Forces in Argentina*, chap. 6. For the emigration estimates, see Ernesto Garzón Valdés "La emigración argentina," in Waldmann and Garzón Valdés, *El poder militar*, p. 179.
20. The definition of literacy is a controversial subject, and many consider that the 30 percent figure, based on the number of school dropouts, is exaggerated. The World Bank standards are easier, resulting in a figure of only 6 percent illiteracy.
21. Unión del Centro Democrático, *Plataforma de gobierno* (Buenos Aires: El Cid, 1983), p. 25.
22. For the party line, see ibid., p. 35. Alsogaray's comments appeared in *Tiempo Argentino*, 2 April 1985, p. 10; and *Clarín*, 3 April 1985, p. 8.
23. See *La Razón*, 6 February 1985, p. 14, for Alsogaray's opposition to Frondizi in the 1950s.
24. Partido Ingransigente, *Aportes para el proyecto nacional* (Buenos Aires: Edigraf, 1983), pp. 40–41.
25. Ibid., pp. 21–23.
26. *La Nación*, 11 January 1985, p. 5.
27. In introducing the second phase of the Austral Plan, President Alfonsín commented on those who criticized him for not unilaterally suspending payments on the debt:

> Let us be clear in this respect. They are demanding of us nothing more nor less than a measure that no government in the world—capitalist or socialist—has adopted until now; and we are covered with opprobrium for our resistance to converting ourselves into an extravagant world exception to a rule whose evident inviolability has its *raison d'être*.

Quoted in *La Nación*, 10 February 1986, p. 3, International Edition. John Kenneth Galbraith was more sanguine in writing on Argentina; he noted that default on international debt was historically common and without lasting disadvantages. "A Journey to Argentina," *The New Yorker* (21 April 1986) p. 70ff.
28. For a top-to-bottom attack of the Alfonsín government, see Frondizi interview in *La Nación*, 12 April 1985, p. 7, where he claims that Radical policies were leading the country toward "chaos and anarchy."
29. See Peter H. Smith, *Argentina and the Failure of Democracy: Conflict Among Political Elites, 1904–1955* (Madison: The University of Wisconsin Press, 1974), p. 95, and Anne Louise Potter, *Political Institutions, Political Decay and the Argentine Crisis of 1930* (Ph.D. dissertation, Stanford University, 1978).
30. Interview with Deputy Héctor Basualdo, *Siete Días*, 12 September 1984, p. 12.
31. Quoted in *La Nación*, 23 November 1984, p. 7.

CHAPTER 7

1. See Carlos Calvo, *El derecho internacional teorico y practico* (Buenos Aires, 1868), 6 vols. Calvo argued that the economic, military, and political advantages of Europe and North America over Latin America led the Latin governments to grant privileges to foreigners that placed Latin Americans "in a position of legal inferiority in their own countries." To redress that inferiority, Calvo proposed that foreigners in Latin America should receive equal treatment to that accorded Latin American nationals, effectively nullifying foreigners' special benefits. See James Leavy, "The Calvo Doctrine in Latin American Loans," *International Financial Law Review* (October 1985): 31–34.

2. Although the 1949 Peronist Constitution permitted presidential reelection, and it is quite likely that Perón would have run again in 1957, at least then he might have lost. That would have destroyed the Peronist image of electoral invincibility.

3. Frederick E. Snyder, "State of Siege and Rule of Law in Argentina: The Politics and Rhetoric of Vindication," 15 *Lawyer of the Americas* 3 (Winter 1984).

4. Germán Bidart Campos, *Derecho Constitucional* (Buenos Aires: Ediar, 1966), 2: 573 ff.

5. The Supreme Court decisions were *Carlos Mariano Zamorano*, 282 *Fallos* 441 (1977); *Inés Ollero*, 300 *Fallos* 457 (1978); and *Jacobo Timerman*, 300 *Fallos* 816 (1978), 301 *Fallos* 771 (1979). In the latter stages of the Process, a few Supreme Court decisions tried to limit the abuse of Article 23 powers. The one appellate judge who, in 1981, held the application of the state of siege to be unconstitutional immediately left the country. Frederick E. Snyder coined the phrase "discourse of rationality" in "State of Siege and Rule of Law," p. 520.

6. José María Rosa, *La fetiche de la constitución de 1853* (Buenos Aires: Ave Fénix, 1984), p. 35.

7. Alberdi, *Bases y puntas de partida para la organización politica de la Républica Argentina*, 4th ed. (Buenos Aires: Plus Ultra, 1984), pp. 233–34. This belief led Alberdi to promote immigration aggressively, drafting constitutional provisions (articles 14 and 20) that granted full civil and economic rights to foreigners, whether or not resident in Argentina.

8. Rosa, *La fetiche*, ch. 5.

9. See the Constitution, articles 95, 96 and 100. The last provides an exception to Supreme Court jurisdiction in cases arising under certain legal codes promulgated by Congress; see also art. 67, para. 11.

10. 158 *Fallos* 290 (10 September 1930). The Court argued that when the provisional government has already been constituted and possesses the military forces and the police necessary to perform its functions, then a de facto government will be recognized, despite the unconstitutionality of its origin.

11. Carlos Santiago Nino, coordinator of the panel and later chairman of Alfonsín's commission on constitutional reform, described the conclusions in *La Nación*, 12 December 1984, p. 9.

12. John Gunther, *Inside South America* (New York: Harper and Row, 1967), p. 201.

13. Unión Cívica Radical, *Plataforma de gobierno* (Buenos Aires: El Cid, 1983).
14. This decision was ratified by Congress in the form of amendments to the Code of Military Justice, *Ley No. 23.049.*
15. *Buenos Aires Herald,* 31 January 1984, p. 1.
16. Foreign Broadcast Information Service, *Daily Report-Latin America* 6:009 (13 January 1984), p. B2.
17. The Supreme Court decision was reported in 109 *El Derecho* 6037 (27 July 1984): 1 *et seq.* The lower court (the Criminal Court of Appeals of Buenos Aires) had ruled that charges concerning the disappearances fell outside the Military Code of Justice. The court thus refused to dismiss civilian charges against General Bignone in the case of the disappearance of conscripts from the Military College. The judge reasoned that under Argentine constitutional law, abduction remains a crime until it is solved. Thus the cases of the thousands of *desaparecidos* still unlocated after the September cutoff date for exclusive military jurisdiction would be covered by the prospective amendments to the code that conferred civilian jurisdiction for common crimes committed under military aegis. The decision was reported in the *New York Times,* 28 March 1984.
18. Text of President Alfonsín's remarks quoted from *Daily Report - Latin America* (trans. FBIS), 31 October 1985, p. B1–B4.

CHAPTER 8

1. Economic statistics for Argentina abound. Official sources include the annual reports of the Central Bank and the frequent publications of the National Institute of Statistics and Census (Instituto Nacional de Estadística y Censo, or INDEC). More accessible is the *World Development Report,* published annually by the World Bank. For historical perspectives, see Carlos F. Díaz Alejandro, *Essays on the Economic History of the Argentine Republic* (New Haven: Yale University Press, 1970), and Gary W. Wynia, *Argentina in the Postwar Era* (Albuquerque: University of New Mexico Press, 1978).
2. Morgan Guaranty Trust Company, *World Financial Markets* (February 1985): 2.
3. In his own defense, see José A. Martínez de Hoz, *Bases para una Argentina moderna, 1976–80* (Buenos Aires: n.p., 1981); República Argentina, Ministerio de Economía, *Evolución económica de la Argentina, abril 1976-diciembre 1980;* and his farewell address as economy minister, in *Boletín semanal del Ministerio de Economía: Anexo, no. 382* (23 March 1981): 757–70.
4. Domingo Cavallo, *Volver a crecer* (Buenos Aires: Sudamérica Planeta, 1984).
5. See Morgan Guaranty Trust Company of New York, *World Financial Markets* (February 1986): pp. 2–6.
6. Karl W. Deutsch explained how rising mass expectations can lead to political disintegration in *Tides Among Nations* (New York: The Free Press, 1979), pp. 192–94.
7. The clearest exposition of libertarianism appears in Robert Nozick, *Anarchy, State & Utopia* (New York: Basic Books, 1974).

8. World Bank, *World Development Report 1983* (New York: Oxford University Press, 1983), p. 201.

9. The growth rate is taken from Morgan Guaranty, *World Financial Markets* (February 1985):3.

10. The terms of trade statistics appeared in Daniel Heymann, "El Plan Austral: una experiencia de estabilización de shock," *Tres ensayos sobre inflación y políticas de establización: documento de trabajo 18* (Buenos Aires: Comisión Económica para America Latina y el Caribe, February 1986), statistical annex chart 10. The grain comparison was provided by secretary of agriculture, livestock, and fisheries, Ing. Lucio G. Reca, quoted in *La Nación*, 24 February 1986, p. 6, International Edition.

11. Martínez de Hoz, *Bases*, pp. 134–35. Martínez de Hoz told the author that the bankruptcies were a necessary step in the development of a modern, efficient economy. Companies that cannot survive competition should not stay in business.

12. For the achievements of developmentalism, see Rogelio Frigerio, *Crecimiento y desarrollo*, 2d ed. (Buenos Aires, n.p., 1984).

13. On state enterprises, see Alberto J. Ugalde, *Las empresas públicas en la Argentina* (Buenos Aires: El Cronista Comercial, 1984), and Enrique A. Bour and Adolfo C. Sturzenegger, *Empresa pública e interés público: rol y regulación de la empresa pública en Argentina*, 3 vols. (Buenos Aires: Sindicatura General de Empresas Públicas, 1984).

14. Domingo Cavallo used this phrase in *Volver a crecer*, p. 26.

15. The Italo purchase gave rise to the congressional investigation mentioned above, at the end of chapter 6. For the expansion of the state enterprises in this period, see Ugalde, *Empresas Públicas*, pp. 168–76.

16. Of course, overvaluation is but one of many causes of the problem. For instance, high domestic wine prices plus cheap credit led Mendozan vintners to overinvest in cheap wines. These wines soon glutted the domestic market, but were too poor to succeed as exports.

    Various export promotion programs have tried to facilitate regional exports, but with limited success. See Ley 23,101 (1984), regulated by Decreto 176/86, and the elements of the second phase of the Austral Plan detailed in speeches by President Alfonsín and Economy Minister Sourouille, the texts of which were reprinted in *La Nación*, 10 February 1986, pp. 3–5, International Edition.

17. *Buenos Aires Herald*, 2 January 1985, p. 7.

18. *Clarín*, economic supplement, 3 February 1985, p. 7.

19. Arnoldo Spitta, "El 'Proceso de Reorganizacíon Nacional' de 1976 a 1981: los objetivos básicos y su realización práctica," in Peter Waldmann and Ernesto Garzón Valdéz, eds., *El poder militar en la Argentina, 1976–1981* (Buenos Aires: Galerna, 1983), pp. 88–90.

20. The service sector has grown rapidly in recent years. In 1980 it comprised 53 percent of the gross domestic product. By 1984, that share had increased to 64 percent. World Bank, *World Development Report*, p. 153, and Morgan Guaranty, *World Financial Markets* (February 1985): 8.

21. The phrase "small savings" and "peso deposits" became synonymous after the sweet money stopped, because anyone with large savings invested in other currencies to prevent the constant wasting of assets. Peso deposits were only taken out by people who had too little to invest in foreign currencies, or needed the pesos back within the month to make purchases, or were ignorant.

22. This 1949 speech was quoted in Juan D. Perón, *Conceptos políticos* (Buenos Aires: Volver, 1982), p. 19. For landowners' complaints over the pro-agricultural policy of the Liberating Revolution, see Gary Wynia, *Argentina in the Postwar Era.*, pp. 155–58.

CHAPTER 9

1. The "safeguards" administered by the International Atomic Energy Agency include systems of material accounting (analogous to cash flow accounting), physical controls, and inspections. Safeguards cannot *prevent* the diversion of nuclear materials to weapon use; their purpose is to provide "timely warning" that there has been a diversion so appropriate responses may be taken to deter the would-be nuclear power from going that route.

2. For other grounds not to ratify the treaty, see *Nucleonics Week*, 30 May 1985.

3. See Daniel Poneman, "An Argentine Bomb," *New York Times*, 29 June 1983, p. A23.

4. Others argue that the more nations with nuclear weapons, the safer the world would be. They believe that the United States and Soviet Union have only avoided full-blown war since 1945 because the nuclear weapons of each has deterred the other. If *every* nation had nuclear weapons, then every nation would be deterred from launching even a conventional attack. The weakness of this view is that it assumes all leaders behave rationally.

5. El Poder Ejecutivo Nacional, *Decreto No. 302* (1979).

6. For the definitive work on this intriguing episode, see Mario Mariscotti, *El Secreto Huemul* (Buenos Aires: Suramerica Planeta, 1985). For a general history of the Argentine nuclear program, see Daniel Poneman, *Nuclear Power in the Developing World* (London: Allen & Unwin, 1982), ch. 4.

7. Naval officers often were appointed to the bureaucratically strategic position of chief of logistics for the commission. Army officers also received choice assignments. During Castro Madero's tenure, one army lieutenant colonel ran the reprocessing program and another ran the research reactor division.

8. See Richard Kessler, *Nucleonics Week,* 15 November 1984. Kessler's reports in *Nucleonics Week* provide the best continuing coverage of the status of Argentine nuclear projects and politics.

9. For further remarks by Castro Madero and Alfonsín on the subject of the enrichment breakthrough, see "CNEA Chairman Makes Announcement," *TELAM* 2102 GMT (18 November 1982), trans. Foreign Broadcast Information Service.

10. For a more measured treatment, see *New Scientist* (8 December 1983), p. 718.

11. Argentina's heavy water needs were reduced when West Germany sent it 143 tons of heavy water originally supplied to the Germans by the United States.
12. The CNEA, for instance, chose a never-produced German reactor model for its Atucha-2 station over the tried-and-true CANDU reactor from Canada, at a $500 million premium. This decision significantly reflected considerations of independence. See Castro Madero's "Statement at the Signing of Decree No. 2441," (n.d.); and Poneman, *Nuclear Power in the Developing World*, chap. 4.
13. Public Law 95–242. The Non-Proliferation Act imposed strict preconditions to U.S. nuclear suppliers, eventually requiring the termination of all major nuclear cooperation to governments that refused to accept IAEA safeguards over all of their facilities, whether imported or built with domestic technology.
14. Poneman, *Nuclear Power in the Developing World*, chap. 4.
15. Krishan Kant, "Must We Be Taught Another Lesson?", *World Focus* 2:6 (June 1981): 21–22.
16. *Convicción* (Buenos Aires), 17 May 1982, p. 11.
17. For a more detailed analysis of this incident, see Poneman, "Argentine Nuclear Prospects," *Orbis* (Winter 1984).
18. Quoted in *Chicago Tribune*, February 1, 1978, p. 9.
19. See Alfonsín's remarks at his first presidential news conference, 15 January 1984, in República Argentina, Presidencia de la Nación, *Discursos presidenciales* (Buenos Aires: Secretaría de Información Pública, 1984).
20. See Kessler's articles in *Nucleonics Week*, 31 July 1986, p. 1, and 11 September 1986, p. 9.
21. Ibid., 11 September 1986, p. 5.
22. Personal interview, 5 March, 1985.

CHAPTER 10

1. Domingo F. Sarmiento, *Travels in the United States in 1847*, trans. Michael A. Rockland (Princeton: Princeton University Press, 1970).
2. Domingo F. Sarmiento, *Facundo*, 8th ed. (Buenos Aires: Losada, 1981), pp. 29, 33–34.
3. Raúl Alfonsín, "Address at the Dinner of Camaraderie of the Argentine Armed Forces," Buenos Aires, 5 July 1985.
4. Max Weber, *Theory of Social and Economic Organization*, trans. Talcott Parsons (New York: Free Press, 1947).
5. José Sarney, "Brazil: A President's Story," *Foreign Affairs* (Fall 1986):115.
6. *The Economist*, 17 August 1985, p. 13.

Selected Bibliography

Abós, Alvaro. *Las organizaciones sindicales y el poder militar 1976–1983.* Buenos Aires: Centro Editor de América Latina, 1984.

Acevedo, Domingo E. "The U.S. Measures against Argentina Resulting from the Malvinas Conflict." *American Journal of International Law* 78:2. April 1984. pp, 323–44.

Aga, Carlos, *et al. El proyecto argentino y el desarrollo nuclear.* Buenos Aires: EDIGRAF, 1985.

Alba, Víctor. *Nationalists without Nations.* New York: Praeger, 1968.

Alberdi, Juan Bautista. *Bases y puntos de partida para la organización política de la República Argentina.* 4th ed. Buenos Aires: Editorial Plus Ultra, 1981.

Alfonsín, Dr. Raúl R. "Address delivered by the president of the Argentine Republic in the Meeting on Peace and Disarmament." New Delhi: 28 January 1985.

――――. *Ahora, mi propuesta política.* 4th ed. Buenos Aires: Editorial Planeta S.A.I.C., 1983.

――――. *La cuestión argentina.* Buenos Aires: Torres Agüero Editor, 1984.

――――. *¿Qué es el radicalismo?.* 2d ed. Buenos Aires: Editorial Sudamericana, 1983.

Allub, Leopoldo. *Social Origins of Dictatorship and Democracy in Argentina.* Ph.D. dissertation: University of North Carolina, 1973.

Alonso, Gerardo López. *1930–1980: Cincuenta años de historia argentina.* Buenos Aires: Editorial de Belgrano, 1982.

Andersen, Martin. "Dateline Argentina: Hello, Democracy." *Foreign Policy.* Spring 1984.

Aráoz, Julius. "Desarrollo y política nuclear." *Clarín,* 30 October 1984, pp. 16–17.

Baily, Samuel L. *Labor, Nationalism and Politics in Argentina.* New Brunswick, N.J.: Rutgers University Press, 1967.

Barisani, Blas. *Formación moral y cívica III.* Buenos Aires: Editorial Estrada, 1981.

Barnes, John. *Evita First Lady: A Biography of Eva Perón.* New York: Grove Press, Inc., 1978.

Beladrich, Norberto O. *El Parlamento suicida.* Buenos Aires: Ediciones Depalma, 1980.

Bidart Campos, Germán J. *Derecho constitucional.* 2 vols. Buenos Aires: EDIAR, 1966.

――――. *Educación cívica I y II.* Buenos Aires: Angel Estrada y Cía., S.A., 1985.

_____. "La Ley 23.049 analizada constitucionalmente por la Corte." 109 *El Derecho* 6037. 27 July 1984.

Bittel, Deolindo F. *Qué es el Peronismo*. Buenos Aires: Editorial Sudamericana, 1983.

Borrini, Alberto. *Política y publicidad: Cómo se hace un presidente*. Buenos Aires: Ediciones El Cronista Comercial, 1984.

Bour, Enrique A., and Adolfo C. Sturzenegger. *Empresa pública e interés público: rol y regulación de la empresa pública en Argentina*. 3 vols. Buenos Aires: Sindicatura General de Empresas Públicas, 1984.

Bravo, Héctor Félix. *Educación popular*. Buenos Aires: Centro Editor de América Latina, 1983.

Camps, Ramón J.A. *Caso Timerman, punto final*. Buenos Aires: Tribuna Abierta, 1982.

Canavese, Alfredo Juan, Luisa Montuschi, and Víctor J. Elías. *Sistema financiero y política industrial para la Argentina en la década de 1980*. Buenos Aires: Ediciones El Cronista Comercial, 1983.

Cárdenas, Emilio J. "El conflicto de las Islas Malvinas. Más reflexiones externas." III *El Derecho* 6123. 28 November 1984.

Carranza, Ambrosio Romero, Alberto Rodríguez, and Eduardo Ventura. *Manual de historia política y constitucional argentina 1776–1976*. Buenos Aires: AZ Editora S.A., 1983.

Catterberg, Edgardo R. *Political Attitudes, Social Background and Consensus among Argentine Elites*. Ph.D. dissertation: University of North Carolina at Chapel Hill, 1973.

Cavallo, Domingo F. *Volver a crecer*. Buenos Aires: Sudámerica/Planeta S.A., 1984.

Cavarozzi, Marcelo. *Autoritarismo y democracia*. Buenos Aires: Centro Editor de América Latina, 1983.

Centro Energético Peronista. *Los lineamientos de Sourrouille: La energía al servicio de la dependencia; Nuestra Propuesta: Concertación energética para la independencia*. Buenos Aires, 1984.

Centro de Estudios Legales y Sociales. *Testimonio sobre el centro clandestino de detención de la Escuela de Mecánica de la Armada Argentina (ESMA)*. Buenos Aires: Ed. CELS, 1984.

de Dios, Horacio. *El tema es la democracia*. Buenos Aires: Editorial de Belgrano, 1983.

de Paula, Alberto S.J., María Haydée Martín, and Ramón Gutiérrez. *Los ingenieros militares y sus precursores en el desarrollo argentino 1930–1980*. Buenos Aires: Dirección General de Fabricaciones Militares, 1980.

De Tocqueville, Alexis. *Democracy in America*. Two vols. Trans. Henry Reeve. Rev. Francis Bowen. New York: Knopf, 1976.

del Barco, Ricardo. *El régimen peronista 1946–1955*. Buenos Aires: Editorial de Belgrano, 1983.

del Carril, Bonifacio. *Memorias dispersas: El Coronel Perón*. Buenos Aires: Emecé Editores, 1984.

SELECTED BIBLIOGRAPHY

Díaz Alejandro, Carlos F. *Essays on the Economic History of the Argentine Republic.* New Haven and London: Yale University Press, 1970.

di Tella, Guido. "The Economic Policies of Argentina's Labour-based Government 1973–1976." In *Inflation and Stabilisation in Latin America.* Edited by Rosemary Thorp and Laurence Whitehead. London: Macmillan, 1979.

Domínguez, Carlos Horacio. *La nueva guerra y el nuevo derecho.* 2 vols. Buenos Aires: Círculo Militar, 1980.

Ecabert, R. "The Heavy Water Production Plant at Arroyito, Argentina." *Sulzer Technical Review.* No. 3, 1984.

Empresa Nacional de Telecomunicaciones. *Telecomunicaciones para el desarrollo: la transformación tecnológica argentina.* Buenos Aires: Rotog, 1980.

Escudé, Carlos. *Gran Bretaña, Estados Unidos y la declinación argentina 1942–1982.* 2d ed. Buenos Aires: Editorial de Belgrano, 1983.

Farrés, María Teresa, Jorge A. Jaroslavsky, and Emilio F. Mignone. *Elecciones y participación.* Buenos Aires: CODEPE, 1984.

Federación Argentina de Trabajadores de Luz y Fuerza. *La salud y las obras sociales.* Buenos Aires, 1985.

Ferns, H.S. *Argentina.* London: Ernest Benn, Ltd., 1969.

Ferrer, Aldo. *¿Puede Argentina pagar su deuda externa?* Buenos Aires: El Cid Editor, 1982.

————, et al. *La economía argentina.* Buenos Aires: Editorial de Belgrano, 1977.

Frenkel, Leopoldo. *El Justicialismo.* Buenos Aires: Editorial Legasa, 1984.

Frigerio, Rogelio. *Crecimiento económico y democracia.* 2d ed. Buenos Aires: Paidós, 1983.

Frontalini, Daniel, and María Cristina Caiati. *El mito de la guerra sucia.* Buenos Aires: Ed. Cels, 1984.

García Lupo, Rogelio. *Mercenarios y monopolios en la Argentina.* 5th ed. Buenos Aires: Editorial Legasa S.R.L., 1984.

Hassan, Farooq. "The Sovereignty Dispute over the Falkland Islands." *American Journal of International Law* 23:1. Fall 1982: 53–72.

Hastings, Max, and Simon Jenkins. *The Battle for the Falklands.* New York: W.W. Norton & Company, 1983.

Helio, Juan Zarini. *Historia e instituciones en la Argentina.* Buenos Aires: Astrea, 1981.

Herring, Hubert. *A History of Latin America from the Beginnings to the Present.* 3d ed. New York: Knopf, 1968.

Hodges, Donald C. *Argentina 1943–1976: The National Revolution and Resistance.* Albuquerque: University of New Mexico Press, 1976.

Hope, Adrián F. J. "Sovereignty and Decolonization of the Malvinas/Falkland Islands." 6 *Boston College International and Comparative Law Review* 2. Spring 1983: 391–446.

Huntington, Samuel P. *Political Order in Changing Societies.* New Haven: Yale University Press, 1969.

Imaz, José Luis de. *Los que mandan.* Buenos Aires: Eudeba, 1964.

Irazusta, Julio. *Perón y la crisis argentina*. 3rd ed. Buenos Aires: Editorial Independencia S.R.L., 1983.

Jones, Leroy P., ed. *Public Enterprise in Less Developed Countries*. Cambridge: Cambridge University Press, 1982.

Kechichian, Roberto N. *Educación Cívica*. 2d ed. Buenos Aires: Ediciones Braga S.A., 1984.

Lanusse, Alenjandro A. *Mi testimonio*. Buenos Aires: Lasserre Editores, 1977.

Ledesma, Dr. Joaquín Rafael. *Cinco años de política economica: April 1976–marzo 1981*. Buenos Aires: Editorial F.E.P.A., n.d.

––––––. *Argentina económica: diagnóstico y propuesta*. Buenos Aires: Editorial F.E.P.A., 1981.

Lernoux, Penny. *Cry of the People*. Middlesex: Penguin, 1982.

Lindsey, John M. "Conquest: A Legal and Historical Analysis of the Root of United Kingdom Title in the Falkland Islands." 18 *Texas International Law Journal*. Winter 1983: 11–35.

Llach, Juan J. "Democracia y economía." 57 *Criterio* (20 December 1984): 689–98.

Luder, Italo Argentino. *El proceso argentino*. Buenos Aires: Ediciones Corregidor, 1977.

Luna, Félix. *Argentina, de Perón a Lanusse 1943–1973*. 2d ed. Buenos Aires: Editorial Sudamericana/Planeta Argentina, 1984.

––––––. *Conflictos y armonías en la historia argentina*. 4th ed. Buenos Aires: Editorial de Belgrano, 1980.

Mallon, R. D., and J. V. Sourrouille. *Economic Policymaking in a Conflict Society: The Argentine Case*. Cambridge: Harvard University Press, 1975.

Mander, John. *The Unrevolutionary Society*. New York: Knopf, 1969.

Mariscotti, Mario. *El secreto atómico de Huemul*. Buenos Aires: Sudamericana/Planeta, 1985.

Martínez de Hoz, José A. *Bases para una Argentina moderna 1976–1980*. Buenos Aires: Compañía Impresora Argentina, S.A., 1981.

Massuh, Víctor. *La Argentina como sentimiento*. Buenos Aires: Editorial Sudamericana, 1982.

McGeagh, Robert. "Catholicism and Sociopolitical Change in Argentina: 1943–1973." Ph.D. dissertation: University of New Mexico, 1974.

Mende, Raúl A. *El Justicialismo: doctrina y realidad peronista*. Buenos Aires: Ediciones Doctrinarias, 1983.

Metra Consulting and International Joint Ventures. *Argentina: Business Opportunities in the 1980s*. London: Metra Consulting, 1979.

Mignone, Emilio F. *Educación cívica I*. Buenos Aires: Ediciones Colihue, 1985.

––––––. ––––––. *Libro del profesor*. Buenos Aires: Ediciones Colihue, 1985.

––––––. *La educación cívica en la escuela media argentina*. Buenos Aires: Comisión Permanente en Defensa de la Educación, 1984.

––––––. *Estudio de la realidad social argentina: primero y segundo año del ciclo básico*. Buenos Aires: Ediciones Coliseo, 1975.

Miguens, José Enrique. *Los neo-fascismos en la Argentina*. Buenos Aires: Editorial de Belgrano, 1983.

Mosconi, Enrique. *El petróleo argentino 1922-1930*. Buenos Aires: Círculo Militar, 1983.

Nosiglia, Julio E. *El Partido Intransigente*. Buenos Aires: Centro Editor de América Latina, 1983.

Ocon, Jorge A. *Historia argentina*. Buenos Aires: Ediciones Coliseo, 1974.

Organización de los Estados Americanos. Comisión Interamericana de Derechos Humanos. *Informe sobre la situación de los derechos humanos en Argentina*. Washington: Organization of American States, 1980.

Oszlak, Oscar. *"Proceso," crisis y transición democrática/1*. Buenos Aires: Centro Editor de América Latina, 1984.

Page, Joseph A. *Perón: A Biography*. New York: Random House, 1983.

Partido Comunista. *Plataforma nacional del Partido Comunista*. Buenos Aires, 1983.

Partido Demócrata Progresista. *77 años PDP, sus principios*. Buenos Aires, 1984.

Partido Intransigente. *Aportes para el Proyecto Nacional*. Buenos Aires: EDIGRAF, 1983.

————. *Plataforma electoral 1983: para que todo cambie*. Buenos Aires, 1983.

Partido Justicialista. *Plataforma de gobierno*. Buenos Aires: El Cid Editor, 1983.

Perón, Eva. *La razón de mi vida*. Buenos Aires: Editora Volver, 1984.

Perón, Juan. D. *Conceptos políticos*. Buenos Aires: Editora Volver, 1982.

————. *Conducción política*. Buenos Aires, 1951.

————. *El Proyecto Nacional: mi testamento político*. 5th ed. Buenos Aires: El Cid, 1984.

————. *La Comunidad Organizada*. Buenos Aires: Editorial Codex, 1974.

Piekarz, Julio A. *Compensación de reservas de efectivo mínimo: La cuenta regulación monetaria*. Buenos Aires: Banco Central de la República Argentina, 1984.

Pinto, Mónica. "Argentina's Rights to the Falkland/Malvinas Islands." 18 *Texas International Law Journal*. Winter 1983: 1-10.

Pla, Alberto J., *et al*. *La década trágica*. Buenos Aires: Editorial Tierra del Fuego, 1984.

Poneman, Daniel B. "An Argentine Bomb." *The New York Times*. 29 June 1983.

————. "Argentina." In *Nuclear Proliferation Prospects*. Edited by Samuel F. Wells, Jr. and Jed C. Snyder. Cambridge: Ballinger, 1985.

————. *Nuclear Power in the Developing World*. London: Allen & Unwin, 1982.

————. "Nuclear Proliferation Prospects for Argentina." 27 *Orbis* 4. Winter 1984.

————. "Latin America." In *The Nuclear Suppliers and Nonproliferation*. Edited by Rodney W. Jones, *et al*. Lexington: Lexington Books, 1985.

Potash, Robert A. *The Army and Politics in Argentina, 1928-1945*. Stanford: Stanford University Press, 1969.

————. *The Army and Politics in Argentina, 1946-1962*. Stanford University Press, 1980.

Potter, Anne Louise. "Political Institutions, Political Decay and the Argentine Crisis of 1930." Ph.D. dissertation: Stanford University, 1978.

Rapoport, Mario. *Gran Bretaña, Estados Unidos y las clases dirigentes argentinas: 1940–1945*. 3d ed. Buenos Aires: Editorial de Belgrano, 1980.

República Argentina. *Banco Central de la Republica Argentina Boletín estadistico*. Various numbers.

————. ————.*Estadística bancaria por partido o departamento y por localidad, prestamos-depósitos*. Buenos Aires, 1984.

————. ————.*Memoria anual*. Various years.

————. *Código de Justicia Militar, Ley No. 14.029*. Buenos Aires: Instituto Geográfico Military, 1984.

————. Comisión Asesora para el Estudio de la Reforma Institucional. *Dictámenes y antecedentes*. Buenos Aires: Ministerio del Interior, 1971.

———— Comisión Nacional de Energía Atómica y Universidad Nacional de Cuyo. *Instituto Balseiro, Centro Atomíco Bariloche, resumen anual 1983*. San Carlos de Bariloche, July 1984.

————. Comisión Nacional de Energía Atómica. *Memoria anual*. Various years.

————. Ministerio de Defensa. Dirección General de Fabricaciones Militares, *Memoria y balance general 1977*. Buenos Aires, 1978.

————. ————. ————.*Memoria y balance general 1976*. Buenos Aires, 1977.

————. ————. Subsecretario de Producción para la Defensa. *Políticas de producción para la defensa*. Buenos Aires, 1984.

————. Ministerio de Economía. *Evolución económica de la Argentina: abril 1976–diciembre 1980*. Buenos Aires, 1981.

————. ————. Secretaría de Hacienda. *Censo nacional de población y vivienda 1980*. Buenos Aires: Instituto Nacional de Estadística y Censos, 1981.

————. ————. Sindicatura General de Empresas Públicas. Dirección General de Fabricaciones Militares, *Estados contables ajustados por inflación al 31 de diciembre de 1983*. Buenos Aires, 1985.

————. ————. Sindicatura General de Empresas Públicas. *El control de las empresas públicas: Documento de divulgación No. 7*. Buenos Aires: SIGEP, 1983.

————. Ministerio de Educación y Justicia. *Política educacional en marcha, período 10 de diciembre 1983/84*. Buenos Aires, 1984.

————. Presidencia de la Nación. La Dirección General de Difusión de la Secretaría de Información Pública. *Reseña de la obra de gobierno*. Buenos Aires, 1984.

————. ————. Secretaría de Planificación. *Escuela permanente de hogares: resultados preliminares*. Buenos Aires: Instituto Nacional de Estadística y Censos, 1982.

————. ————. ————. *Lineamientos de una estrategia de crecimiento económico 1985–1989*. Buenos Aires, 1985.

————. Poder Ejecutivo Nacional. *Terrorism in Argentina*. Buenos Aires, 1980.

Rivera, General Horacio Aníbal. *Fabricaciones Militares: visión de una gran empresa*. Buenos Aires: Analog Publicidad, 1981.

Robledo, Federico, and Antonio Tróccoli, *et al. La Reconstucción de la democracia*. Buenos Aires: El Cid, 1981.

SELECTED BIBLIOGRAPHY

Romero, José Luis. *Breve historia de la Argentina*. 6th ed. Buenos Aires: Editorial Abril, 1984.

———. *Las ideas políticas en Argentina*. Buenos Aires: Fondo de Cultura Económica, 1984.

Rosa, José María. *El fetiche de la Constitución*. Buenos Aires: Ediciones Ave Fénix, 1984.

Rouquié, Alain. *Poder militar y sociedad política en la Argentina II: 1943–1973*. Buenos Aires: Emecé, 1978.

———, ed. *Argentina, hoy*. 2d ed. Mexico: Siglo 21, 1982.

Russell, Roberto. *América latina y la guerra del Atlántico Sur: experiencias y desafíos*. Buenos Aires: Editorial de Belgrano, 1984.

Saavedra, Emiliana López. *Testigos del "proceso" militar/1*. Buenos Aires: Centro Editor de América Latina, 1984.

Sánchez, Pedro. *La presidencia de Illia*. Buenos Aires: Centro Editor de América Latina, 1983.

Sarmiento, Domingo F. *Facundo*. 8th ed. Buenos Aires: Editorial Losada, 1981.

———. *Travels in the United States in 1847*. Trans. Michael A. Rockland. Princeton: Princeton University Press, 1970.

Savio, General Manuel N. *Obras del General Manuel N. Savio*. Buenos Aires: SOMISA, 1972.

Schumacher, Edward, "Argentina and Democracy." *Foreign Affairs*. Summer 1984.

Silvert, Kalman H. *The Conflict Society*. Rev. ed. New York: American Universities Field Staff, Inc., 1966.

Smith, William C. *Crisis of the State and Military-Authoritarian Rule in Argentina, 1966–1973*. Ph.D. dissertation: Stanford University, 1980.

Snow, Peter G. *Political Forces in Argentina*. Rev. ed. New York: Praeger Publishers, 1979.

———. *Radicalismo Argentino*. Buenos Aires: Editorial Francisco de Aguirre, 1972.

Sorondo, Marcelo Sánchez. "Hacia la institucionalización." *La Ley*. 1983 B: 940–950.

Snyder, Frederick E. "State of Siege and Rule of Law in Argentina." 15 *Lawyer of the Americas* 3. Winter 1984: 503–20.

Tedesco, Juan Carlos, Cecilia Braslavsky, and Ricardo Carciofi. *El proyecto educativo autoritario argentino*. Buenos Aires: Facultad Latinoamericana de Ciencias Sociales, Grupo Editor Latinoamericano, 1985.

Timerman, Jacobo. *Prisoner Without a Name, Cell Without a Number*. Trans. Toby Talbot. New York: Vintage Books, 1981.

Ugalde, Alberto J. *Las empresas públicas en la Argentina*. Buenos Aires: Ediciones El Cronista Comercial, 1984.

Unión Cívica Radical. *Plataforma de gobierno: UCR*. Buenos Aires: El Cid, 1983.

Unión del Centro Democrático. *Bases doctrinarias y elementos para la plataforma electoral*. Buenos Aires, November 1983.

Union Industrial Argentina. *Ponencias—informes de las comisiones—conclusiones y conferencias de congreso de la pequeña y mediana industria*. Buenos Aires, 1983.

_____. *Bases para una política industrial argentina*. Buenos Aires, December 1981.

_____. *Memoria y balance 1983*. Buenos Aires, 1984.

Vanossi, Jorge R. A. *El estado de derecho en el constitutucionalismo social*. Buenos Aires: Eudeba, 1982.

Waldman, Peter, and Ernesto Garzón Valdéz. *El poder militar en la Argentina 1976-1981*. 2d ed. Buenos Aires: Editorial Galerna, 1983.

Weil, Thomas E., *et al. Area Handbook for Argentina*. 2d ed. Washington: American University, 1974.

Westerkamp, José F., ed. *Evolución de las ciencias en la República Argentina 1923-1972: Tomo II*. Buenos Aires: Sociedad Científica Argentina, 1975.

World Bank. *World Development Report 1983*. New York: Oxford University Press, 1983.

Wright, Ione S., and Lisa M. Nekhom. *Historical Dictionary of Argentina*. Metuchen, N.J. and London: The Scarecrow Press, Inc., 1978.

Wynia, Gary W. *Argentina in the Postwar Era*. Albuquerque: University of New Mexico Press, 1978.

Zarini, Juan Helio. *Constitución de la Nación Argentina*. Buenos Aires: Editorial Astrea, 1984.

Index

A number in brackets [ ] following a page number refers to a footnote on that page. Most abbreviations are cross-referenced to their meaning. Non-English items are cross-referenced to their English equivalent.

229